DIVORCE AND THE MILITARY II

A Comprehensive Guide
for
Service Members, Spouses, and Attorneys

by

Marsha L. Thole
and
Frank W. Ault

Published by
The American Retirees Association
Post Office Box 2333
Redlands, CA 92373-0781

Research Assistant: MSgt. Paul C. Barth (USAF, Retired)
Technical Editors: MSgt. Melanie L. Barth (USAF) and
    MCPO Thomas L. Koester (USN, Retired)
Legal Consultant: James A. Noone, Esq., Karalekas & Noone,
    Washington, DC
Cover design by Michael Townsend Graphic Designer

This book is not an official publication of the Department of Defense, nor does its publication in any way imply its endorsement by that agency.

Publisher's Cataloging-in-Publication Data
Thole, Marsha L and Ault, Frank W.
Divorce and the Military II: A Comprehensive Guide for Service Members,
    Spouses, and Attorneys
        408 pages. Includes Resources appendix.
        1. Divorce. 2. Military (Family and Divorce). 3. Military Retired Pay
        (and Divorce). 4. Law (Domestic Relations). 5. Uniformed Ser-
        vices Former Spouses' Protection Act. 6. Federal Benefits (in a mili-
        tary divorce).
I. Title.
Library of Congress Catalog Card Number: 98-86922
ISBN 0-9639850-1-9 $19.95 Softcover
Printed in the United States of America

Typesetting and prepress services provided by
Desert Dreams Publishers, 7600 Coulson NE, Albuquerque, NM 87109
Phone/Fax: (505) 857-0285

DISCLAIMER

This book is printed, published, sold, circulated, and distributed with the intention and understanding that the publisher and authors are not engaged in rendering any legal, accounting, or other professional services. State laws relative to domestic relations vary and change frequently. If legal or other expert assistance is required, the reader should consult with competent professionals.

This book is designed primarily to provide general information on the issue of military retired pay as a divisible marital asset. Because of possible unanticipated changes in governing statutes and case law relating to military divorce, all persons or entities involved in the preparation, publication, sale, or distribution of this book disclaim all responsibility for the legal and other consequences (e.g., financial) of any document prepared, or action taken, by relying on information contained in this book. Purchasers and individuals intending to use this book in connection with the preparation of any legal documents are advised to check specifically with competent legal and other counsel on the current applicable state and federal laws in all jurisdictions in which they intend the documents to be used.

ABOUT THE PUBLISHER

The American Retirees Association (ARA) was chartered in California in 1984 as a nonprofit, tax-exempt corporation to deal with inequities in the Uniformed Services Former Spouses' Protection Act (USFSPA), Public Law 97-252, 10 U.S.C. §1408 *et seq.* Its membership includes active duty, reserve, and retired members of the uniformed services, both male and female.

The ARA is headquartered in Redlands, California, and maintains an action office in the national capital area. The ARA is recognized, within the national community of veterans' organizations, as the leader of the USFSPA reform effort.

The goals of the ARA are relief for those military veterans already affected by various inequities in this law and reduction of the threat to future military retirees. The ARA maintains that there must be fair and equitable treatment for *both* members of any military marriage that ends in divorce.

INTRODUCTION

Making the decision to divorce can be extremely difficult. No one plans, when getting married, to end their marriage. Unfortunately, 55 percent of all marriages in this country end in divorce, with the divorce rate for military marriages generally mirroring that of the civilian population. As then Representative Robert K. Dornan (R-CA) said in a prepared statement before the [then] House Armed Services Subcommittee on Military Personnel and Compensation on April 4, 1990, "There is no stereotype of the ideal military marriage or the unfortunate circumstances that lead to separation."

Men and women have been divorcing in this country for more than 300 years. In 1900, the divorce rate was three couples per 1,000. The rate dipped during the Depression, climbed during World War II, and dipped again until the early 1960s. It doubled from 1965 to 1975, and rose to 22 divorces per 1,000 married couples in 1979. In 1994, it dropped to 20 divorces per 1,000 couples. Today, marriage is considered to be in crisis, moving from a period when divorce was viewed as a failure that created hardships, to the current era where unhappiness alone may be considered a serious enough reason to divorce. Economic affluence often has persuaded individuals to focus on their own emotional happiness and expectations to the detriment of the family unit.

Demographics

The Military Family Resource Center (MFRC) in Arlington, Virginia, publishes a yearly *Profile of the Military Community: [year] Demographics.* While it contains numerous statistics (e.g., numbers on married military), it is totally lacking in statistics on the number of divorced military members. In a telephone call to the MFRC, the authors learned that the Center is unable to obtain this data from the Department of Defense (DoD), and has been told that such numbers really do not exist (from DoD). Oddly, DoD provides MFRC statistics on the age and gender of adult dependents, including former spouses, lumped together with parents, grandparents, and disabled older children.

We know that such data does exist from the Defense Finance and Accounting Service (DFAS), since it receives notices to garnish wages for child support, alimony, etc., and pays allowances to divorced members who are supporting dependents, and pays out the spouse's share of retired pay as the court orders. Other sources for demographic data on the Uniformed Services include the following: American Forces Information Service (Alexandria, VA), Defense Manpower Data Center (Arlington, VA), Office of Family Policy (DoD, Pentagon), and the U.S. Bureau of the Census.

Since the USFSPA originally was directed at nonworking spouses, we have chosen to highlight some of the employment statistics for women over the past 20 or so years. The MFRC does list in its *Profile* spouse employment statistics.

The percentage of women age 16 or older in the work force grew from 51 percent in 1979 to 58 percent in 1992 overall. The proportion of military spouses in the labor force increased from 54 percent in 1985 to 65 percent in 1992 (not broken down by age). In 2005, women will make up about 48 percent of the U.S. civilian work force, with the percentage of military spouses in the work force projected to be 63 percent.

Women age 35 to 44 have seen the fastest gains in labor-force participation, from 64 percent in 1979 to 77 percent in 1992. Older married women are more likely to work than previously, while older single women are less likely to work.

Economists are forecasting that labor rates for never-married women age 55-64 may be declining, as they are more likely to have worked and have had a job with a pension plan, thus being able to retire earlier.

Two-income marriages are now becoming the norm. In 1963, 78 percent of married white women between the ages of 18 and 44, and 71 percent of married black women in the same age bracket, were in marriages where the husband provided 70 percent of all the family income. In 1992, according to a large government survey, 47 percent of the 18-44 year-old white wives and 56 percent of the black wives were in co-provider marriages.

The women's movement in the 1970s helped increase the number of women entering the military, thereby increasing the ranks of male non-military spouses. In 1973, male spouses of female service members were finally recognized as bona fide dependents, but it took the U.S. Supreme Court, in the landmark case of *Frontiero v. Richardson*, to do so. The majority of male spouses has some prior military service.

Dual-career couples abound in the military, with 50,343 military men and 43,971 military women married to someone who also is in the active military, Reserves, or Guard (as of December, 1996). In FY 1997, 6.1 percent of active duty personnel were married to other active duty personnel. In FY 1997, 58.2 percent of active duty personnel were married, 38.1 percent were single, and 3.6 percent no longer married (DoD provided the statistics and it is unknown whether these figures include divorced and widowed personnel).

Divorce rates for military members vary. According to 1992 statistics, nearly 40 percent of ranks E-7 to E-9 were divorced. (Note: This was their marital status for that year and does not mean that 40 percent of them divorced in that year.) Approximately 26 percent of officers ranked O-4 (major, lieutenant commander) and above were divorced, and the Air Force had the highest percentage of divorced members.

The Uniformed Services Former Spouses' Protection Act

On September 8, 1982, the Uniformed Services Former Spouses' Protection Act (USFSPA),[1] Public Law 97-252, 96 Stat. 730 (1982), was signed into law. The provisions of the USFSPA are found at 10 U.S.C. §1408 (1982). The effective date was 1 February 1983, but it was made retroactive to 25 June 1981. Courts are authorized to award up to 50 percent of the military member's[2] retired pay (or up to 65 percent including court-ordered child support) in a divorce.[3]

Original Intent of USFSPA Still Laudatory

The original intent of the USFSPA was laudatory and remains so: to provide, in a divorce action, for the faithful spouse who had loyally supported the military member's career. The American Retirees Association has always advocated traditional support for deserving former spouses, as well as a fair and equitable division of the marital assets. But the USFSPA has created mass confusion in the state courts where decisions based on precedent have, in many cases, resulted in great injustices, primarily due to the myriad of interpretations of the USFSPA, nationwide.

It is not believed that Congress ever envisioned the problems the USFSPA has caused: among them, that it has created, in many cases, another class of affected personnel: the military retiree and his[4] or her current family, at the expense of the military member.[5]

How This Book Came About

This book, as well as the first, has come about for two main reasons. First, while there is a lot of information on the USFSPA, the bulk of it was published in the 1982-86 time-frame, primarily in military law publications, law reviews, and family law journals. The military law journals are not readily available to the typical layperson, and even military legal offices do not always carry them. Thus, neither the military member nor the spouse has ready access to the information most needed to learn about and understand how federal law can affect their divorce.

Second, it is not only the experience of the American Retirees Association and its members, but the experience of military spouses as well, that many attorneys know little, if anything, about this law, or worse, do not understand it. Legal counsel's knowledge of this law is, obviously, important. But it should be the cornerstone of an attorney's representation if his or her client is a military member or the spouse of a military member. As part of a military family, the member's or spouse's decision to divorce is complicated by issues (explained in Chapter 8) that civilian couples usually do not have to grapple with. These are issues that arise from circumstances relating to the military member's service.

Our first book could be considered the "macro" approach—history of the law, broad controversies, and general information. This second book is the "micro" approach—details by state, more information to take to your attorney, and more depth on a number of issues that both parties need to know to negotiate their divorce. Input for ideas in this second book has come from thousands of phone calls, letters, faxes, and e-mail that we have received since the publication of the first book.

How You Can Benefit From Reading This Book

Our experience, in hearing from hundreds of military members and their spouses, indicates that the majority of military people, including spouses, have no idea about the law that affects their retired pay in a divorce. And without knowing what the law is and how it could affect your divorce, you run the risk of overlooking the many issues that need to be addressed in your decree, including the appropriate wording. Once the decision to divorce has been made and you begin the process of seeking an equitable dissolution, both your goals and your attorney's goal should be to:

1. Ensure that the decree will not be reopened because of a lack of knowledge or misinterpretation of the USFSPA or the omission of important military issues;
2. Verify that the coverage of military issues insures the decree is recognized by the military finance center as being in conformance with the federal law, obviating the need for subsequent modification or clarification.
3. Identify and disclose all the federal benefits that currently exist so that successful negotiations between both parties can result in a fair and equitable distribution of the assets.

Why We Wrote the Book—Why Not An Attorney?

Certainly, there are qualified attorneys who could write on this subject (and have). But we wanted to give you some insight from our perspective for several reasons.

First, many attorneys have never served in the military and have no idea what it is like to face combat or to be under constraints and restrictions due to military service. They often lack knowledge of military benefits and how these benefits are tied to various service requirements. Thus, it is virtually impossible to empathize with the military member's case. Further, lawyer-client communications are often limited because of the adversarial nature of divorces and the myriad of issues associated with a military divorce that are not usually addressed or adjudicated in a civilian divorce.

Second, ARA has been on the receiving end of many expressions of dismay over the military divorce process and has heard the problems from all sides (including that of the non-military spouse). From that perspective, we regularly hear the "horror stories" of our military members and spouses who occasionally may not have received the best legal representation. As a result, ARA has taken the lead in seeing that military personnel, Congress, veterans' organizations, and the legal community are kept up to date on the issues surrounding the division of military retired pay in a divorce.

Third, we are rather appalled, not so much at the lack of understanding by military personnel and retirement offices of the law in this area, but by the military services' deliberate omission of it, especially since this is a law which can significantly impact their lives in retirement. Indeed, military recruits are not briefed on the USFSPA upon entering the service; nor are those who attend retirement briefings given the information they should have about this law. Consequently, updated information has not been provided to military personnel with any degree of regularity. Even many military lawyers, from our experience, do not know the details of this law and, furthermore, they are rarely military divorce specialists who can tell you how the law is being applied in their states, based on *recent* or precedent-setting cases.

If You Are An Attorney Reading This Book

If you are an attorney, you know that the lack of communication is one of the biggest complaints of clients, and, as such, can quickly sour the attorney-client relationship. Divorce is a highly emotional issue for the client, and any miscommunication can aggravate or stall the proceedings for the divorce.

You may or may not have a client who has already gone through the "emotional" divorce and who is now ready to move on with the "legal" divorce. In any case, you are dealing with a military member who has strong emotional ties to the 20 or more years he or she has served to earn the military retired pay, or you may be dealing with a spouse who feels he or she has made a significant investment in the member's career. You must be able to appreciate what the service member has contributed in service to our country, as well as the feelings of the spouse who believes that he or she has gone through a lot to earn it, too. Often, both parties are dissatisfied with the latitude granted to state courts to treat and divide their assets.

To clear up misunderstandings about military retired pay, and its associated federal benefits, you may want to have your clients read this book for the basics, and then return to address questions based on their newly acquired knowledge. By doing so, you will not have to spend your time, or your client's money, to explain the basics. You may find it more efficient to spend your time explaining what you can and cannot do for them, depending on your state's treatment of the USFSPA.

If you are not as familiar with the USFSPA and its implications as you would like to be, or if your client has a unique situation (e.g., a mix of active duty and reserve time), you may want to call the American Retirees Association. It will refer you to experienced USFSPA attorneys and other professionals who work with other attorneys on the specific military aspects of divorce cases. At the very least, you will find in this book one of the best sources for all the items of discovery that military couples must examine.

SBP and Disability

In addition to the USFSPA, two other issues often arise in military divorce cases. These are the Survivor Benefit Plan (SBP) and disability compensation, where non-disability retired pay is waived to accept VA[6] disability pay.

The SBP is a program designed to provide income protection to spouses, dependent survivors, or former spouses of service members who die in retirement or on active duty after reaching retirement eligibility. The SBP is often a complicated negotiating point in divorces because of its cost to the member. It becomes even more so when there is both a former spouse and a current spouse. Eligibility requirements are not as stringent as for retirement pay. Specific information on SBP is widely available, and ARA has reprinted information on the subject (see Chapter 11) found in various almanacs published by Uniformed Services Almanac, Inc. Two other sources for SBP information include The Retired Officers Association (TROA), Alexandria, Virginia, and the Army Air Force Mutual Aid Association (AAFMA)[7] in Arlington, Virginia.

Except for information regarding VA disability as determined by the *Mansell*[8] decision, the reader is encouraged to seek information on VA disability retirement from the local VA medical center and other veterans' organizations, such as the American Legion and Disabled American Veterans.

Not only is the VA disability compensation tax exempt, allowing the retiree to take home a greater share of retired pay,[9] but the USFSPA provides that VA disability pay is exempt from inclusion in the disposable retired pay awarded to an ex-spouse in a divorce action. Unfortunately, some courts are currently ignoring this prohibition. This book includes the controversy over the awarding of disability retired pay, and you are advised to review the various treatment of same by the states in Chapter 12, *51 Flavors and Counting*.

Why Book II?

There are approximately 10,000 copies of *Divorce and the Military* in circulation. This does not necessarily provide a measure of the scope of interest in the subject. More likely it represents the difficulty of reaching people who need to know that there is an authoritative source of information on the military divorce process and that there exists an organization (viz. the ARA) to which they can turn for advice and assistance. This is not surprising because the DoD does not brief its uniformed personnel on the existence of the USFSPA. Military members and their spouses must rely mostly on word of mouth during their married years and delay a face-to-face encounter with the realities of the USFSPA until after a decision to divorce, when an informed attorney explains the implications of federal intervention in a process (viz. divorce) traditionally reserved for the states.

There are now approximately 85,000 military divorces which have involved a USFSPA award. In addition, there are an uncounted number of divorces, prior to 25 June

1981, where military retired pay was awarded as marital property. More than half of the ex-spouses now receiving a share of their (former) military mate's retired pay are receiving it, via direct payment, from the DFAS. The number of divorces where a USFSPA award is involved is growing at the rate of approximately 600 per month. This, alone, would justify the continued publication of a book which provides authentic, straightforward, unbiased information on the military divorce process—and is useful to BOTH parties and their legal counsel. But there is another consideration.

Despite a constantly growing body of evidence that the history of the USFSPA is replete with examples of discrimination, unfairness, imbalance and inequity, neither Congress nor the Pentagon has shown much interest in reforming it. Indeed, most of the public pronouncements on the subject range from disinterested to actively opposed. This contrasts dramatically with what has been going on behind the scenes.

Since the enactment of the USFSPA in September 1982, the laws pertaining to divorce in the military have been amended 23 times. Only *two* of these amendments were the result of public hearings. The remaining 21 were effectuated by the attachment of obscure riders to mainstream legislation—without public hearings or debate. The results have been overwhelmingly in favor of ex-spouses who have benefited in 18 instances, while military members have benefited only once. This circumstance, alone, warrants an update of the original book in order to shine some light on the products of a process with a material impact on the lives in retirement of military members and those of their spouses, ex or current.

Finally, the authors have added five new chapters: "Federal Benefits," "Financial Management Before and After Your Divorce," "Survivor Benefit Plan," "51 Flavors and

Counting," and "Bits and Pieces." These new topics evolved from the questions and responses we have received since the original book was published. The appendices have also expanded.

What This Book Leaves Out

Associated with military retired pay is a host of entitlements, such as the use of military commissaries and exchanges, and access to military medical services. We have included information on benefits in Chapter 9 to help identify your current financial situation and formulate your negotiating positions, since many of these federal benefits may not be available once the service member retires. Situations vary as to whether such benefits or entitlements extend to a former spouse and even to members in the Reserve or Guard. Details on military benefits can be obtained from any military installation, online, veterans and other military associations, and publications published by the Uniformed Services Almanac, Inc. Military legal offices should be able to provide specifics as well.

The details of various decisions regarding divorce—specific state laws on alimony, child support, and financial planning considerations—are not addressed here. We have included in this book, however, information on various divorce issues as they pertain to each state (see Appendix O). This information is not meant to serve as the basis for any decisions you make and, as always, ARA advises you to seek competent professional assistance.

One last point needs to be stressed. This book will not have the answer to every question that may arise as you gain knowledge in this area or go through your own divorce. It is not a stand-alone, self-help book on how to divorce, or a guide to domestic relations' law, or a substitute for consulting an attorney or other professional.

This book will, however, provide the information you need to recognize whether the federal law will affect your divorce, how to seek competent professional help, and how to organize your papers to work with your attorney and spouse to fully disclose the military and other matters that need to be addressed.

This book will help *educate* the service member, the spouse, and their attorneys. As many have realized throughout history: "Knowledge is power" (Francis Bacon, 1561-1626); "Forwarned, forearmed" (Cervantes, 1547-1616); and finally, "Ignorance of the law excuses no one..." (John Selden, 1584-1654). *You* are in the best position to protect your rights, whether you are the service member or the spouse, when you are fully informed about them.[10]

INTRODUCTION ENDNOTES

1. The abbreviation "USFSPA" is used to refer to the Uniformed Services Former Spouses' Protection Act. The word "Act" and the abbreviation "FSPA" are also used to refer to this public law.

2. The following terms are used interchangeably throughout this book: military member, member, service member, uniformed service member, military spouse, spouse, ex-spouse, former spouse.

3. The term "military divorce" has been coined to mean a divorce in which at least one of the parties is a military member (active duty, reserve, or retired). This term is not legally recognized (a divorce is a divorce), although you will sometimes hear a divorce between a military member and spouse referred to as such for distinction purposes. As used in this book, "military divorce" includes a divorce of a member of *any* of the Uniformed Services.

4. Throughout this book, the impersonal pronouns "he" and "she" are used to refer to either the member or spouse. They are understood to mean "he" or "she." The USFSPA applies equally to male and female members, although the 1980s congressional hearings focused on the spouse who was the "wife."

5. See Chapter 16, "Legislative Environment," for an update of the legislation that has benefited the former spouse only.

6. The Veterans Administration was elevated to department level and is now called the Department of Veterans Affairs. The abbreviation "VA" is still used to refer to various veterans' benefits and programs.

7. See Appendix P of this book for information on AAFMA and TROA.

8. *Mansell v. Mansell*, 104 L.Ed.2d 275, 109 S.Ct. 2023, 10 EBC 2521.

9. A bill was introduced in 1992 that would allow the military retiree to keep the disability compensation without having to forfeit a like amount of regular retired pay. The "concurrent receipt" bill died, but was revived in the 103rd Congress. Since then numerous other bills have been introduced but have gone nowhere.

10. Readers may find references to inequities in the USFSPA as they relate to the military member. It is not the intent of the publisher to offend the spouse, military member, or the attorneys, but rather to cite the facts.

CONTENTS

federal retirement programs...#4—The spouse is always treated as the "innocent" party...#5—Award of retired pay based on rank at retirement, not at time of divorce... #6—Circumvention of the USFSPA's protection of disability pay...#7—Restrictions associated with receiving retired pay apply to the retiree but not the spouse...#8—Impact of civil service employment on USFSPA award...#9—USFSPA payments survive remarriage of the ex-spouse... #10— Separation bonuses...#11—No statute of limitations...#12—Early retirement

Truth and consequences...The legal morass...Legal and other precedents...The bottom line

Female military must get in line behind the nonmilitary wife...DACOWITS...Times have changed...Career discrimination

Reservists are not always compensated with money...Does the "plight" apply to spouses of reservists...Reserve retirement system...Creditable service...Active duty for retirement eligibility purposes...Computation of Reserve retired pay...Reservists and the USFSPA...Reservists have fewer benefits than ex-spouses...Bottom line for reservists—you are subject to the USFSPA, however...

"Military" divorce vs. "civilian" divorce...Issues unique to a military divorce...Military benefits an important consideration...20/20/20 and 20/20/15 spouses...Abused Military Dependents Act...Dependent support...SBP—Don't ignore

the pre-retirement notification requirements...Social Security...Jurisdiction...Timing can work to both the military member's and spouse's advantage...Do's and don't's... Compliance with the law is in your best interests

Allowances...Bonuses...Child care...Civil Service employment...Combat-zone and other operations exclusion benefits...Commissary benefits...COLA...Dental benefits...Dual compensation and pay...Early or forced retirement...Educational benefits...Employment benefits...Exchange shopping privileges...Federal tax advantages...Financial resources—retirement funds ...Hardship duty pay...Hazardous duty and hostile fire pay...Health benefits...Homeowner assistance...Incentive and special pay...Leave...Life insurance...PCS relocation reimbursements... Promotions...Retired pay...Separation pay and bonuses...Social Security benefits for divorced spouses...Space-available travel...Temporary disability retirement list...Temporary duty...Transition benefits...Bottom line

Alimony ...Allowances...Automobile insurance...Bank and other financial accounts...Bonuses...Children...Credit cards...Education...Employment with the Federal government...Health insurance...House...Legal fees...Life insurance...Moving expenses...Property transfers...Retired pay--conditions under which you could lose it...Separation date—marital...Separation date—military...Separation pay and SSB/VSI bonuses—Reserve and Guard...Social Security...Spouse preference...Support payments...Tax considerations...Wills...Post-divorce financial management...In summary

benefits... 9. Consider a separation agreement... 10. Don't forget SBP, life insurance, and other survivor benefits... 11. Keep yourself informed... 12. Get organized and know when to cut your losses...One final note about records...Summary

Visible legislation...1990 Hearings...Retroactivity finally laid to rest...Disposable pay redefined...Stealth legislation...Ex-Spouse gets first call on SBP...Protection for abused military dependents and former spouses...Prevention of circumvention of court order by waiver of (military) retired pay to enhance Civil Service retirement annuity...Former spouse access to disability pay...Political flak vest...Fairness amendments...On the legislative horizon

What and where...If you need information...The ARA's platform...ARA's proposals for reform of the USFSPA...Afterthought

Why no further equity changes to the USFSPA?...Civics 101—Congress does not have to be consistently fair...Read it in your military newspaper first!...NIMBY syndrome...Ignorance or apathy?...The military member is not the lone ranger...What you can do

When the service member might lose retired pay...Keeping your military status current...Disbursement of retired pay...Pension funds to which you may be entitled...Soldiers' and Sailor's Civil Relief Act...Don't stir the pot...One final thought or two

Book Order Form

Membership Application

FOREWORD

Both members of any military marriage headed for a divorce, as well as those already divorced, need to understand the federal laws relevant to their interest in military retirement benefits. These include the Uniformed Services Former Spouses' Protection Act, the Survivor Benefit Plan, and the laws related to medical benefits, base privileges and other entitlements which may be affected by divorce. Equally important is that the information obtained be current since the laws are constantly changing.

Unfortunately, many military couples enter into the divorce process with little or no understanding of their respective rights and those aspects of a military divorce which distinguish it from the divorce process in the civil sector. Even worse is the possibility that legal counsel for either or both parties is unaware of these distinguishing characteristics and must either go through a learning experience at the client's expense or recommend a less-than-ideal settlement for either or both.

Marsha Thole and Frank Ault have done an outstanding job for both parties and their attorneys, an evenhanded presentation of the vital information unique to a military divorce. It truly qualifies as a "don't leave home without it" piece of work. *Divorce and the Military II* builds on the foundation of the original book, first published in 1994, providing a complete update on legislative and other changes impacting the military divorce process. Five new chapters and an expanded compilation of appendices greatly enhance its utility as a standard reference text.

In my experience both military members and their spouses are often poorly informed—and, therefore, poorly prepared—to make the decisions necessary to achieve the fair and equitable treatment of both parties to the divorce process. Often, especially in the case of enlisted personnel, military retirement benefits represent the principal assets of the marriage. Even when this is not the case, the possibility of the contemporaneous award of military retired pay, alimony, child support and the other assets of the marriage presents formidable challenges to both parties and their attorneys in achieving a satisfactory settlement. Divorce frequently creates a "pay now" or "pay later" situation. Many of my clients have, unfortunately, fallen into a "pay later" situation and have hired me to try to correct the deficiencies in a poorly crafted divorce decree in which the unique aspects of a military divorce were not properly addressed. In most cases, these are the result of the lack of timely, accurate information, either on the part of counsel or clients who were not sufficiently informed to evaluate the legal advice they were provided.

Attorneys should purchase a supply of *Divorce and the Military II* to give their clients in order to improve the quality of client-counsel communications. For their part, clients should insist that their lawyers are conversant with the contents of the book. In divorce, payment is an almost inevitable consequence. The objective is to avoid the "pay later" outcome because then the situation may be beyond retrieval. This book can be a major factor in the "pay now" divorce settlement: for military members, their spouses, and their attorneys.

James N. Higdon
Capt. USNR (Ret.)

James N. Higdon is a partner in Higdon, Hardy & Zuflacht, San Antonio, Texas. His experience in divorce cases involving military members and their spouses is extensive, and he is a member of the

State Bar of Texas, Sections on Family Law, Litigation, Military Law, and ADR. He is also board certified in Family Law, and a Fellow with the American Academy of Matrimonial Lawyers, among other memberships. He is the author of numerous professional legal articles, and has presented numerous speeches, seminars, and continuing education classes in all aspects of military retirement, including the Soldiers' and Sailors' Civil Relief Act, SBP, Voluntary Separation Benefit Programs, and division of retired pay.

1

WHAT YOU DON'T KNOW
CAN
HURT YOU

Imagine for a moment the following scenario:

You were taken prisoner of war and sent to a North Vietnam POW camp from the fall of 1967 until repatriation in 1973—seven years. You were released and returned home only to be served with divorce papers. Then picture being told by a court that it has found that the "date of separation" from your spouse was April 1, 1970, and she did not have to repay any of your pay and allowances that she spent after the date of separation, that she was entitled to your accrued leave pay, monies paid to you under the War Crimes Act for inhumane treatment, and she was entitled to your remaining pay, even though California law stated that earnings and accumulations after the date of separation were separate property. This was on top of the fact that she openly had affairs during the time you spent in the North Vietnam prison. The court also awarded her your home, your car, and 42.7 percent of your military retired pay, and you were ordered to pay child support and spousal support (despite her marriage to one of the attorneys who represented her in the divorce). And, despite your four children all telling the court they wanted to live with you, you received custody of only the two older children.

This, unfortunately, is not the product of someone's imagination. It happened to a military member. Consider the following other actual cases:

A staff sergeant served in combat with the Marine Corps during Operation Desert Storm. Upon return to his duty station in Twenty-Nine Palms, California, with plans to retire after 20 years of honorable military service, he found his wife of 19 years cohabitating with another man. In May 1991 his wife abandoned him and their three children and filed for a no-fault divorce in California. The divorce was final in January 1992, with the spouse receiving half the property of the marriage plus 47.5 percent per month of the sergeant's military retired pay. The payments will continue until his death or hers, even if she remarries.

A U.S. Marine Corps sergeant major served 25 years in the military. He was married in 1949 and divorced in 1970. The California court found the wife to be an "unfit mother" and awarded custody of the five minor children to the military mem-

ber (husband). He was remarried in December 1970 to a woman who also had five children, and they raised all ten. His ex-wife remarried, and then sued in 1987 for retroactive award of his retired pay. In November 1988, the court awarded his ex-spouse 38 percent of his retired pay for life.[1]

An Air Force colonel retired in 1970 after serving 28 years. He was married for 23 years. No military retired pay was awarded at divorce, in accordance with the state law. In May 1987 the ex-spouse filed retroactively for (and received) 50 percent of his retired pay. The ex-spouse remarried another military husband; he died and she receives survivor benefits from the second marriage. She was married a third time to a retired USAF officer. The ex-spouse now receives military retired pay from one prior husband and survivor benefits from another, while sharing the retired pay of the third military (retired) member.

An Air Force master sergeant served 20 years in the military, including two tours in Vietnam. He and his wife were married the last 16 years of his military career. While stationed in Alaska, and entering his last year before retirement, he was sued for divorce by his wife (who had found a boyfriend) and thrown out of the house. The Alaska court awarded his ex-spouse 40 percent of his retired pay as property and 27 percent as child support. Out of his monthly $851 retirement check (at the time), he received $130 after taxes. The ex-spouse at the time was making $34,000 a year and living with her boyfriend (who was earning $26,000).

A doctor (lieutenant colonel) in the Air Force who had returned to active duty in 1985 had previously been divorced in Fairfax County, Virginia, in 1980. He remarried and had a second family. At the time, he had been paying alimony of $6,000 per month until he was forced to close his private practice. His ex-wife was employed as a nursing supervisor, earning $35,000 per year, with her own wealth and assets in excess of $2,000,000. In May 1987 his ex-wife garnished his wages for $90,000 per year, with the Fairfax courts stating he had to "keep his ex-wife in the style to which she had become accustomed; that his joining the USAF had made her suffer." There was lack of proper notification and legal representation prior to garnishment.

*The wife of a USAF colonel divorced him in 1964 and remarried shortly thereafter. She was awarded alimony, and received 75 percent of the marital assets. He remarried in 1971 and retired in 1972. The former spouse sued him for arrearages in 1987 plus prospective payments; she requested but was denied an annuity for a like amount of prospective payment for her estate. The military retiree and his second wife of 18 years had already spent $40,000 in legal fees when a judgment was entered in 1989, awarding the former spouse two years' arrearages and 33 percent of **gross pay**[2] for the colonel's life based on his full 30 years' service and subsequent promotion (they were previously married 19 years out of the 21 years of his active duty time at the time of separation).*

Unfair but Legal

If these cases sound unfair or outrageous to you, please be advised that they are entirely legal and strictly routine for Vietnam, Desert Storm, and other military veterans. Most veterans have not been informed by their military leadership about a law that will materially reduce the amount of military retired pay they will receive. Whether they are retired and already receiving retired pay or on active duty and expecting to receive full retired pay, they need to be informed about this law.

Treatment of Retired Pay—the Result of Two Major Legal Actions

In accordance with federal law, divorce courts may treat military retired pay as a marital property asset. Worse, it may be treated either as property or as income, or both, and be subject to division, with a subsequent award to the ex-spouse. This unique treatment of military retired pay is the result of two major legal actions.[3]

The first is the U.S. Supreme Court decision in *McCarty v. McCarty* (453 U.S. 210 [1981]). On 26 June 1981, the Court ruled that "the military retirement system confers no entitlement to retired pay upon the retired member's spouse and does not embody even a limited community property concept." The court further stated that "the application of community property principles to military retired pay threatens grave harm to clear and substantial Federal interests." In its decision, however, the court recognized that the situation of an ex-spouse of a retired military member could sometimes be a serious one, possibly resulting in destitution or some other unfair predicament, and invited Congress to legislatively review and change the situation.

And change the situation it did. Congress inserted a rider to the Defense Authorization Act for FY 1983, which is known as the Uniformed Services Former Spouses' Protection Act (USFSPA). This public law (97-252) was passed in September 1982, with an effective date of 1 February 1983, and backdated to 25 June 1981, one day before the *McCarty* decision. Thus, the USFSPA circumvented but did not supersede the *McCarty* ruling by providing that "a (state) court may treat disposable retired pay payable to a (military) member for pay periods beginning after 25 June 1981, either as property solely of the member or as property of the member and his[4] spouse in accordance with the law of the jurisdiction of such court."

States Had Been Dividing Retired Pay in Divorces

Up until this time, some states had already been including and treating military retired pay the same way they treated civilian pensions, and making an award of this marital asset to the spouse. Now, with the passage of the USFSPA, the state courts could treat military retired pay as both pay and property, using it, in addition, as a source of alimony as well as child support.

Although you may conclude, after reading this book, that the *McCarty* decision should go down in history as one of the more important and controversial decisions of the Supreme Court, we must report that it did not make the top 100.[5] The intricacies of a "military" divorce and division of military retirement benefits are usually neither known nor understood by military people who contemplate divorce. Moreover, knowledge of *McCarty* and its consequences is not widespread in the civilian legal community or in Congress. This makes it imperative that both parties—husband and wife—and their attorneys be informed. This book has been written to do just that.

Problems Not Foreseen

Many military members do not think that Congress envisioned the problems that are now occurring. The USFSPA states that state courts *may* divide a military member's retired pay in a divorce action. But, in reviewing its history, the USFSPA has operated in *theory* as an *option*, but, in *practice*, as a *mandate*. Its track record provides irrefutable evidence that the USFSPA unfairly discriminates against divorcing military members who manifestly do not enjoy protection under the law equal to that provided their civilian counterparts. So long as courts continue to automatically make lifetime awards of military retired pay to former spouses, regardless of whether the ex-spouse remarries or is financially or economically stable, the courts will continue to create a class of affected individuals other than the spouses it was designed to assist: the military retiree and his or her current family.

We realize that for every "horror" story military members can cite, former spouses' groups can cite one, also. Nevertheless, honorable military veterans have never subscribed to the theory of the "throwaway spouse" and readily agree that the proper goal of a divorce settlement is the fair and equitable treatment of *both* members of a military marriage, with the recognition, as well, of nonmonetary contributions of both parties. The American Retirees Association (ARA) believes that this is possible, even in the era of the no-fault divorce, and taking into account the substantial social, economic, and cultural changes that have altered the status of military families since the early 1980s.

CHAPTER ENDNOTES

1. Up until November 1992, a former spouse could petition a court to reopen the divorce case to apply for retroactive division of the retired pay if the divorce occurred before 25 June 1981. This unfair loophole was closed with the passage of Public Law 101-510, §555 in November 1990. The case is used as an illustration of the inequities that existed in the USFSPA, and to show that, with perseverance, a law can get changed.

2. At the time, the federal law allowed for an award of only *net disposable retired pay.*

3. Another very important decision handed down by the U.S. Supreme Court in 1989, *Mansell v. Mansell,* exempted disability pay, waived in lieu of retired pay, from being divided in a divorce.

4. The USFSPA applies equally to male *and* female military members.

5. Reference is made to the book, *The Supreme Court: A Citizen's Guide,* by Robert J. Wagman (New York: Pharos Books, 1993). The book cites the 100 most significant decisions the court has made.

2

WHAT USFSPA IS AND WHAT IT IS NOT

Many military members, their spouses, and even attorneys, are either uninformed or ill informed when it comes to the provisions of the Uniformed Services Former Spouses' Protection Act. As a result, they can get "blindsided" by not knowing what this law means to them. Thus, some discussion of basic precepts is in order. Subsequent chapters of this book elaborate on those concepts.

What Does the USFSPA Do?

Simply stated, this federal law authorizes state courts to treat military retired pay as property and to award up to 50 percent of it to a former spouse in a divorce.

Who USFSPA Applies To

USFSPA is applicable to both male and female members of the Uniformed Services, Regular and

Reserve Components, who are on active duty, in the reserves, or already retired, in the following:

- Army
- Navy
- Air Force
- Marine Corps
- Coast Guard
- National Guard and Reserve
- Public Health Service
- National Oceanographic and Atmospheric Administration.

Where USFSPA Applies—Locations

USFSPA is applicable in any court of competent jurisdiction in the following:

- The 50 states
- District of Columbia
- Commonwealth of Puerto Rico
- Guam
- American Samoa
- Virgin Islands
- Northern Mariana Islands
- Trust Territory of the Pacific Islands
- Any foreign country with which the United States has an agreement to honor its court orders.

USFSPA Characteristics

The basic characteristics of USFSPA are as follows:

- Applies to all military divorces* subsequent to 25 June 1981.

---

* "Military divorce" is the term used throughout this book to define a divorce between a member of any "uniformed service" and his or her spouse (who may or may not also be a military member).

- Prohibits some, but not all, retroactive awards of military retired pay prior to 25 June 1981.
- Permits military retired pay to be classified as *property* (as opposed to income) for purposes of a divorce settlement.
- Permits the ex-spouse to receive up to 50 percent of the military member's retired pay, directly from the finance center, based on the number of years married concurrent with military service.
- Ignores fault, merit, need, ability to pay, or respective financial circumstances.
- Prohibits courts from ordering a military member to retire in order to commence USFSPA payments (but does not prevent the courts from ordering spousal support payments to begin before the service member is actually retired (see Chapter 12).
- Does not allow courts to order a military member to begin making USFSPA payments before the member has actually retired.
- Requires the establishment of a court's jurisdiction for a partitioning under the USFSPA.
- For divorces final before 5 February 1991, it defines "disposable pay" as the total monthly pay, less:
  - existing debts to the government
  - amounts of retired pay forfeited due to court-martial
  - waivers for VA disability (Title 38), Civil Service Pay (Title 5) or DoD disability (Chapter 61, Title 10)
  - SBP premiums when the former spouse is the beneficiary
  - amounts withheld for federal, state, or local income taxes
- For divorces final on or after 5 February 1991, "disposable pay" has been redefined and *does not* in-

clude subtractions for personal debts or taxes. All of the other above listed exemptions remain in effect.

- Provides for payments of retired pay to the abused ex-spouses of military personnel whose entitlement to retired pay has been terminated or denied.

No-Fault Feature

- The military member appears to wear the "black hat"—i.e., the member is considered to be at fault, given that the award of military retired pay (as defined in the federal law) is not based on merit, need, or ability to pay.

Misconceptions about USFSPA

Many military members are ill informed or uninformed when it comes to the applicability of the USFSPA. *Many military members wrongly believe that the USFSPA:*

- Returned a "pre-existing right" (to divide military retired pay as marital property) to the states.

  As confirmed by *McCarty*, the states did not have such authority prior to the USFSPA. The USFSPA now allows the state courts to consider military retired pay in the same way they apply state law to other "pension plans."

- Is automatically a part of the military divorce process.

  Just as the state courts retain authority to establish settlement agreements involving other property and income, they retain the right to determine whether military retired pay should be included or excluded as property of either party.

- Precludes the court from concurrently ordering alimony or child support.

  Since the state may treat the military retired pay as "property," a state could exclude it from consideration as a source of alimony and child support *in addition to* the award of the retired pay. However, the award of the share of the military retired pay does not preclude the contemporaneous award of alimony or child support payments, or both, whether retired pay is the only source for these payments.

- Applies only to male military members.

  While it is true that male military members significantly outnumber the female members, USFSPA is gender neutral and applies equally to both sexes.

- Does not apply to Reserves (and Guard).

  This law applies to active duty, retired, and reserve/guard (whether active duty, inactive status, or retired), pay and nonpay categories.

- To qualify for payments, the benefiting ex-spouse must be married to the military member at least 10 years.

  The marriage need not have lasted 10 years for the spouse to acquire a share of or interest in the military member's retired pay. The marriage *does*, however, need to have lasted 10 years (during 10 years of creditable military time) in order for the ex-spouse to receive a direct payment (irrevocable) from the DFAS.

- Permits partitioning of active duty pay prior to retirement.[1]

   The USFSPA does not apply to active duty pay. A court, however, can order the active duty military member to pay alimony or other support, including child support, from whatever source it deems appropriate, and then order the commencement of USFSPA payments upon retirement. Some states have ordered payment if the service member has the requisite 20 years to retire but remains on active duty. California and New Mexico are two of these states.

- Includes partitioning of disability pay.

   The USFSPA prohibits the partitioning of certain disability pay. Moreover, the U.S. Supreme Court confirmed in the *Mansell* decision that military disability pensions are not marital property subject to division. However, the member's disability pay is being divided by some state courts,[2] in violation of that Supreme Court decision and, indeed, the provisions of the USFSPA itself.

- Is in addition to Survivor Benefit Plan premiums.

   The award of the Survivor Benefit Plan (SBP) to a former spouse is exclusive from an award of retired pay under USFSPA. In other words, an ex-spouse might not get any portion of the retired pay but might be named as the SBP beneficiary (as could children and others). SBP premiums are, however, deductible from the amounts involved in USFSPA payments to the same ex-spouse.

- Is the only recourse of the spouse of a military member in a divorce proceeding.

  Individuals married to military members have always had (and still have) access to all the remedies and protections available to non-military couples in divorce court.

Problems and Pitfalls

The military is unique and not just for its mission. Just as the military is singled out in a number of ways, some positive and some not so positive [e.g., frequently proposed cost-of-living-allowance (COLA) reductions in retired pay], so it has been with the USFSPA. These issues, as listed below, are explained further in Chapter 3.

- This law was not grandfathered.
- Payments continue after remarriage of the former spouse.
- USFSPA does not preclude contemporaneous awards of alimony, child support, or other support.
- USFSPA provides windfall benefits to the ex-spouse, often at the expense of a second spouse who has been married to the military member longer than the first spouse was.

- USFSPA does not preclude further garnishment of the military member's pay.[3]
- The military member has continuing federal obligations; the benefiting ex-spouse does not.[4]
- There is no statute of limitations on when the former spouse must file to receive the retired pay, thus leaving the service member in "financial limbo."

Two other problems need to be highlighted, as they have perhaps the greatest potential for affecting both partners' financial outcome in a military divorce:

- Military members are not being informed of this law.
- The civil legal community is generally not familiar with the complexities of this law.

It is important to know how this law can affect the service member's retired pay, and that the courts can give lifetime awards of a part of the military retired pay to the former spouse, based on the member's pay grade at retirement and *not at the time of divorce*, regardless of whether the ex-spouse remarries or is financially or economically stable. The next chapter addresses the various implications and problems that have arisen as a result of this law.

CHAPTER ENDNOTES

1. A July 1993 New Mexico court decision, *Ruggles v. Ruggles*, has ruled that a spouse can be awarded immediate payment of a *vested* pension, even though the other spouse has not begun receiving it. This applies to military retirement. While this appears to violate and preempt federal law, until a military divorce case is appealed in New Mexico, we do not know what

and restructuring, a 20-year career is no longer guaranteed. Despite what the federal law says (that payments under USFSPA cannot begin until the service member is receiving retired pay), other states are ignoring this provision. See Chapter 12 for other states that are ordering payment of retired pay before the service member has retired.

2. California and New Mexico are two of those states where courts have divided disability pay in violation of the *Mansell* decision. See Chapter 12 for other states' treatment of disability pay.

3. Under the USFSPA, specifically excluded from the definition of "disposable retired pay" that courts can consider as community property is (i) retired pay waived in order to receive disability pay from the Department of Veterans Affairs under Title 38 of the U. S. Code and (ii) disability pay received from DoD at the time of retirement under Chapter 61, Title 10, of the U. S. Code. However, some states are ignoring these specific exclusions in the USFSPA and are dividing disability pay (see Chapter 12). Moreover, pursuant to provisions in the Social Security Act, 42 U.S.C. 659, VA disability pay can be garnished to provide child support or alimony payments.

4. More than 4000 retired military members were recalled to active duty in 1991 during Operation Desert Storm. USFSPA beneficiaries were not subject to (recall to) active duty. Retirees have also been recalled as recently as March 1998 to support operations in the Middle East.

3

WHERE WERE YOU IN '82? (THINGS THE RECRUITER DIDN'T TELL YOU)

Historical Look at Community Property

First, a short historical look at the subject of community property is in order.[1,2] In earlier times, the man typically owned and controlled the wealth in a marriage. A divorce could leave the wife in a destitute state, and often did. Recognizing this unfairness, state laws gradually came to include a more balanced view of the assets acquired in a marriage. The concept of recognizing that each party contributes to the marriage is treated somewhat differently in each state; however, it can generally be said that states are either community property states (i.e., each party has a 50-50 property right to all that was acquired during the marriage) or adhere to a principle of equitable interest/distribution (may not necessarily be 50-50, but it is equitable).[3]

19

Just because one party brings home the paycheck does not mean the other party's non-monetary contributions do not deserve to be recognized. The Maryland courts have addressed this subject head-on:

> *The Commission does not believe that the people of Maryland today hold the view that a spouse whose activities within the marriage do not include the production of income has never contributed anything toward the purchase of property acquired by either or both spouses during the marriage. Its members believe that non-monetary contributions within a marriage are real and should be recognized in the event that the marriage is dissolved or annulled. As homemaker and parent and housewife and handyman (of either sex), as a man and a woman having equal rights under the law united into one family unit, in which each owes a duty to contribute his or her best efforts to the marriage, the undertakings of each are for the benefits of the family unit. In most cases, each spouse makes a contribution entitled to recognition, even though the standards or methods of quantifying a spouse's non-monetary contribution are inexact.*[4]

Tracing the history[5] of the matter of military retirement benefits as an asset in a divorce is not easy. Thus, only a narrative summary is presented here.

Landmark McCarty Decision—Precursor to the USFSPA

On 26 June 1981, the U.S. Supreme Court ruled 6-3, in *McCarty v. McCarty*, 453 U.S. 210 (1981), that federal law precluded the award of military non-disability retirement benefits as marital property upon divorce because a conflict was found between the property right issue for the spouse and the federal interests in the military retirement statutes. The issue was whether federal statutes granting non-disability military retirement benefits preempted California courts from dividing such benefits upon divorce.

The court's own words, in holding that federal law precludes a state court from dividing military retired pay according to state community property laws, were:

> *There is a conflict between the terms of the federal military retirement statutes and the community property right asserted by the appellee. The military retirement system confers no entitlement to retired pay upon the retired member's spouse, and does not embody even a limited community property concept. Rather the language, structure, and history of the statutes make it clear that retired pay continues to be the personal entitlement of the retiree.*

> *Moreover, the application of community property principles to military retired pay threatens grave harm to clear and substantial federal interests...In addition, such a division has the potential to interfere with the congressional goals of having the military retirement system serve as an inducement for enlistment and re-enlistment and as an encouragement to orderly promotion and a youthful military.*

There followed much turmoil, as many retirees quit paying former spouses the "community property" share of their military retired pay. Concomitantly, state courts, citing concepts of *res judicata*,[6] denied any application for cases already decided. Outraged ex-spouses had military members ordered back into court to make up and continue payments as well as to pay court costs and legal fees for both sides. Federal courts denied jurisdiction and appeals courts supported the divorce courts. For divorces during this period, the state courts had no choice but to find that the military retired pay was not community property.

Thus, the *McCarty* decision was not without controversy, with cries of unfairness not only from the military retiree but from the nonmilitary spouse of long-term marriages, and a "taking back" from the states of the power and authority (they had assumed they had) to divide military retirement benefits.

Supreme Court "Invites" Congressional Action

In the *McCarty* decision, the court "invited" congressional action, by making it clear that the source of any change in military retirement policy rested with Congress. The outcome of efforts to overrule *McCarty* was the signing into law on 8 September 1982, of the Uniformed Services Former Spouses' Protection Act,[7] Public Law 97-252, 96 Stat. 730 (1982). The provisions of the USFSPA, which counteract the *McCarty* decision, are found in 10 U.S.C. §1408 *et seq.* (1982). The effective date was 1 February 1983, but it was made retroactive to 25 June 1981, one day prior to the *McCarty* decision.

While the *McCarty* decision addressed only community property principles applicable to military retirement, it has been for all intents and purposes applicable to the division of marital property in equitable distribution jurisdictions. Our research has shown, however, that the more complicated, controversial, and complex cases have come out of California and Texas (both community property states), states where there is a heavy military representation, both active duty and retired. One must understand, however, that *McCarty* did not permit either community property or equitable distribution jurisdictions to classify military non-disability retired pay as community or marital property. And the USFSPA does not impinge on *McCarty* in that it does not prevent a court from awarding alimony or child support, or both, in addition to the retirement benefits.

USFSPA presents some unique situations because of the dates for the U.S. Supreme Court decision, the passage of USFSPA, and the retroactivity of USFSPA. Application of the law varies on when the divorce took place and whether the disposition of military retirement benefits was decided at that time. Thus, a case (up until the 1990 change to the law) may be decided based on (1) pre-*McCarty* state law (before 26 June 1981); (2) modification of a prior favorable judgment, due to a retroactive application of *McCarty*; (3) the gap period (from June 1981 to February 1983) during which federal law preempted state community property laws; or (4) retroactive application of USFSPA to allow the division of benefits paid during all pay periods after 25 June 1981 (the day before the date of the *McCarty* decision).

Mass Confusion in State Appellate Courts

Both *McCarty* and USFSPA created mass confusion in the appellate courts, and decisions based on precedent were, in many cases, ignored, primarily due to myriad interpretations given to *McCarty* and USFSPA. Retroactivity was extensively litigated (and still is today, but much less than before). USFSPA did not prohibit the reopening of cases, it merely permitted state courts to reconsider judgments in light of marital property and procedural laws without the presence of *McCarty*.

A cursory review of any cases in any state code will show that, nationwide, courts of appeals in the same state have taken almost as many different approaches to the problems of adjudicating military retirement benefits during the problematic *McCarty*-era and post USFSPA-era as there are reported cases on the subject.

How the Law Was Passed

The USFSPA permits the states to treat the military retired/retainer pay as they treat civilian pensions, with certain exceptions. The Act attracted little attention at the time it was passed, probably because it was a rider to the annual Department of Defense Authorization Act.

Sponsored by now-retired Rep. Patricia Schroeder (D-CO), the bill was intended to help former spouses left destitute by their military mates (assumed to be the husband) and to repay them for years invested in helping further the spouse's military career. It has done the opposite in many cases, creating hardships for military members and their second families, and former spouses who have had to return to court.

Many felt this law was unnecessary. Military spouses have always had the same range of divorce remedies as any other spouses, including garnishment of pay. Now, the military member feels as if he or she is being blamed for the breakup of the marriage. There is no requirement for the spouse to prove economic or financial need, or "contribution to the military member's career." Moreover, the law can (and has) "reward(ed)" miscreant spouses.

Unlike other retirement plans, the military plan has unique requirements. In order to receive retired/retainer pay, the military member must have served no less than

20 years of active creditable service. For the former spouse to receive direct payment from DFAS of up to 50 percent (65 percent to honor a garnishment for child or spousal support) of the disposable net retired pay, the marriage need only have lasted at least 10 years during which the member performed at least 10 years of creditable service.

The division of pay is considered separate from any alimony or child support. Further, because it is considered "property," the pay continues even after remarriage of the former spouse, unlike alimony and most other forms of spousal support. This has not precluded the states from awarding other amounts (including half of the retired pay) in cases where the military marriage lasted less than 10 years.

Post-USFSPA Enactment Problems Not Envisioned

It appears that Congress did not envision the problems that have occurred since the law was enacted. By automatically allowing lifetime awards of the military retirement check to former spouses, regardless of whether the ex-spouse remarries or is financially or economically stable, Congress has created a situation where it is possible that the military member or former spouse will have to return to court for clarification or modification issues.

As the reader will see in Chapter 16, nothing happened in Congress to change the law from 1982 forward until 1989 (with the exception of changes to 10 U.S.C. §1448 *et seq.*, the Survivor Benefit Plan).

CHAPTER ENDNOTES

1. In researching this subject, one may find references to its similarity with the pension laws of the Foreign Service and Central

Intelligence Agency. These two federal agencies' retirement plans are not addressed here.

2. Please note that this book addresses primarily the issue of non-disability military retirement benefits as divisible marital property. See Chapter 12 for states that are dividing disability retired pay.

3. Only an in-depth study of the results of a society with many two-income families could determine whether the concept of 50-50 should be more universally applied.

4. Report of The Governor's Commission on Domestic Relations Laws, at 3 (1978), as quoted in *Harper v. Harper*, 284 Md. 54, 448 A.2d 916, 920 (Md, 1982).

5. Prior to 1975 the federal government did not get involved in divorces vis-a-vis military retirement. In 1973, then Rep. Patricia Schroeder (D-CO) drafted legislation that became Public Law 93-647 and attached it to the Social Security Act. It allowed state courts to garnish active and retired pay for child support. In 1975 section 459 was effective to provide for garnishment of retired pay for alimony. Public Law 95-30 limited the amount of retired pay that could be garnished. Public Law 95-366 authorized the assignment of retired pay of a civilian employee to a former spouse in a community property settlement. In 1981 Rep. Schroeder proposed H.R. 3039 and H.R. 1711 for court-awarded military retirement benefits. Senator Dennis DeConcini (D-AZ) proposed S. 1453 to distribute military retirement benefits following divorce.

6. *Black's Law Dictionary* defines *res judicata* as: A matter adjudged; a thing judicially acted upon or decided; a thing or matter settled by judgment. Rule that a final judgment rendered by a court of competent jurisdiction on the merits is conclusive as to the rights of the parties and their privies, and, as to them, constitutes an absolute bar to a subsequent action involving the same claim, demand or cause of action.

7. This has sometimes been known as the "Schroeder Amendment," as it was initially introduced and sponsored by then Rep. Schroeder.

4

CONTROVERSY
APLENTY

Background

On the surface, it would not appear that the basic thrust
of the USFSPA—allowing state courts to treat military
retired/retainer pay as they treat civilian pensions, with
certain exceptions—would create problems. The law that
was enacted was intended to help former spouses left "destitute" (language in the Congressional hearings) by their
military mates and to repay them for years invested in
helping the spouse's military career. Unfortunately, it has
done the opposite in many cases.

These unique requirements have created a number of
controversies surrounding the USFSPA, as shown below,
many of which have been cited in divorce case appeals.
It is not our intent to resolve these controversies by discussion in this book, but rather to make you aware that
they have and continue to create problems as they are interpreted by each court. Further, while courts have usually rendered decisions based on "precedent," this has not

always been the case, even within the same jurisdiction, when it comes to military divorce judgments. See Chapter 12 for how the various states have treated this law.

Controversy #1 — Definition of Retired Pay and Its Treatment by the Courts

Perhaps the most talked about controversy is the anomaly created by the definition of military retired pay. The Department of Defense views military retired pay as reduced pay for reduced services. Military retired pay is defined in federal statutes as income, it is treated as income in a tax court, and it is treated as income in a bankruptcy court. But for purposes of USFSPA, state courts **may** treat it as *property* in a divorce action. Nowhere in statute or case law is military retirement compensation defined as either a pension or as property. One way to look at this controversy from the other side, and one of the ways it was seen when the law was enacted, is that military retired pay may be the only major asset that a military couple has. Military members in earlier days moved from one base or post to another every two years or so, making the acquisition of a house or other tangible marital assets somewhat out of the question. This is no longer always the case, as couples own real estate (often in more than one state), IRAs, and other investments.

This unique treatment of *military* retired pay is, to be sure, just that. No comparable federal law for non-military former spouses exists. Indeed, Congress grandfathered certain employees in the Foreign Service and Central Intelligence Agency for similar retirement programs. Payments to those former spouses do not come out of the retiree's retirement check. Rather, payments are made by the federal government.

Controversy #2 — Retroactivity (still causing problems)

Another controversy that has been addressed by Congress, but not necessarily ended, is that of retroactivity. USFSPA did not grandfather any military member who had been divorced prior to the enactment of the law. (Congress did, however, grandfather retirees in six other federal retirement programs.) This meant that the law changed *after* many military members had already retired. Thus, a military member who had been retired, for example, for 15 years and perhaps remarried with a second family might find himself or herself facing a judgment for back retired pay plus half of all future retired pay. Because grandfathering was not done, some retirees were forced into bankruptcy as the state courts applied this law retroactively and required the payment of arrearages.

While it is not unusual for Congress to *not* grandfather every piece of legislation, in this case Congress stated, in a conference report, that the USFSPA was not intended to allow courts to reopen divorce cases. Unfortunately, that statement was not codified into the law itself. Much to the surprise of Congress and state courts, former spouses did, indeed, suddenly reappear with court orders and judgments for arrearages and prospective retired pay. Retroactive reopenings or partitionings were finally halted with the passage of Public Law 101-510, Section 555.

Even then, however, the 1990 amendment required military members to continue to make USFSPA payments for a period of two more years (until 5 November 1992) before they were relieved of the problem of retroactive reopenings. The 1990 amendment did not apply to divorces prior to *McCarty* wherein an award of retired pay had already been made or a court had reserved jurisdiction over a future distribution of retired pay.

The problem of retroactivity was never foreseen. Indeed, in a letter to the ARA Executive Director, Lawrence

J. Korb (former Assistant Secretary of Defense) acknowl-
edged that "it was not [his] view nor that of DoD that
such a law be allowed to be retroactive in its application,
and it was [his] understanding that grandfathering was, in
fact, incorporated from the start to prevent after-the-fact
disenfranchisement of military personnel."[1]

Although payments on some retroactively reopened
cases ceased in November 1992, retroactive applications
of the USFSPA are still causing problems because some
state courts are ignoring the 1990 amendment to the
USFSPA.[2] Moreover, as mentioned above, the law provided no relief in the case of those pre-*McCarty* divorces
where retired pay had already been awarded or jurisdiction to award had been retained by the court.

Controversy #3 — Treatment Disparate from Other Federal Retirement Programs

A third controversy is that of the disparity between the
military and their retired pay and that of other groups of
federal employees and their retired pay. For example,
CIA and Foreign Service retirees were grandfathered when
similar legislation was passed that affected the division
of retired pay in a divorce settlement. Requirements for
spousal support under those systems included filing limitations, no retroactivity, and termination of payments upon
remarriage before a certain age.

Controversy #4 — The Spouse Is Always Treated as the "Innocent" Party

Another controversy that causes a lot of consternation
for military members is that the law implies that it is always the spouse who is the "innocent" party and the military member who is the "heavy"—the guilty party. Just
as it is not always the military member who is the plain-

tiff in a divorce action, so it is not always entirely the member's "fault" in the breakup of a marriage. The USFSPA, however, allows the states to ignore fault or need in rendering awards and, thus, often "rewards" miscreant spouses.

Controversy #5 — Award of Retired Pay Based on Rank at Retirement, Not at Time of Divorce

A continuing controversy, and one of the main objectives of attempts to amend the USFSPA, is that it does not specify that the computation and subsequent award of retired pay is to be based on the rank/pay grade of the member at the time of the divorce. This is illustrated in the following example:

The military member who is a captain (O-3) at the time of divorce is divorced at the 10-year point. Assume that Spouse Number 1 is awarded 50 percent of his retired pay in the divorce settlement. There are no children. He remarries at the 13-year point, has two children, and continues to serve for a total of 30 years. He retires at the rank of colonel (O-6). It could certainly be said that Spouse Number 2, if you interpret the original intent of USFSPA, "contributed" more to his career than did Spouse Number 1, by virtue of having been married to him longer (17 years vs. 10 with the first wife).

Yet, as a result of USFSPA, the finance center will compute the share of retired pay to Spouse Number 1 at the rank of colonel, not captain.[3] Spouse Number 2 and the children are the ones who are shortchanged here. What did spouse Number 1 do to contribute to his career after they were divorced? The answer is "nothing."

Thus, courts generally have interpreted the law to read that the amount to be awarded to the former spouse is to be based on the military member's rank and years of service at the time of retirement. Only infrequently have courts said it is to be calculated on the basis of the date of the divorce. The argument is that an ex-spouse is unfairly benefiting from the increased retired pay as a result of longevity or promotions. Indeed, if a second spouse has been married to the member longer than the first spouse, it could be the second spouse who has "contributed" more to the member's career than the former spouse.

Controversy #6 — Circumvention of the USFSPA's Protection of Disability Pay

Some courts, in violation of the U.S. Supreme Court decision in *Mansell*[4] and, indeed, the USFSPA itself, divide the military member's disability compensation (received from DoD or the VA in lieu of regular retired pay). Section (a)(4) of 10 U.S.C. §1408 defines "disposable retired pay," *inter alia*, as "...the total monthly retired pay to which a member is entitled less amounts which—

(B) are deducted from the retired pay of such member . . . as a result of a waiver of retired pay in order to receive compensation under . . . title 38;

(C) in the case of a member entitled to retired pay under chapter 61 of this title, are equal to the amount of retired pay of the member under that chapter computed using the percentage of the member's disability on the date when the member was retired (or the date on which the member's name was placed on the temporary disability retired list); . . ."

The previous excerpt requires translation for the layperson. The reference in subparagraph (B) is to disability pay received from the Department of Veterans Affairs, provided for in Title 38 of the U.S. Code. Title 38 provides that in order to receive VA disability pay, the retired member must waive a like amount of regular retired pay. The total amount of compensation remains the same.

The reference in subparagraph (C) is to disability pay

received from DoD. Chapter 61 of Title 10 of the U.S. Code provides for the payment of disability pay directly by DoD to retired members.

In either case—whether disability pay is paid by the VA or DoD—the clear language and intent of the USFSPA is that it not be divided by the courts as property in divorce proceedings. The reason for this is that, by its very nature, disability pay is absolutely personal to the individual receiving it, i.e., the person suffering the disability.

The simplest means of circumvention has been, simply, to ignore the provisions (above). This leaves the military retiree, most often already financially distressed by the court's decision, with the problem of locating funds to appeal it.

A second means of circumvention—and one frequently used when the member is 100 percent disabled—is to award alimony, disregarding the member's source of financial resources (not to mention totally ignoring what the service member had to endure to become disabled) which may, indeed, be restricted to disability pay. Since alimony is not "marital property," the subject of "disposable pay" is neatly side-stepped.

Public Law 104-201, enacted in September 1996, amended the USFSPA to provide what only can be called "back door access" to disability pay by providing that an ex-spouse can obtain payment of unsatisfied obligations to pay alimony or child support or both through garnishment, or other means under either 10 U.S.C. §1408 or 42 U.S.C. §659. Experience to date with these two statutes has been that whenever conflicts have arisen as to applicability, courts have generally ruled that the provisions of 42 U.S.C. §659 supersede those of 10 U.S.C. §1408.

It is worth noting that one of the objectives of the ex-spouse community is the elimination of the statutory protection of disability pay. Public Law 104-201 might well be viewed as just the first of what could be many changes in the legislation. While there are hopes that the enactment of "concurrent receipt" (of disability and non-disability pay) legislation would ease the ex-spouse pressure, it is more likely that such legislation would result in the declaration of an open season on an ex-spouse share of BOTH payments.

Controversy #7 — Restrictions Associated with Receiving Retired Pay Apply to the Retiree but Not the Spouse

Further adding to the debate on this issue are a host of duties, obligations, and restrictions to which the military retiree is subject. You will find these in the "small print" in the papers the member receives at retirement. For starters, retirees are subject to recall to active duty (physical condition permitting). They also remain subject to the Uniform Code of Military Justice (UCMJ) and are restricted in certain post-service activities. Contingency Mobilization Plans include the recall of between 22 and 86 percent of the retired force, depending on the service. In other words, retired members continue to serve.

Other restrictions pertain to employment. Retirees who want to accept employment with a foreign government are required to have prior approval of the Secretary of State and the Service Secretary. Acceptance without approval would result in reduction or forfeiture of retired pay. In addition, a retiree is forbidden to accept employment with a defense contractor within three years of retirement if the member worked on projects in which the contractor was also engaged.

Based on their active duty assignments, some retirees are restricted from traveling to specific foreign countries without prior approval from the Service Secretary. Again, they are subject to the UCMJ if they violate such orders.

The remaining restrictions pertain to dual compensation limits on federal employment salary, publications of military experiences, lectures on sensitive military sub-jects, and conduct while in uniform.

Ironically, the former spouses, who are drawing from the same retired pay envelopes, are not subject to any of the above obligations or restrictions. Indeed, the non-military spouse frequently has more right to military re-tired pay than a military spouse of a military member.[5] Specifically, an ex-spouse is entitled to the military member's retired pay after a marriage of any length. Unless divorced, a military spouse married to a military member has to serve at least 20 years to qualify for mili-tary retired pay on his or her own.

Controversy #8 — Impact of Civil Service Employment on a USFSPA Award

Until 1 January 1997 there existed a "loophole" whereby a retired military member could reduce or eliminate the size of the USFSPA payments being made to the ex-spouse by acceptance of federal civil service employment. Pub-lic Law 88-448, The Dual Compensation Act, revised, *inter alia*, the laws governing the employment of retired military personnel in federal civilian positions. The pro-visions of particular interest are:

- All retired military personnel who take federal ci-vilian jobs are entitled to receive the full pay of the position.
- All retired military officers are allowed to take fed-eral civilian jobs.
- Retired regular officers and warrant officers receive only a portion of their military retired pay plus 50 percent of the remainder. At present, this portion is $10,104.46 for retirees who commenced their mili-tary service prior to 1 August 1986, and $9,170.26 for those whose military service commenced on or after 1 August 1986.[6]

- Retired reserve officers, all retired enlisted personnel (both reserve and regular), and regular officers
retired for combat disability, keep all their retired
pay while in federal civilian jobs. An exception is
those who retired after 11 January 1979 whose combined retired pay and civil service salary exceed a
cap based on the salary rate for Level V of the Executive Schedule.

During the 104th Congress Sen. Carol Moseley-
Braun (D-IL) sponsored legislation that, in due course,
emerged as Section 637 to the Defense Authorization
Bill for FY97: Public Law 104-201. This amendment
provides that

> *"If after 1 January 1997 an employee or Member
> waives retired pay that is subject to a court order for
> which there has been effective service on the Secre-
> tary concerned for purposes of section 1408 of title
> 10, the military service on which the retired pay is
> based may be credited as service for purposes of this
> chapter only if the employee and Member authorizes
> the Director to deduct and withhold from the annuity
> payable to the employee and Member under this sub-
> chapter an amount equal to the amount that, if annu-
> ity payment was, instead, a payment of the employee's
> or Member's retired pay, would have been deducted
> and withheld and paid to the former spouse covered
> by the court order under such section 1408. The
> amount deducted and withheld under this paragraph
> shall be paid to the former spouse."*

What this legal language boils down to is that for those
divorced, retired military members who accepted federal
civilian employment on and after 1 January 1997, they
will continue to make USFSPA payments to an ex-spouse,
even if the amount of military retired pay received thereafter is reduced or surrendered. This legislation protects
the ex-spouse's interest in the retired pay.

Since the impact of civil service employment has, in the past, frequently been a reason for litigation, there is no reason to expect a diminution in the number of cases based on the pre-1 January 1997 situation. Section 637 may, in fact, intensify efforts to bring pre-1997 cases in line with Sen. Moseley-Braun's amendment. Regardless of the outcome, the time and costs of litigation could be worrisome.

Many military members feel this is just one more instance where restrictions are placed on the service member and not the spouse (particularly the dual compensation restriction), limiting and denying the service member freedom to seek other employment as he or she sees fit. Also, non military members do not see their salaries decreased when they choose to retire from one company, collect a retirement, and go to work for another company. Once again, service members are singled out with restrictions that do not apply to other retirees or spouses.

Controversy #9 — USFSPA Payments Survive Remarriage of the Ex-Spouse

Since its enactment in 1982, the USFSPA has contained no provision terminating payments of retired pay to former spouses despite the remarriage of those former spouses. This is unfair to retired military members for the following reason:

It discriminates against retired military members in that it is inconsistent with the treatment of former spouses under all other federal government retirement and survivor benefit systems.

This disparate treatment of the military is illustrated below. The remarriage consideration is included in all other federal retirement benefit programs, thereby discriminating against military members.

Retirement Annuities

- **Foreign Service** — Under both the Foreign Service Retirement and Disability System (FSRDS), covering employees who began service before 1 January 1984, payments of retirement annuities to former spouses terminate upon remarriage of the former spouse before age 55 if the remarriage occurred on or after 8 November 1984, or before age 60 if the remarriage occurred prior to 8 November 1984. Under the Foreign Service Pension System (FSPS), covering employees who began service after 1 January 1984, payments of retirement annuities to former spouses end upon remarriage of the former spouse before age 55. FSRDS, 22 U.S.C. §4068; 4069a(6) FSPS, 22 U.S.C. §4071j(a)(1)(B).
- **Central Intelligence Agency** — §4068, 4069a(b); Annuities payable to former spouses are terminated upon remarriage of the former spouse before age 55. 50 U.S.C. §403 note, §224(b), Central Intelligence Agency Intelligence Agency Retirement Act of 1964 for Certain Employees.

Survivor Benefits

- **Military** — Under the Survivor Benefit Plan applicable to all military members, annuities to widows, widowers, or former spouses terminate if the recipient remarries before age 55. Payments may resume if the remarriage ends in death, divorce, or annulment. However, if the recipient is also entitled to an annuity, he or she must elect which one to receive. 10 U.S.C. §1450(b).

- **Veterans Benefits** — Under Title 38 of the U.S. Code, for purposes of payment of retired pay to surviving spouses and dependency and indemnity compensation, a "surviving spouse" is defined as one who has *not remarried.* 38 U.S.C. §101(3).

- **Civil Service** —Under both the Civil Service Retirement System (CSRS), covering employees who began service before 1 January 1984, and the Federal Employees' Retirement system (FERS), covering federal employees who began service on or after 1 January 1984, survivor benefits to former spouses are terminated upon remarriage before age 55. CSRS, 5 U.S.C. §8341(h)(3)(B); FERS, 5 U.S.C.§8445(c)(2).

- **Social Security** — Under the Social Security system, benefits for former spouses terminate upon remarriage of the former spouse. 42 U.S.C. §402(b)(1)(H) and (c)(1)(H).

Abused Spouses

- Section (h) of 10 U.S.C. §1408, added in 1992, provides that the spouse or former spouse is eligible to receive payments of the retired pay of a military member whose entitlement to retired pay is terminated as a result of misconduct by a member involving abuse of a spouse or dependent child. Payments are made by the government and continue so long as the former spouse remains unmarried. This means that, within the same Act, a dichotomy exists in that payments (made by the government) to an abused spouse cease upon remarriage, while payments (made by the military member) to an ex-spouse who was not abused survive remarriage. *This inconsistency (a clear case of discrimination against the military member) begs for resolution.*

Customary Notions of Spousal Support

- Continuation of payments beyond remarriage of former spouses overrides any aspect of financial need. Usually, remarried former spouses attain financial security by virtue of (1) the income of their new marriage partner, or (2) the combination of their own income and that of the new marriage partner. By contrast, many retired military members whose pay has been divided also support second families. The inequitable result is that a remarried retired member, most often in need of his or her retired pay, must continue making payments to a remarried former spouse, who should no longer need those payments for financial security.

- As currently written, the USFSPA is inconsistent with customary notions of spousal support in U.S. domestic relations law. An obligation to pay alimony as support for a former spouse generally ceases upon remarriage of the former spouse. This has been standard legal doctrine since the founding of this country, based on the rationale that in a remarriage there is a transfer of spousal support responsibility to the new spouse.

Multiple Payments

- Currently under the USFSPA, a former spouse can acquire more than one award of retired pay by divorcing after a remarriage and remarrying again. Not only is this unfair to the retired member(s) whose pay is being divided on behalf of that former spouse, but it is a situation that encourages divorce. Such cases are not rare.

Controversy #10 — Separation Bonuses

A new controversy hit the scene as a result of defense downsizing. The issue revolves around the bonuses service members receive when they agree to cut their careers short in exchange for the lump-sum Special Separation Benefit (SSB) or the Voluntary Separation Incentive (VSI) annuity. These separation payments are in lieu of retirement; thus, a service member forfeits the right to retired pay.

Obviously, if the divorce has already occurred while on active duty, and a portion of the retired pay was awarded prospectively to the former spouse, then the court order to divide retired pay as part of a divorce settlement becomes worthless to the ex-spouse if the military member takes an early out.

Currently, there is no law or provision in the USFSPA that precludes a court from awarding a former spouse a portion of the separation bonus. However, legislation was introduced by former Rep. Schroeder that would allow state courts to divide, *as property,* monies received by military members as separation bonuses or incentives. (See Chapter 16 for more details.) More and more states consider severance pay to be marital property.

The subject of separation bonuses has become another legislative tug-of-war, not unlike the controversy of the "income vs. property" label put on retired pay. One of the most obvious areas is the potential for accusing the military member of intentionally evading compliance with a divorce decree that orders the member to pay the former spouse a share of the retired pay. Unfortunately, many members must make some very difficult decisions on whether to take the bonus and leave, or face the possibility that another promotion passover or congressional downsizing action may put them out on the street with no bonus whatsoever. Periodically, the various military *Times* publications have published a listing of career fields and statistics showing whether a career field is expanding or contracting, and the chances of reaching field grade rank or senior enlisted status.

The separation bonus, just like other assets acquired during the marriage, is subject to the domestic family laws of each state. As such, there should be no need for Congress to pass new legislation when judges now have the authority to divide such an asset according to the state law. The military member's concern should be the potential for having to defend his or her decision to leave active duty prior to completing the mandatory years for retirement, and not merely avoiding or appearing to avoid USFSPA payments to the ex-spouse.

Controversy #11 — No Statute of Limitations

Under the law as currently written, there is *no* limitation on the time during which former spouses may seek a share of a member's retired pay. Therefore, divorced military members who may be subject to a claim under the USFSPA must live under a shadow of uncertainty about their retired pay during the lifetime of their former spouse. Not only is this unfair to retired members, but it is inconsistent with common legal practice. Almost every legal action, civil or criminal, has a statutory time beyond which the action may not be brought. Moreover, a statute of limitations *is* provided under other federal retirement systems:

- **Foreign Service** — To be recognized as valid under the Foreign Service Retirement and Disability System (FSRDS), a court order directing payment of an annuity to a former spouse must be issued within *24 months* [authors' emphasis] of the date of the final divorce. 22 U.S.C. §4054(a)(4).

- **Central Intelligence Agency** — Court orders for payments from a retirement fund to former spouses must be issued within *12 months* [authors' emphasis] after the divorce becomes final. 50 U.S.C. §403 note, Section 222(a)(7). Central Intelligence Agency Retirement Act of 1964 for Certain Employees.

Controversy #12 — Early Retirement

Since the late 1990s, taking an early retirement—more than 15 years of service but less than 20 years—has been an option for some military members, primarily those in over-strength fields or careers that are no longer critical. Retired pay under such plans is reduced pro rata.

While early retirement should pose no problems under those circumstances where the parties divorce after such a retirement, problems can occur if the divorce takes place before the service member has made such a decision. If a specific dollar amount or formula is used that is based on a 20-year retirement, the service member could be paying an unfair amount at his or her expense to the advantage of the former spouse. Such problems can be avoided by carefully wording the computation for award of retired pay in the divorce decree. Keep in mind, however, that retired pay for more than 15 but less than 20 years of service *is* divisible under the USFSPA.

CHAPTER ENDNOTES

1. Letter, dated 20 March 1990, to the Executive Director, American Retirees Association, from Lawrence J. Korb, Director of the Center for Public Policy Education, The Brookings Institution. While serving in the Pentagon during the Reagan administration, Korb was one of the key framers of the Department of Defense position on USFSPA.

2. The Lambert Gonzales case (*Gonzales v. Roybal*, DR89-00908, Second Judicial Court, County of Bernalillo, State of New Mexico; and No. CIV 93-1302 MV/DIS, U.S. District Court for the District of New Mexico, filed 31 July 1995, Santa Fe) is an example of this. Gonzales petitioned New Mexico's Second Judicial District Court, Bernalillo County, to terminate USFSPA payments on the basis of the 1990 congressional amendment. On 29 June 1993, the court ruled against Master Sergeant Gonzales, reasoning that, under New Mexico law, there is a "limited reservation of jurisdiction" that is incorporated into every NM divorce decree. Under this rationale, the conditions of the congressional amendment did not apply—and can never apply—in New Mexico. The decision flies in the face of the intent of Congress and is in direct violation of federal law.

3. This computation could be considered the "default" method, in accordance with the literal reading of 10 U.S.C. §1408. Of course, the court can also specify a different amount and method. Thus, each person's final decree may differ.

4. On 30 May 1989, the U.S. Supreme Court in a 7-2 decision ruled that a veteran's disability benefits were not subject to property division in a divorce proceeding. The case stemmed from the 1979 California divorce of retired Air Force Major Gerald Mansell and his wife, Gaye. (Mansell's request in 1983 to modify the divorce decree to exclude disability pay was rejected.) Please note that this ruling does not preclude a court from ordering the member to pay a portion of the retired pay award from other income. 109 S.Ct. 2023 (1989), 104 L.Ed.2d 675 (1989), 57 U.S.L.W. 4567, 10 E.B.C. 2521. On remand *In re Marriage of Mansell* (1989, 5th Dist) 216 Cal.App.3d 937, 265 Cal.Rptr. 227, 1989 Cal.App; 217 Cal.App.3d 319, 1989 Ca.App. (History: 487 U.S. 1217, 101 L.Ed.2d 904, 108 S.Ct. 2868).

5. See Chapter 6 for a discussion of the impact of USFSPA on female military members.

6. This provision, in particular, created problems for USFSPA beneficiaries because their share of military retired pay was/is being reduced proportionately to that of the military spouse's.

5

IS IT INCOME
OR IS IT PROPERTY?

While there are continuing controversies surrounding USFSPA, as pointed out in the previous chapter (some of which will probably never get resolved), there is one controversy that has gotten more attention than most.

Truth and Consequences

Inarguably, the most controversial feature of the USFSPA is its reclassification of "pay" as "property." The law, 10 U.S.C. §1408(c)(1) states: "Subject to the limitations of this section, a court may treat disposable retired pay payable to a member for pay periods beginning 25 June 1981, either as *property* solely of the member or as **property** of the member and his spouse in accordance with the law of the jurisdiction of such court." [bold type provided]

While postulating that the principal purpose of Congress, in enacting the USFSPA, was to remove the "fence" around military retired pay placed there by *McCarty*, it is also reasonable to surmise that only a handful of legislators appreciated the full implications of the "property" treatment. Foremost among these is that an award of property under the USFSPA survives the remarriage of the benefiting ex-spouse. This is inconsistent with customary notions of support in U.S. domestic relations law.

It should be noted that Congress could have removed the "*McCarty* fence" around military retired pay simply by legislating that it *could* be used as a source of alimony and child support in a divorce proceeding, but as **pay**, not property. Military veterans may well wonder whether the underlying motivations were vindictiveness and greed, not equity and need—particularly since the USFSPA does not preclude contemporaneous awards of alimony, child support, USFSPA payments, and other assets of the marriage. The astounding result is that state courts are arbitrarily classifying military retired income as "pay" for some purposes and "property" for others.

The Legal Morass

Divorced military retirees comprise the only class of U.S. citizens which has its income classified, by federal statute, as *both* pay and property. It is believed by many military retirees that this dichotomy derives principally from the response of an inconsistent Congress to the strident demands of feminist pressure groups and the incessant search for "political correctness."

The USFSPA circumvented, but did not supersede, *McCarty*. Congress attempted to imply that it did by taking the unprecedented step of **backdating**[1] the USFSPA to one day prior to *McCarty*. Nevertheless, the core of the *McCarty* ruling (namely, the military retirement system confers no entitlement to retired pay upon retired members' spouses and does not embody even a limited community property concept) still stands. Corroborating evi-

dence of this has been provided by the USFSPA's principal congressional sponsor who regularly introduces legislation to provide an automatic, statutory entitlement to
military retired pay to anyone who marries a military member, from the wedding date onward.

The USFSPA abetted the public misconception of retired pay as a pension, despite the fact that federal statutes
and case law have historically and consistently regarded
military retired pay as *reduced compensation for reduced
services* with no attributes of a pension. This position has
been taken by the Comptroller General, the Defense Department, the Internal Revenue Service, and the U.S. bankruptcy courts. A serious (and, possibly, litigious)
anomaly exists in that divorced military members and
their ex-spouses are required to pay federal and state
income taxes on **pay** legally reclassified, by the
USFSPA, as **property**.

Legal and Other Precedents

Notwithstanding the fact that Congress can do anything
it likes (albeit, subject to Supreme Court review), the following are citations of legal and other precedents that further fuel the "income vs. property" issue.

1. Since the USFSPA was not grandfathered, its effect
   was to retroactively change the military retirement
   compensation system. Military members already retired or eligible for retirement were caught unexpectedly by a law which they had no reason to anticipate. The failure to grandfather was a failure to
   provide equal protection under the law for a group
   of American citizens (divorced military veterans)
   whose lives in retirement were devastated without
   prior notice and with no compensatory relief. It
   could be argued that the USFSPA does, in fact,

constitute "unjust taking" in violation of protections provided by the Fifth Amendment of the U.S. Constitution.

2. The Armed Forces Voluntary Recruitment Act of 1945 (Public Law 79-190), Section 4, states: "Whenever any enlisted man of the Regular Army shall have completed not less than twenty or more than twenty-nine years of active service, he may upon his own request, *be transferred* to the Enlisted Reserve Corps. An enlisted man so transferred and retired shall receive, except with respect to periods of active duty **he may be required to perform**, until his **death, annual pay**." [bold type added] There is like status for officer personnel. This law clearly defines military pay as wages. If pay is taxed as wages, how, then, can it be property?

3. Retirees have no rights to benefits not yet paid. A lawsuit brought by the National Association of Retired Federal Employees (NARFE) contended that a 3.1 percent COLA became a vested entitlement on 1 December 1985, and, therefore, its cancellation by Gramm-Rudman-Hollings (The Balanced Budget and Emergency Deficit Control Act of 1985) on 12 December 1985, made it illegal. A federal 3-judge panel ruled that retirees have no property rights to benefits not yet paid. This was, essentially, upheld by the U.S. Supreme Court by its refusal to hear the appeal.[2]

4. A military retiree's position is unique in that the military retiree is subject to both civil law *and* the Uniform Code of Military Justice (UCMJ), for the remainder of his or her retirement. No other U.S. wage earner is subject to such a commitment as a prereq-

uisite for continued compensation. The elements of a lifetime agreement with the government for continuing reduced pay for reduced services, as defined in *McCarty*, are present and obvious.

5. Article 1, Section 9 of the Constitution specifically states, "No Bill of Attainder or *Ex Post Facto* Law will be passed . . ." Section 10 states that Congress may not "Pass any Bill of Attainder, *ex post facto* law, or Law impairing the obligation of Contracts . . ." [emphasis added] The Fourteenth Amendment reinforces those sections by stating, in part, "nor shall any state deprive any person of life, liberty, or property, without due process of law; nor deny to any person within its jurisdiction the equal protection of the laws." Whether the agreement began and concluded under a law *or* as an agreement, there can be no difference. When one makes an agreement in good faith and spends time in the execution of that agreement, then the government must honor that agreement. A new Congress must uphold the integrity of the old; otherwise, the continuity of congressional commitments is broken and the word of Congress is worthless. Enactment of the USFSPA by the 97th Congress clearly changed a course set for retired military veterans by earlier Congresses.

6. The U.S. Supreme Court in *Buchanan v. Alexander*, 45 U.S. 20 (1846), ruled that money owed by the United States to the individual service member belongs to the Treasury until it is paid to that individual. Essentially, the Supreme Court held that courts *cannot* tell a federal disbursing official what to do since it would defeat the purpose for which Congress appropriated the money. If the specific reason Congress appropriates funds for the retired mili-

tary member after 20 years of active duty is not as compensation for continuing military obligations, what, then, is its reason? What law provides other reasons? The USFSPA provides that a former spouse may receive military retired pay directly from a military finance center, without sending the money to the military member first.[3] Clearly, this circumvents pay directly to the individual who earns it.

7. The U.S. Supreme Court in *United States v. Tyler*, 105 U.S. 244 (1881), ruled that when the status of the military member changes from active duty, compensation is continued at reduced rate and the connection of the member to the military is continued, with reduced duties and responsibilities. The USFSPA provides that a former spouse may receive up to 50 percent of the monies the military member is paid for fulfilling continuing obligations to the federal government. This money is paid without any corresponding responsibilities whatsoever on the part of the benefiting ex-spouse, who draws from the same pay envelope.

8. Certain sections of the Internal Revenue Code imply that military retirement qualifies as wages and is considered taxable income. Indeed, retirees must report their retired pay as income and pay tax on it. Although 26 U.S.C. §3401(a), Chapter 24 (Collection of Income Tax at Source of Wages), defines "wages" to mean "...all remuneration..., including the cash value of all remuneration (including benefits)...," there appears to be no provision in the Code flatly stating that military retired pay qualifies as wages and is taxable income.

9. The General Accounting Office, in a letter dated 23 February 1990, to an ARA member, stated:

    Dear ——:
    This is in response to your letter regarding the use of the term pension when referring to retired pay received from a military service.

    This office has always maintained that retired service members receive retired pay rather than pensions because they continued to serve after retirement from active duty. In our letter [decision] B-236084, 31 July 1989, concerning Oliver North's retired pay (copy enclosed), we said that military retired pay constitutes current reduced pay for current reduced services, rather than a pension for past services rendered. We have stated this in our decisions since the first volume of published Comptroller General decisions (see 1 Comp.Gen. 700 (1922)).

    Our decisions follow the reasons of the Supreme Court in United States v. Tyler, *105 U.S. 244 (1881), in which the Court said that after a member's retirement, 'compensation is continued at a reduced rate, and the connection [of the member to the military] is continued, with a retirement from active service only.'*

    We share your concern that the news media sometimes inaccurately refer to military retired pay as a pension.

10. The term "property" describes one's right to possess, use, and dispose of a thing as well as the object, benefit, or prerogative which constitutes the subject matter of that right (*Barron's Law Dictionary, 1984*). Since it has been ruled that a military retiree has no vested interest in his/her retired pay (it cannot be sold, given away, or passed on to

heirs), it fails the test of legal property: that of disposability by its owner. It is subject to the terms of enlistment or employment, and thereafter, the terms of retirement.

11. For any law within the United States to be truly valid, it must, first, meet the requirements of the Constitution and become effective only from its actual date of passage. It cannot be postdated. To be fair, it must also be universally applied, non-discriminatory, consistent in its application, and equitable in its considerations. The applications of and the passage of the USFSPA itself meet *none* of these requirements.

The Bottom Line

If there is a "bottom line" on the *income vs. property* issue, it is that military retired pay fails the legal test of property: that of disposability by its owner. Military retired pay cannot be sold, transferred, or passed on to heirs. Furthermore, the military member is not *vested* in the retired pay the way a civilian employee is. The member must usually serve[4] at least 20 years of honorable service.[5]

Surrounding this fundamental failure is a plethora of conflicting and confusing statutes, court decisions and precedents. The legal arena is rich with opportunities for litigation, either to repeal the USFSPA or to amend it to bring it into conformance in the numerous arenas where it is in conflict.

The most notable relevant litigation to date is the "Unjust Taking" case which was ruled on by the U.S. Court of Appeals for the Federal Circuit on 16 July 1990 (see Appendix E). The ruling deftly sidestepped the constitutional (and other) issues involved.

The principal determinants for further litigation are:
- a conviction that it would be successful and have the curative effects desired;
- the legal talent to prepare and successfully argue the case; and
- the financial resources to pay for it.

The ball, while clearly in the court of those current USFSPA-affected members who have the will and the resources to litigate, is also in the court of every military member who wishes to preserve the constitutional principles underlying retired pay (notwithstanding fair divisions of marital assets in a divorce action). Little, if any, financial help can be expected from any other veterans' organizations, if for no other reason than they may consider other veterans' issues more important than repeal or reform of the USFSPA. However, an overwhelming majority of the national community of veterans organizations strongly supports USFSPA reform.

In the meantime, service members must continue to look to Congress to right the wrongs it has wrought with this unbalanced and discriminatory law. For their part, state divorce courts will continue to make the awards of military retired pay—as property—that the USFSPA empowers them to make.

CHAPTER ENDNOTES

1. Mike Causey, who writes "The Federal Diary" column in *The Washington Post*, said it best in his feature titled, "Give and Take on Benefits" (10 May 1993, p. D2), in response to those who contend "Congress *cannot* change the system because it wouldn't be fair or right" [in reference to lowering survivor benefits for federal retirees]. He goes on to say: "Let's go back to Civics 101. Congress can do most anything it wants. It changes laws and rules all the time....Just because a proposed

change may be wrong, or unpopular, doesn't mean it can't happen. Citizens are entitled to fight for or against changes. But they are wrong when they say Congress *cannot* [Causey's emphasis] do something."

2. Source: *Air Force Times*, 12 January 1987.

3. For the spouse to receive *direct* payment from the military finance center, the marriage has to have lasted at least 10 years during which the military member performed 10 years of creditable service.

4. Spouses, however, become entitled to a direct payment of a share of the member's retired pay after only **10** years, according to the USFSPA. See Chapter 6 for a discussion of this anomaly of female military members married to other members. Early retirement plans enacted in the late 1990s allow certain members to retire with at least 15 and less than 20 years, and to receive retired pay on a pro rata basis.

5. Recent changes related to the Defense Department downsizing have resulted in an early retirement offer, which comes with many restrictions. (There are also exceptions for members who are medically retired.)

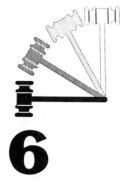

6

WOMEN
IN UNIFORM

When the USFSPA was first introduced into Congress, early debates centered on the "plight of the military wife" and recognized her important contributions to military life in deference to her husband's career and to the detriment of her own. And, although USFSPA is gender neutral—it applies to all people in uniform, both men and women —the concern was not, as the testimony clearly points out, for the civilian male with a military *wife*.[1] In fact, the only pronoun appearing in the USFSPA itself in connection with military retired pay is "his."

There are approximately 1,106,600 female military veterans in the United States. This is exclusive of the number of women currently on active duty and in the National Guard, Reserve, and Coast Guard. Women comprise 13.7 percent of the active duty forces. It is only recently that female married military members are beginning to be affected by the USFSPA, as the percentage of women entering the Armed Forces and staying in for a career increases.

Female Military Must Get in Line Behind the Non-Military Wife

It is the female military member, however, who must get in line behind a nonmilitary wife. Perhaps the anomaly of this situation can best be summed up in the words of then ARA member Major (then Captain) Kimberly K. Power, MSC, who wrote in a letter to Congress:[2]

> *Under USFSPA MY CONTRIBUTION TO THIS NATION'S SECURITY IS FAR MORE VALUABLE IN MY ROLE AS MILITARY WIFE THAN IN MY ROLE AS A MILITARY OFFICER [capitalization by letter's author]. According to USFSPA, I am vested in 15 years' worth of my husband's retirement benefits [having been married for that length of time currently], yet after my ten years of service I have no entitlements to my own retirement. I must serve a full 20 years to receive anything based on my own military career. The lack of logic and fairness is mind boggling.*

DACOWITS

The civilian organization known as the Defense Advisory Committee on Women in the Service (DACOWITS) has, as its charter, the responsibility to address the needs and welfare of women in the military. It meets at least twice a year. For two years running, Major Power was instrumental in bringing the USFSPA issue to the attention of DACOWITS as it relates to women military members.

In her address to the DACOWITS spring conference on 24 April 1991, Major Power said that it was "high time the DACOWITS treat the concerns of military women as being of higher priority than the interests of civilians previously married to military personnel."[3] From the perspective of national security, certainly there can be no argument that the contributions of women in uniform far surpass those of most women in mufti.[4]

To date, DACOWITS has refused to take a stand supporting military women on this legislation, despite the fact that USFSPA has been the biggest blow to women in the military in many years, "outranked," perhaps, only by the women in combat issue. Perhaps if one of the criteria for being on the committee were prior military service, the USFSPA issue would get the attention it deserves.

Times Have Changed

If you were to read the original testimony of the hearings held before Congress in 1982, you would find that the typical civilian spouse of a military member was portrayed as a nonworking wife who devoted her full time to her husband and family and needed lifetime support because she was incapable of working.

This concept is inconsistent with the social and economic realities of the 1990s and as we enter the 21st century. Given the constantly growing presence of women in the workplace and their contributions to society as a whole (not just to the military family), the "plight of the military spouse," as advertised during Congress' 1982 pro-USFSPA debate/discussion, may no longer be valid, if it ever were.

Today's military spouse is a "working" spouse. Indeed, the number of working military spouses in the labor force increased from 54 percent in 1985 to 65 percent in 1992.

Career Discrimination

Many women in uniform who are informed on this issue feel this law obstructs the careers of America's military women and deprives them of earned entitlements. In the words of Major Power, "We have worked too hard for the gains made to allow any law to discourage our female officers and NCOs from seeking full and rewarding careers."[5]

As more women join the Armed Forces, this issue may take on new importance as more and more *men* are added to the ranks of USFSPA beneficiaries.

In the interim, as mentioned earlier, female military members might be well advised to note that the only pronoun appearing in the USFSPA in connection with military retired pay is "HIS." Perhaps it is time that a female military member argued, in divorce court, that the USFSPA does not apply to "HER."

Concomitantly, members of Congress should be informed that the "fem fear" which has led them to continue to tighten the USFSPA noose may, indeed, backfire if they continue to legislate in favor of female civilians married to military members while discriminating against females serving the nation in uniform.

CHAPTER ENDNOTES

1. Were the situation reversed, we find it hard to think that Congress would have been so sympathetic toward the male who would give up his career to be the "backbone of the military family."

2. Letter, dated 14 May 1991, to the Honorable Beverly B. Byron, then chairperson of the House Armed Services Subcommittee on Military Personnel and Compensation.

3. The same can be said of reservists—they too have fewer rights and benefits than ex-spouses enjoy. See Chapter 7.

4. Likewise, the contributions of reservists will surpass those of the ex-spouse.

5. See endnote #2 above.

7

THE RESERVES AND THE GUARD

There are several issues that are unique to a military divorce which can make the process much more difficult than a divorce between civilians. Adding to the complications is the uniformed member's status if he or she is a reservist. (Unless specifically noted, members of the National Guard are also included in this discussion.)

When the uniformed member is a reservist, the calculation of the amount of retired pay due a former spouse is often complicated. For members whose entire military career was spent on active duty, the calculation of the pro-rata share of retired pay is based simply on the number of years married concurrently with active duty, divided by the number of years on which the payment of retired pay is based, times the percentage awarded the spouse by the court, up to 50 percent.[1]

Reservists Are Not Always Compensated with Money

The problem for reservists starts with basic differences in the retirement system for regulars and reservists. The active duty member earns money for every day of active duty. Both the active duty time (which is usually consecutive) and the pay earned are considered in divorce settlements. The reservist, on the other hand, may be in a non-pay category or status and still be required to put in the time (i.e., work).

It has been argued that it is mainly the reservist's efforts that are involved and not the "community efforts" frequently claimed by the spouses of career military members. Yet, the reservist's retired pay will be divided on the basis of the law and not on the merits of the peculiarities associated with reserve duty. While most reserve duty is performed on the weekend, many reservists also perform their duty during the week by taking personal leave from their own jobs. Others put in extra time in the evenings, quite often for no pay.

Does the "Plight" Apply to Spouses of Reservists?

Some have opined that the 'hardships' claimed by the spouses of active duty members, particularly those attributable to long or frequent deployments, are not applicable to the spouses of reservists. Indeed, it has been argued, it is the reservist who experiences the 'hardship' because he/she works outside a regular job, sometimes for no pay. Such distinctions are being progressively blurred as reductions in force levels of active duty personnel require increasing reliance on the Reserve Components.

In the final analysis, such arguments have been shown to bear little weight in divorce court. Courts have generally not seen fit to distinguish between active duty retired pay and reserve retired pay in determining whether a former spouse should receive a pro rata share. Divorced reservists should expect that when they reach age 60 and are eligible to receive retired pay, they, almost always, would be required to share it with their ex-spouses.

Reserve Retirement System[2]

The Army and Air Force Vitalization and Retirement Equalization Act of 1948 (Public Law 810, 80th Congress, codified at 10 U. S. C. 1331-1337, now 10 U. S. C. §12731-12740 established a retirement system for members of the Reserve. Title III of this Act provides that any member of the Reserve Components who accumulates 20 years of creditable service, with the last eight years of qualifying service in a Reserve Component, and reaches age 60, is entitled to retired pay computed on the basis of the number of retirement points he or she has accumulated.

Public Law 103-37, the FY95 Defense Authorization Act (10 U.S.C. §12731(f)), reduced the number of years of Reserve Component qualifying service from eight to six years for members retiring from 1 October 1994 to 30 September 1999.

Federal civil service retirees may credit active military service in computing both civil service retirement and reserve retired pay. However, active military service performed after 31 December 1956, is not creditable for civil service annuity purposes beyond age 62 if the reservist then qualifies for Social Security retirement benefits. Administrative procedures and policies are established by each of the services.

Retired pay normally begins on the retiree's 60th birthday. Even if application is made after age 60, pay is retroactive. There is a six-year statute of limitations. If the retired pay application is filed more than six years after age 60, one day's retired pay is deducted for each day's delay.

A reservist's retired pay is exempt from the restrictions imposed by the Dual Compensation Act of 1964. However, the Civil Service Reform Act of 1978 requires reduction of military retired pay if the combined and annual income from federal civil service employment plus military retired pay exceeds that of Executive Level V.

Reservists may, under certain circumstances, qualify for early retirement when they are involuntarily separated with at least 15 years of service but with less than 20 creditable years. The pay is at a reduced rate and cannot be collected until age 60. The pro rata share of retired pay is based on a 20-year retirement minus a percentage for the number of years served less than 20. Other benefits apply to involuntarily separated reservists (see Chapter 9).

Creditable Service

Stipulations governing creditable service devolve from two periods of service, either before or after 1 July 1949.

Prior to 1 July 1949, 10 U.S.C. §12732, provides that one year of creditable service, to be counted toward a member's 20 or more creditable years, accrues from each year of service in 10 organizations.

After 1 July 1949, a reservist is entitled to one year of creditable service for each one-year period in which he or she has been credited with at least 50 retirement points. How the points are credited varies by Service. Some service may not be counted as creditable service for determining reserve retirement eligibility.

Service in the *National Guard* is treated as Reserve Component service if the person concerned was later appointed to the National Guard, Army National Guard, Air National Guard, or the Army or Air Force Reserve, and served continuously in the National Guard from the date of Federal recognition in the Guard to the date of appointment.

U.S. Public Health Service

A reservist is entitled to one year of creditable service for each year of active service in the Commissioned Corps of the Public Health Service during such time as it was a military service pursuant to Presidential declaration under section 217 of the Public Health Service Act (42 U.S.C. §217).

National Oceanic and Atmospheric Administration

A reservist is entitled to one year of creditable service for each year of active commissioned service in the National Oceanic and Atmospheric Administration, including Coast and Geodetic Survey during such time as he or she transferred to the service and jurisdiction of a Military Department pursuant to section 16 of the Act of 22 May 1948 (33 U.S.C. §853).

Crediting Former Service in Regular Components

A former member of the regular components of the Armed Forces who counts active duty service as creditable service for retirement eligibility purposes cannot have served in the last eight qualifying years in the Regular Components, the Fleet Reserve, or the Fleet Marine Corps Reserve, according to 10 U.S.C. §12731 (a). These last eight years of qualifying service do not have to be consecutive. This period of qualifying years is reduced to six years from 5 October 1994 to 30 September 1999 by the FY95 Defense Authorization Act, 10 U.S.C. §12731(f).

Each Service and, within the Service, sub-agencies, may issue directives that specify the activities which may or may not earn points. For example, a Category E reservist in the Air Force Reserve may earn only one point total for a physical examination that is required, even though the required examination may take an entire day or more. In another example, designing and developing a course of instruction is limited to two points, even though anyone who has ever designed a course knows that the research and preparation it takes to write a course take much longer than that. The bottom line here is that each reservist must be thoroughly familiar with the activities that earn points and make sure that such participation is documented and credited.

Retirement points are credited only in the year in which they are earned. That is, if the reservist earns 72 retirement points (normal for a drilling reservist who performs an annual tour) in one year and only 40 points the next year, he cannot shift 10 of those 72 points over into the next year to make it a qualifying year (which is 50 points).

Regardless of your Service or grade, we cannot stress enough the importance of each individual reservist keeping meticulous records of his or her yearly point accounting and to make sure that he or she earns at least the minimum number of points to have the year qualify as a "good [creditable] year." The reservist has to juggle the earning of those points to coincide with fiscal year requirements AND his or her retirement/retention year requirements. In most cases, these are not the same and often the overlap is such that the length of time to earn a good year's worth of points is fewer than 12 months. Reservists have only themselves to blame if they get a "bad" year.

Active Duty for Retirement Eligibility Purposes

No member of the Armed Forces may be ordered to active duty solely for the purpose of qualifying him or her for reserve retired pay. However, the provisions of 10 U.S.C. §§12646 and 1176 provide that a reserve commissioned officer or reserve enlisted member who has completed 18 or more but less than 20 years of creditable reserve service may not be discharged or transferred from an active reserve status (and thereby lose eligibility for retirement for having fewer than 20 years of creditable service) until the earlier of the following dates:

1. The date on which he or she is entitled to be credited with 20 years of creditable reserve service, or
2. The third anniversary of the date on which he or she would otherwise be discharged or transferred from active reserve status (with at least 18, but not less than 19 years of service) or
3. The second anniversary of the date on which he or she would otherwise be discharged from active service (with at least 19, but fewer than 20 years of service).

This provision of law protecting a reservist's retirement eligibility does not apply to members discharged from active status because of disability or age.

Computation of Reserve Retired Pay

Retired pay under the Reserve system is computed by totaling all points credited in all years, whether creditable for retirement eligibility, dividing by 360 (one year) and then multiplying by 2 1/2 percent to determine the benefit multiplier. The multiplier is applied to the basic pay rate in effect for the grade and longevity held at the time of request for retired pay. The longevity includes all years in military service, whether active, reserve, or retired reserve status and is not limited to the years of creditable service for retirement purposes. In the case where a member elects discharge from the Reserves instead of transfer to the retired reserve, the multiplier is applied to the basic pay rate in effect for the grade and longevity held at the time of discharge. (The pay can also be computed by referring to the multiplier for the grade and longevity listed in tables published by the Reserve Components.)

Reservists and the USFSPA

Whether the USFSPA applies to reservists is addressed in detail in an article written by Captain Karen A. MacIntyre in 1983.[3] Despite the date of the article, the logic of the information is, for the most part, still relevant.

The point to be made here is that the 'hardships' and inequities that were originally cited as the main reasons for enacting the USFSPA do not necessarily exist when the military member is a reservist. Captain MacIntyre has examined in detail the "language" of the original statute to determine whether reservists were ever meant to fall under this law. (The article does not, however, address the issue of a "good year" in accounting for the time on which the reservist's eventual retired pay will be based. In the case of the reservist, it may take more than one year to accumulate enough points to equal one good year for retirement purposes.)

To understand the problems in calculating the share of retired pay that will go to the ex-spouse, look at the following example.

A reservist, age 50, married 12 years, has just retired with "20 good years" for retirement purposes and has accumulated 2860 points. But it actually took him 24 years to get 20 years with sufficient qualifying retirement points (i.e., at least 50 points in each of those years). He won't begin (by law), however, to draw retired pay until age 60. The entire time he has been married he has been a reservist. He divorces at age 55. How is the retired pay awarded the ex-spouse calculated? Is it based on one-half of 20 years' retirement? 24 years? Or is it based on a pro rata share based on points earned while married and, if so, how calculated?

It can be argued that the fairest means of determining an ex-spouse's share of the member's retired pay would be to credit her/him with the number of points accrued during the marriage and then divide that number by the number of points credited for retirement purposes and multiply by the percentage awarded the spouse. This is the most frequently used method by the courts to determine the ex-spouse's pro rata share. For example, if the reservist (above) retired with 2840 points, 1400 of them accumulated while married, the former spouse's share would be 1400 divided by 2840 times 50 percent, for 24.6 percent (if the spouse is awarded 50 percent) of the community's retired pay.

This is not to say that a year-based determination method should not be used. It may, however, be more complicated than a point-based method and more likely to be contested on the basis that it is not fair to the ex-spouse. A division of retired pay that is demonstrably fair[4] to both parties is less likely to result in extended litigation.

Reservists Have Fewer Benefits Than Ex-Spouses

Just as the USFSPA is unfair and discriminatory in some respects toward active duty members or regular retirees, so it is with its application for reservists. One of the major changes required concerns benefits for reservists in the "gray area," those who are on the retired list awaiting age 60 to receive retired pay. The benefits reservists receive during that period are considerably less than what they had available while in an active reserve status. Now, while waiting to collect retired pay, reservists have fewer rights and benefits than ex-spouses from a 20/20/20 marriage. For example, that ex-spouse can use the commissary 365 days a year. Yet the gray area retired reservist (as do all reservists) can only use the commissary 24 times a year!

Reservists deserve rights and benefits at least equal to those the ex-spouse receives.

Bottom Line for Reservists—You Are Subject to the USFSPA, however....

Members of the Reserves, National Guard, Public Health Service, and NOAA are subject to the mandates of the USFSPA. And, if you qualify for retired pay and are divorced, your ex-spouse could be awarded up to 50 percent of it.

There is, however, a stop-payment exception, although not necessarily an avidly sought one. Retired members who are recalled to active duty no longer receive retired pay during the period of their active duty services. Since there is no longer any retired pay to divide, USFSPA payments to an ex-spouse are suspended until the member is, once again, receiving retired pay. Precedent for this was well established during Operation Desert Storm in 1991 by DFAS, which suspended payments to the ex-spouses of military retirees recalled to active duty. Members making USFSPA payments out-of-pocket who emulated the DFAS action were, if and when their actions were contested in court, able to prevail.

One final situation that reservists need to be aware of is the issue of separation bonuses if they took one while on active duty. There is a recoupment formula for those who took the Special Separation Benefit (SSB) or Voluntary Separation Incentive (VSI). If the member later retires from the Reserves or National Guard, he or she will have to repay the government for that exit bonus. It is absolutely essential that members who are divorced on active duty know what the payback obligations are if they have any intention of joining the Reserves or Guard, particularly if the bonus was included as an award of assets in the divorce.

CHAPTER ENDNOTES

1. This methodology has not been codified and is not part of the USFSPA. It is, instead, the normal practice of many courts and is widely cited as precedent. The USFSPA as written (literally) permits the award of 50 percent of a member's retired pay for a marriage lasting only a matter of minutes. (The ARA is not aware of any case where this has happened.) There is growing pressure to amend the USFSPA to provide that an award of retired pay will not be made unless the marriage has lasted at least 10 years. There is a "10-year clause" in the USFSPA but it applies to the minimum number of years the ex-spouse must have been married in order to qualify for direct payments by DFAS.

2. Portions of this chapter were extracted from publications by Uniformed Services Almanac, Inc. For a complete treatment of military retirement for Reserve Component members, readers are advised to consult the current edition of *Retired Military Almanac* or one of the other three books published annually by Uniformed Services Almanac, Inc., P.O. Box 4144, Falls Church, Virginia 22004. Copies are available in military exchanges nationwide.

3. Captain Karen A. Macintyre, A Legal Assistance Symposium Division of U.S. Army Reserve and National Guard Pay Upon Divorce. 102 Mil.L.Rev. 232 (Fall, 1983).

4. The ARA functions on a platform of fairness and equity for

BOTH parties to any military marriage that ends in divorce. Use of either method of calculation of pro-rata share is probably acceptable, provided that it is defensible on those grounds. We have also heard reports from attorneys where the active duty retired pay schedule was erroneously used for the reservist. This is one area where the reservist and spouse need to ensure that he or she is receiving adequate counsel.

8

ALL DIVORCES ARE NOT ALIKE: WHAT YOU NEED TO CONSIDER

This chapter, indeed, this book, is not meant to be a treatise on domestic relations law. The military member and spouse need to be aware, however, of the many issues that can affect their divorce.

"Military" Divorce vs. "Civilian" Divorce

Military divorces are, in many respects, no different from other (civilian) divorces. While one might argue that military couples are faced with more and greater hardships than the average civilian couple, making it difficult to maintain a marriage and family life, military divorce will, nevertheless, involve procedural requirements, property distribution, and perhaps child support or maintenance. It is the problem of the division of military retired pay, the basis for this book, that presents some unusual considerations in military divorces.

Issues Unique to a Military Divorce

There are numerous issues that are unique to a military divorce which can render the process much more difficult than a civilian divorce. They include:

1. Status of the military member at the time of divorce: active duty, reserve/guard, retired.
2. Pay grade of military member at time of divorce.
3. Divorce that is initiated when one or both spouses are overseas.
4. Previous military divorce.
5. Direct payment versus an allotment for payment to ex-spouse.
6. Entitlement of military member to disability pay.
7. Disposable vs. gross retired pay (for calculation purposes).
8. Type of discharge from the service.
9. Domicile issue (for jurisdiction purposes).
10. Due process requirements for the military member still on active duty and the Soldiers' and Sailors' Civil Relief Act of 1940.
11. Pre- and post-retirement employment (and dual compensation restriction).
12. Length of marriage during the military career as a determinant for receiving military benefits (such as medical care, commissary and exchange privileges).
13. Status of military member after divorce (active duty, already retired, disabled retiree, reservist, dual compensation in case where retiree returns to work for the federal government)—officer, en-

listed, regular, or reserve.
14. Survivor Benefit Plan for former or current spouse.
15. Military member as single parent (custody of children that requires designating a guardian during deployment of a military member).
16. Conversion of military retirement time with subsequent federal civil service employment (to receive a Civil Service pension).
17. Treatment of separation bonuses (SSB and VSI) in a divorce proceeding.
18. Treatment of abused military spouses.
19. Early retirement (before 20 years).
20. Date of entry into military service (to determine which retirement system applies).[1]

Military Benefits an Important Consideration[2]

Members of the military and their families are entitled to numerous benefits. Depending on the length of the marriage, military spouses may also be entitled to benefits based on the retirement status of their marital partners. Minor children's entitlements are not affected by the divorce. We have chosen to address these benefits because they can become part of the pre-divorce negotiations[2] and, indeed, in many cases, should be addressed in the divorce decree (e.g., whether or what portion of the retirement remains the military member's, and what share goes to the former spouse; whether the military member retains the choice of beneficiary for SBP).

The benefits that may be extended to the former spouse include commissary, exchange, and medical. Based on the length of the marriage, combined with the military member's active duty time, the ex-spouse may be entitled to continue receiving these benefits. In fact, it may be in the military member's best interests, if very close to the

20-year point, to remain married in order for the spouse to continue to receive all the benefits he or she is currently receiving. Given that some military families do not amass any extensive list of assets or retirement vehicles (stocks, bonds, etc.), the military benefits may end up being the major assets that an ex-spouse receives. As the saying goes, "Timing is everything."

20/20/20 and 20/20/15 Spouses

The term 20/20/20 is one that you will see often in any discussion of USFSPA. A former spouse may qualify for certain benefits and privileges, depending on the length of the marriage, the number of years of military service creditable for retired pay, and the overlap of marriage and military service. To qualify for all benefits at the time of divorce, an unremarried former spouse must have been married for at least 20 years to a military member who performed at least 20 years of service creditable for retired pay, and there must also have been a 20-year overlap of marriage and military service (20/20/20). A 20/20/15 spouse is one where there was an overlap of at least 15 years.

If a former spouse is covered by an employer-sponsored health plan, medical care is not authorized (medical care may be reinstated when the former spouse is no longer covered by an employer-sponsored health plan). A former spouse who qualifies for 20/20/20, who lost eligibility because of remarriage, and who subsequently became unmarried through divorce or death of the spouse, is entitled to reinstatement of commissary, base exchange, and theater privileges only. No medical care is authorized (Public Laws 97-252, 98-525, and 100-565). There are other rules governing a 20/20/15 marriage where the divorce occurred before 1 April 1985, or on or after 30 September 1988.

There have been continuing attempts to provide PX/BX and commissary privileges to ex-spouses who do not meet the 20/20/20 or 20/20/15 criteria. If shopping privileges are an issue in your divorce, you should contact the American Retirees Association Internet web site (www.americanretirees.com) to ascertain the status of current legislative activity in this arena.

The Abused Military Dependents Act

If a military member is charged with domestic violence under the Abused Military Dependents Act (AMDA) of 1992,[3] he or she could lose their retired pay altogether, but their dependents may not. The AMDA requires the military services to pay an annuity, based on the retired pay to which a military member may have lost entitlement by reason of abuse of dependents, to eligible spouses and former spouses.

Eligibility ceases if the benefiting ex-spouse remarries. The original (draft) legislation provided for the loss of benefits if the abused spouse resumed cohabitation with the abuser. Since this was not retained in the amendment as enacted, it must be presumed that an abused spouse may continue to receive payments of retired pay if she does not divorce and remarry—or, in short, resumes legal cohabitation with her abuser.

Notwithstanding the obligation and need to support the military dependents when such abuse cases arise, here we have in the same section of Title 10 of the U.S. Code conflicting provisions on the remarriage of ex-spouses receiving military retired pay. It is worth noting also that the AMDA, when it originated in the Senate, included a statute of limitations provision which was eliminated in the subsequent House-Senate conference committee. This is yet another example of the sloppy legal work which has characterized the crafting of the USFSPA since its inception in 1982, and is discussed in more detail in Chapter 16.

Dependent Support

Another area that can cause trouble is that of dependent support. Again, it is not worth the possibility of extended litigation (where the court takes matters into its own hands) to get in trouble over basic entitlements or privileges. The military expects its members to support their dependents and, based on marital status, gives them extra money to do so, courtesy of the U.S. taxpayer. For example, if the military member is receiving a housing allowance at the "with dependents" rate, based on the status of being married, then it would be foolish to withhold that housing allowance from the spouse. To do so could be considered a change in status—if dependents are not receiving the allowance, then the military member does not need it.

It is **illegal** for a military member to refuse to support his dependents while receiving allowances at the "with dependents" rate. Refusing to do so could result in any number of actions, not the least of which is a court-martial and a discharge! Further, if there is a court order to pay support, the dependents could have the military member's pay (active duty, reserve, or retired) garnished.

Child custody can be complicated, since a dilemma is posed between what is best for the child (e.g., the military member is the one entitled to the benefits) and how the military member will be able to fulfill all his or her military obligations. The service member is required to have a guardian for the children so that the member is free to be sent worldwide without notice for national security purposes.

Married members and those with dependents actually do receive more money just for having a spouse or dependents. Single members do not share in additional funds.

Military members who are divorced may, under certain circumstances, be entitled to a housing allowance at the "with dependents" rate, even though they may be divorced.

SBP—Don't Ignore The Pre-retirement Notification Requirements

Approximately 90 days prior to retirement, active duty members are briefed on the Survivor Benefit Plan. Military members will have the choices of declining it, accepting it with full base coverage (see Chapter 11 on SBP, and for sources on SBP, Appendix P), or accepting it with some other amount of base coverage. *If the military member declines SBP or accepts less than full base coverage, the spouse must concur in writing.* The fact that a military member might be undergoing a divorce does not relieve the Services of their legal obligation to notify the spouse. If the military member refuses to let them notify his or her spouse, and the spouse does not agree with the choice, the law says that the military member will be enrolled at the maximum amount (for which a 6.5 percent premium is deducted from the gross retired pay). The survivor receives 55 percent of the selected base amount of the member's retired pay.

How does this affect divorcing members? The problem occurs when the couple goes to negotiate the terms of the divorce settlement. The first spouse has first call on SBP. If the court ends up ordering the military member to carry SBP on that spouse, then that premium could be for the *full* base coverage unless the spouse agrees to a lower coverage amount.

Example

Assume retired pay is $2500 a month. The monthly SBP premium will be $162.50 (the mili-

tary member gets a tax break, however, as it is deducted before taxes are figured). Moreover, whatever amount the member pays as the SBP premium for an ex-spouse is deducted from the gross pay in figuring disposable pay.

Let's now say that the military member had consulted the spouse and she might have agreed to a less-than-full base coverage amount of $1000 (she would receive $550 per month upon the member's death). The premium would then be only $65 each month. However, since the law only allows the military member to use the amount in effect at the time of retirement (in this case, the member refused to process the paperwork), the military member would be required to elect full base coverage. It may be possible *to increase the coverage during open season,* when there is one, but it cannot be decreased, once it is selected.

Thus, it would behoove the member to (1) not ignore the paperwork just because he might be angry with his spouse; and (2) discuss the matter with his spouse or through her attorney, *before* he officially retires.

The decision to act promptly and maturely in this matter could save the military member a lot of money. Failure to act prudently may also mean that the court may order the military member to pay the premium.

It is very important, then, that the military member understand the requirements of SBP and consult with the spouse or through the spouse's attorney. Remember, SBP may be an important element of any pre-divorce negotiations. It is a very valuable asset which could be offered in exchange for other considerations during a divorce settlement.

One final point to remember—if the spouse prior to the divorce is the SBP beneficiary of record and will also be after the divorce, the spouse will have to reapply for SBP coverage after the divorce. Coverages does not automatically carry over.

Social Security

Although not exclusively a military benefit, Social Security may figure importantly in a military divorce action. The ex-spouse of a member is entitled to the same benefits he or she would get if still married to the member, which is a sum equal to half of the member's check if the member is still alive, or to the full amount if the member has died, *provided that*:

1. The couple was married at least 10 years.
2. The ex-spouse is not currently married.
3. The ex-spouse did not earn enough on the job to be eligible for a benefit equal to or greater than the military spouse's.
4. The military member has filed for Social Security benefits, or else the ex-spouse is over age 62 and has been divorced for more than two years. (The 2-year waiting period is waived if the military member was entitled to Social Security benefits before the divorce.)

The ex-spouse's benefit does not affect that of the military member. Similarly, if the military member remarries, the subsequent spouse's benefits do not affect those of the divorced ex-spouse. If the ex-spouse remarries, he or she can choose whether to apply on the account of the former or current marital partner.

With all the hue and cry about "the plight of the military spouse," Social Security benefits are frequently overlooked in calculating what an ex-spouse will receive, thus bolstering claims to USFSPA payments, child support, other marital assets, and whatever else may be assessed and divided from a session in divorce court.

Jurisdiction

The issue of jurisdiction in a military divorce is also complicated, since meeting residency requirements and notifying the other spouse may present problems. Frequent moves may mean that not enough time has transpired for the service member to be considered a resident. The usual proof for establishing residency is often lacking, such as length of residency, owning a home, paying taxes in the state, voting, etc. Some states may, however, have special requirements that allow service members to divorce even though they are not legal residents in the traditional sense of the word.

In most divorces, property is divided. In a military marriage, this often may not include a house, or even substantial financial assets. The military member's retirement benefits may be the only asset worth dividing.

Timing Can Work to Both the Military Member's and Spouse's Advantage

The uniqueness of the military, thus, presents some interesting, if not unusual, considerations in divorces, particularly in the areas of general benefits, child custody, jurisdiction for filing purposes, and retired pay. It may be more advantageous for the military couple to separate rather than divorce for the time being, particularly if the couple is approaching the 20-year point, when the member will become eligible for retired pay. By doing so, the military spouse remains eligible for military benefits, and some of the major issues usually raised in a contested divorce might be avoided.

Timing becomes even more important when Defense is downsizing its active and reserve forces, and subsequently initiating early-outs (voluntary), and causing involuntary separation or reductions in force (RIFs), and involuntary retirement based on a selective early retirement board (SERBs), and early retirement (the new 15-year-plus retirement eligibility).

Thus, it is even more critical that the military member know that there are issues unique to a military divorce, just as timing in a civilian divorce can be critical to successful financial planning and each party's subsequent share of the marital assets. The list cited at the beginning of this chapter should serve as a checklist of items the military member and spouse may need to discuss with their attorneys.

Do's and Don't's

The divorce process is bad enough without further complicating it, but sometimes service members are their own worst enemies. There are numerous stories about military members who refused to do certain things. For example, if the service member retires and is separated from his spouse, the spouse must get a new identification (I.D.) card to reflect the member's retired status.[4] The member must sign the paperwork for the spouse to get a new I.D. card—do not refuse to do so.

Likewise, if either party is relocating when the divorce occurs, with the member going to one location and the spouse to another, the member must not refuse to file any loss or damage claims for the spouse's household goods that were (or will be) moved under the member's orders.

The military member is the sponsor, and the spouse is

dependent on the sponsor for a number of things. Some of these things may create problems for the member who does not want to cooperate. For example, the member may be held liable for costs incurred if the ex-spouse is hospitalized in a military facility, because the member will be identified on his or her I.D. card (now) as the sponsor, along with the member's Social Security number. Failure to comply will require time and, perhaps, money to extricate oneself.

Refusing to comply with entitlements that are due the spouse only aggravates an already difficult situation. Needless to say, the service member does not look very good in the eyes of his or her base personnel or finance center either, not to mention their commander. In fact, such a service member would appear rather immature and petty. Members are only hurting themselves when they fail to carry through with regular actions that are expected of them.

Compliance with the Law Is in Your Best Interests

One last comment is in order. Whether you are a member or a spouse, do not withhold any support and do not refuse to execute all paperwork for the entitlements which your dependents would normally receive. To do so is asking for trouble and could jeopardize your divorce settlement. It just plain isn't worth it.

CHAPTER ENDNOTES

1. The amount of retired pay that a uniformed service member may receive after completing 20 or more years of active service depends on the beginning date the person first became a member of a uniformed service. There are three systems under which the retired pay may be computed. (1) The <u>Final Pay Plan</u> covers members who entered the service before 8

September 1980. The amount of retired pay is 50 percent of basic pay after 20 years of military service, plus 2.5 percent for each additional year up to 75 percent. An annual cost-of-living allowance (COLA) is also provided, and varies with the Consumer Price Index (CPI). (2) The High-three Plan covers members who entered between 8 September 1980 and 31 July 1986. The amount is 50 percent of the average of the "high-three" (36 months) of base pay for 20 years, and 2.5 percent for each additional year up to 75 percent. (3) The Military Retirement Reform Act (also known as "redux") covers members who enter after 31 July 1986. Retired pay is computed using 40 percent of the "high-three" years of service for 20 years of service, with an additional 3.5 percent for each additional year up to 75 percent. The COLA adjustments are one percentage point less than inflation, as measured by the CPI. Further adjustments are then made when the service member reaches age 62.

2. See Chapter 9 for a listing of the benefits and other issues that need to be considered or negotiated in a military divorce.

3. Public Law 102-484, FY93 Defense Authorization Act. This law has been added as subsection (h) to 10 U.S.C. §1408 (USFSPA).

4. As any military member or spouse knows, your status is a factor in the use and receipt of military privileges and benefits. For example, some bases will not provide medical care to military retirees' dependents because they don't have enough trained personnel or staff. Dependents must seek medical care through the TRICARE system.

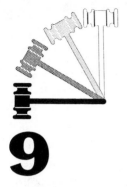

9

FEDERAL BENEFITS:
Here Today and May
Be Gone Tomorrow

Upon retiring, service members frequently find that the gap between military and civilian sector pay which they have heard about throughout their military careers is not so wide as they had been led to believe. While part of this may be attributable to what is being paid in the civilian sector for work comparable to military duties, a contributing factor is often the loss of benefits which terminated upon separation or retirement. It is important that, in calculating the current status of the family finances and in projecting the financial futures of both parties, federal benefits—current and projected—be included in the calculations. These should cover the entire gamut of possibilities, ranging from remaining on active duty to being permanently retired.

To that end, this chapter identifies the benefits which must be considered in planning for divorce. Some of them will disappear when the divorce takes place; others will remain available to one party but not the other; a few (e.g., payments of retired pay under the USFSPA, or DoD I.D. cards if the ex-spouse is a 20/20/20) will be available to both parties.

A factor which has impacted military divorces in recent years is the force reduction activity of the DoD. Military members and their families who had been counting on at least a 20-year military career may become involuntary civilians with only SSB or VSI as remuneration. Others with at least 15 years of service may be awarded retired pay but at a rate below what had been anticipated for 20 or more years of satisfactory service. Those receiving retired pay are subject to a division of it under the USFSPA. Attempts have been made to amend the USFSPA to include VSI and SSB but without success as yet. There have been, however, several awards of shares of SSB and VSI in divorce courts around the nation so that case law now exists justifying similar awards in the future.

In evaluating the relevance of the following benefits and entitlements, the reader must ascertain whether they apply to active duty, separation, or retirement. Concomitantly, it must be determined whether they extend to a current spouse, former spouse, or any children. Finally, some benefits may apply to certain elements (e.g., Reserves, Guard) and not to others. Since the benefits picture is a constantly changing one, it is imperative that current status be verified by a visit to the nearest military personnel office.

Attorneys should find this chapter on benefits helpful in the discovery process which normally accompanies a divorce action.

ALLOWANCES

The allowances that have been paid to service members have undergone various changes throughout the years. The more recent changes affect those who are moving or stationed overseas and separated from their families. In nearly all cases, these changes have not reduced the amount of money going to the families.

Basic Allowance for Housing (formerly BAQ & VHA)—Active Duty

The basic allowance for quarters—known as BAQ—was redesigned 1 January 1998 and merged with the variable housing allowance, or VHA, to create the new Basic Allowance for Housing, or BAH. The old system, which was linked to increases in basic pay, has been replaced with a system that is linked directly to the cost of housing. Family size will not make a difference, but rather the typical housing costs for civilians with comparable salaries. The new allowance does, however, distinguish between "with dependents" and "without dependents." Service members will continue to pay an average of nearly 20 percent of their housing costs out of their own pockets, but that is expected to improve in future years (assuming Congress approves the money to pay for it). The allowance will be based on the duty location, regardless of where the service member lives. The BAH is not taxed.

Basic Allowance for Housing (BAH)—Reserve Component

Reservists who perform duty away from home and who reside in government quarters or who must be billeted off base will receive something like BAH, but it is called a temporary housing allowance. Rates for 1998 are 2.8 percent higher than those for 1997 BAQ. Beginning in 1998, reservists on active duty or supporting contingencies of 140 days or more will receive the full BAH. All of the other current housing allowance rules for reservists still will apply in 1998. The BAH is not taxed.

BAH and Divorced Members Paying Child Support

A housing allowance differential has been paid to members who reside in government quarters and who pay child support. They receive a differential that is halfway between the housing allowances at the "with" and "without dependents" rate for their rank.

Keep in mind that previous military rulings have determined that there is no burden on the service member to show that he or she is actually supporting his or her spouse, by giving dependents their share of the allowances. Such entitlements are based upon a presumption of family support.

Basic Allowance for Subsistence (BAS)

This cash allowance is paid in lieu of in-kind subsistence (i.e., eating in military dining facilities), and is not taxed.

Dislocation Allowance

This allowance offsets moving expenses and is paid at two different rates. When service members move, they receive an amount equal to 2½ times their monthly amount they would receive in BAH for their rank and dependency status. If they are required to move a second time in the same year, they are paid at a rate double their BAH.

Family (Temporary) Separation Allowance

This allowance, which is not taxed, is paid at two rates, and may or may not be linked to the BAH rate. The most common form of this allowance is called Type 2, and is an extra monthly payment of $75 (as of 1998) that goes to members overseas who are separated from their families but who live in government housing, and to those serving on ships or on temporary duty for more than 30 days. The other form, Type 1, is linked to BAH, and goes to service members, also separated from their families, who are stationed overseas and unable to live in government quarters. They still receive their BAH at the "with dependents" rate. They cannot (by law), however, receive two BAHs to cover their housing in non-government quarters. Therefore, they receive a Type 1 separation allowance that, in essence, is an extra monthly BAH at the "without dependents" rate. These allowances are being redesigned, and the service member will receive the new merged allowance. Overseas, the new change has merged the BAH with the Overseas Housing Allowance.

Temporary Lodging Expense—CONUS

This allowance is paid to service members to cover housing and food costs during a move to stateside posts. The number of days allowed to move and live under temporary conditions varies by location. The amount paid has increased over the years and it is taxed.

Temporary Lodging Allowance—Overseas

This is a local per diem rate that is adjusted regularly, and authorized in 10-day increments. It is not taxed.

What to Look for in the Future

While military families may complain about the lack of adequate pay, keep in mind that at any time Congress may approve special allowances for specific periods and operations to make up for the sacrifices service members must endure, or to keep certain members from exiting the service. For example, be aware of the possibility of the following: (1) payments to service members called away unexpectedly, (2) increases in the family separation allowance, (3) hazardous-duty pay (the countries in which service is paid this amount change constantly, including the length of time for which it is paid), (4) and bonuses to retain various career fields, such as pilots.

BONUSES

Enlistment Incentive—Overseas Extensions

The FY98 Defense Authorization Act increases the incentive lump-sum bonus to $2,000 for certain enlisted members who extend their overseas tours by 12 months. This bonus is payable to those members serving unaccompanied 12- and 15-month tours or split tours of either 24 months accompanied or 12 or 15 months unaccompanied.

Service members at long-tour locations serving in critical or imbalanced career fields are also eligible. These include the Airborne Communications Systems, Combat Control, and Safety specialties.

Reenlistment for Active Duty Personnel

Bonuses are paid from time to time in various services for various career fields and as reenlistment or retention incentives for both officer and enlisted career fields. For example, a selective bonus averaging nearly $6,000 over a 4-year term has been authorized for enlisted security-force members. The calculation is obtained by multiplying the monthly base pay by a multiplier (which is designated as 1 for security troops) and then multiplying that by the number of years of the reenlistment. Bonuses vary by career field, term of service, rank, and location.

Other reenlistment bonuses range up to $45,000, with half paid in a lump sum and the balance in installments over the reenlistment period.

Reserve and Guard Bonuses

Public Law 105-85 extends various bonuses and pays as follows: (1) Reserve component enlistment, reenlistment, and affiliation bonuses through 30 September 1999. (For example, categories include nurses, and special incentives to recruit and retain dental officers.) (2) Extends authority through 30 September 1999 for special pays and the repayment of educational loans to reservists possessing critical skills who serve in the Selected Reserve. (3) Expands the Reserve Affiliation Bonus to include Coast Guard Reserve (for separating active-duty personnel who agree to serve in a unit of the Coast Guard Reserve). (4) Conforms the separation pay of NOAA Commissioned Corps officers to that of the other uniformed services.

The Pentagon proposed (March 1998) legislation to pay selective reenlistment bonuses to eligible reservists on permanent active status, bonuses which are now restricted to active duty personnel. The Navy is currently spearheading this effort, since its greatest shortage is in its Reserve Forces, especially among its propulsion and mine-sweeping specialties. While the Air and Army National Guard and Army Reserve are not seeking reenlistment bonuses at this time (as of publication of this book), they would be eligible to do so under the proposed legislation.

As of April 1998, the Air Force Reserve Command (AFRC) has authorized 40 Air Force specialties to receive bonuses under the command's enlisted incentive program. The AFRC revises this list every six months based on shortages in career fields command wide. Thus, a shortage at one location may not apply at another, as bonus lists are generated locally. This list can be reviewed in the unit's military personnel flight office. Active duty bases usually have a reserve support office within the active duty personnel flight office where the list can also be reviewed.

Special bonuses or retention incentives may also be paid to medical personnel such as doctors and dentists (up to $30,000), and flying personnel, such as pilots.

CHILD CARE

The cost of military child care—that provided by the military—remains below that of comparable nonmilitary facilities. Fees vary from base to base and by income range (gross income, even though part of it may be non taxable or excluded for federal or state reporting purposes). Installations in high-cost areas may also charge special fees. Consider who will take the deduction for the children on their taxes, as well as the elimination of this tax credit when the taxpayer's income exceeds allowable amounts.

CIVIL SERVICE EMPLOYMENT

For military divorces prior to 1 January 1997, the payments of retired pay under the USFSPA were reduced proportionately to the extent that military retired pay was either reduced or surrendered in order to accept post-military employment in the civil service.

During the 104th Congress, Senator Carol Moseley-Braun (D-IL) sponsored legislation that emerged as Section 637 of the Defense Authorization Act for FY97. This legislation provides that whenever there has been prior effective service under 10 U.S.C. §1408 (i.e., the USFSPA), the former spouse covered by the court order will continue to receive the entire amount awarded via withholding from the (now) civil servant's pay or annuity.

It is possible that former spouses whose payments were reduced by the "civil service employment loophole" in divorces prior to 1 January 1997 may go to court to sue for the payment, in full, of amounts as originally awarded, including arrearages. The principal defense is that the situation *now* existing is attributable to the law *then* existing. Any decision unfavorable to the military member should be appealable.

COMBAT-ZONE AND OTHER OPERATIONS EXCLUSION BENEFITS

Officers and enlisted personnel may receive an amount which is tax-free (limited for officers), while serving in declared zones. Enlisted and warrant officers' entire military pay is exempt from federal income taxes while serving in a combat zone.

Benefits go to those serving in various zones and, while there might not be an actual declaration of war, service members as well as civilians deployed to such declared areas are eligible for a host of pays and benefits. Among them may be: standard benefits such as medical and dental care, commissary and exchange visits, imminent-danger pay, certain-places pay, daily incidental expenses, free mail, telephone service, tax-filing extension, special-leave accrual, and re-employment protection (for Reserve Components). An example of tax-free benefits are those provided service members serving in Bosnia-Herzogovina, Croatia and Macedonia. All the pay for enlisted and warrant officers in those areas is excluded from taxes. And, the former limit of $500 monthly (dating back to 1966) has been increased to more than $4,000 for commissioned officers.

COMMISSARY BENEFITS

Active Duty and 20/20/20 Former Spouses

Active duty members and their dependents have unlimited access to military commissaries, where discounts average 25 percent and more for similar items in civilian stores. Commissary benefits are available immediately to ex-spouses of a 20/20/20 marriage to an active duty retiree.

Reserves and Guard

Reservists and Guard personnel were, until late 1998, limited to 12 visits to the commissary, in addition to any visits eligible as a result of active duty orders (and only for the duration of the orders). The number was raised to 24 visits after closed-door negotiations between the House and Senate on the FY99 Defense Authorization Bill. Dependents must show a valid I.D. card and a copy of the military member's orders when using the commissary, or the sponsor's commissary privilege card (which is then stamped by commissary personnel).

The 24-visit limit also, unfortunately, applies to retired reserve members in the "gray area," awaiting age 60 to receive retired pay. This is one benefit that gives the ex-spouse (of a 20/20/20 marriage) more benefits than the reservist (365-day access to the commissary for former spouses vs. 24 days for reservists, including retirees in the "gray area"!).

COST-OF-LIVING ALLOWANCE (COLA)

To give military members a stateside level of buying power to compensate for currency fluctuations and other effects of overseas assignments, DoD pays members a COLA. The COLA indices are multipliers to basic pay. The COLA is paid monthly and varies by duty station, number of dependents and pay grade. The amount also varies by month due to fluctuations in the overseas currency.

Situations where members receive a "COLA Unique" would include areas that require a costly car inspection (e.g., Japan, where an inspection costs hundreds of dollars versus the typical U.S. rate of $25). Members stationed in England must register and pay license fees on televisions. All members are reimbursed equally for such special situations based on average expenses for such unique items during their tour of duty.

DENTAL BENEFITS

Dependent Dental Insurance Plan

Active duty service members receive free dental care at military facilities. Those with families can buy dental insurance, with the government subsidizing the program.

Retirees are mostly on a space-available basis. The Military Retirees' Dental Plan, however, does not include former spouses.

In January 1998 the new DeltaSelect USA/TRICARE Retiree Dental Program became available to military retirees and their family members. The retiree pays a premium for the services and costs rise incrementally, dependent on the number of family members enrolled. These are currently in the neighborhood of $14 per enrollee per month. Coverage commenced in February 1998. Premiums for the first four months must be paid at the time of enrollment. Thereafter, premiums are automatically deducted from monthly payments of retired pay by DFAS. Once enrolled, participants must remain in the program for a minimum of two years. Detailed information on the program may be obtained from: DeltaSelect USA/TRICARE Retiree Dental Program, P.O. Box 537008, Sacramento, CA 95853. Telephone (888) 838-8737. Tap into their web site at: http://www.ddpdelta.org. The program does not cover all dental procedures. It would be wise to compare it with dental programs being offered by several veterans' organizations before committing.

Reserve Components

As of December 1997, DoD implemented its dental plan (TRICARE Selected Reserve Dental Plan—TSRDP) for members of the Selected Reserve. Reserve organizations are lobbying for this program to be extended to actively participating members of the Ready Reserve, many of whom receive no pay and who drill with active units for retirement points only. At the present time, this benefit does not extend to reservists' dependents.

DUAL COMPENSATION AND PAY

Post-retirement employment with the Federal Government for regular retired commissioned officers and warrant officers is affected by the Dual Compensation Act of 1994. For members who joined the uniformed services before 1 August 1986, the formula (as of 1 December 1995) for reduction of retired pay is one-half of the annual retired pay in excess of $10,104.46. For members who joined on or after 1 August 1986, it is one-half of the annual retired pay in excess of $9,170.26. Reserve officers and enlisted personnel are exempt.

In applying the dual compensation formula, the amount of any VA disability compensation is deducted from the amount of the gross retired pay, reducing the dual compensation reduction. An exemption from dual compensation restrictions is granted to those retired for a combat-incurred disability or whose disability retirement was due to an instrumentality of war incurred during a period of war.

Further, the Civil Service Reform Act of 1978 places a pay cap on all uniformed services personnel (regular, Reserve, and enlisted) who retired on or after 11 January 1979. The combined annual rate of retired pay and federal salary is limited to the salary rate of Executive Level V.

EARLY OR FORCED RETIREMENT

Active Duty

In 1988, the Air Force began to conduct selective early retirement boards, or SERB, to reduce the number of senior officers on active duty. The boards were used during the height of the drawdown to determine who among colonels and lieutenant colonels would stay and who would have to leave. All those considered by the boards were eligible to retire. Leaving was not voluntary. These SERB boards may be used in the future.

Reserve Components

The FY95 National Defense Authorization Act authorized a proportionately reduced retirement at age 60 for medically disqualified reservists who have between 15 and 20 years of satisfactory service. This Reserve Transition Assistance Program will expire at the end of FY99.

Reservists out of a job because of realignment or other force reductions may be entitled to involuntary separation pay; early qualification for retired pay; Reserve Special Separation Pay; extended GI Bill educational benefits (for 10 years); and an extension of commissary, exchange, morale, welfare, and recreation benefits for a period of two years. Separation may be the only option for such members, as transferring to another position in the Reserve or Guard is not easy, or may not be possible. Units throughout the Reserve and Guard are experiencing forced drawdowns (1600 jobs in 9 states in May 1997 alone), and units may not have openings in the career field sought. Switching to a Guard unit is not without its problems. Since it is a state-run organization, getting into a Guard unit may be difficult without good, personal local contacts. Transferring to a reserve unit is easier. (See "SEPARATION PAY" below as it applies to Reserve Components.)

To qualify for early retirement, Reserve Component personnel must be involuntarily separated and have at least 15 years of creditable service, with the last six in the Selected Reserve. As with the regular Reserve retirement, retired pay cannot be collected until age 60 and will be reduced to reflect the years served for early retirement.

EDUCATIONAL BENEFITS

While on active duty, service members can receive a 75 percent reimbursement for tuition. Other educational benefits for active duty members vary by service, as well.

For those leaving active duty or retiring, educational benefits, commonly known as the "GI Bill," are also available and have increased to reflect higher costs of acquiring an education, although the increases have not always been enough to cover all educational costs.

For anyone entering the service between 2 January 1977 and 30 June 1985, the Veterans Educational Assistance Program (VEAP) was available, providing a maximum of $225 per month benefits for a total contribution of $2,700, and a maximum cap of $8100 in paid-out benefits. The old Montgomery GI Bill (MGIB) provided a maximum (1997 figures) of $428 in return for a $1,200 contribution, with a cap of $15,403 on total payments. (These figures were adjusted for inflation yearly.) Service members had an opportunity to convert to the old GI Bill in 1997. Service members with families received a higher benefit. Benefits for qualifying reservists under Chapter 1606, MGIB benefits, exceed $200 per month for full-time students.

National Guard

Most states provide some form of tuition assistance to their National Guard members (and in some cases, their dependents), though none for many other Reserve members.

Reserve Eligibility

Certain benefits are available to selected reservists (IMA and unit). However, if they are unsatisfactory participants (among others, have accumulated five unexcused absences or do not earn the minimum number of points each year) or request reassignment to an inactive status, they lose educational benefits and will be required to pay back benefits they received. Reassignment to inactive status suspends their eligibility to receive GI Bill benefits, with eligibility terminating *prior* to the effective reassignment date. Eligibility can also be suspended for reservists requesting reassignment for temporary reasons (e.g., personal, overseas and unable to attend school, etc.). Upon incurring a six-year reserve service obligation, earning a high school diploma, and completion of initial active duty for training, a reservist is eligible under Chapter 1606 of the MGIB, but is limited to completing that education in 10 years.

Reservists and guard members should contact their reserve personnel center (or local unit) to determine eligibility on educational benefits. For example, Air Force Reservists would direct their questions on education to the ARPC Education and Training Division, at HQ ARPC/RMT. Toll free at 800-525-0102, Ext. 330; commercial 303-676-6396; DSN 926-6396. Write: 6760 E. Irvington Place #6000, Denver CO 80280-6000. E-Mail: ed-tng@arpc-emh1.den.disa.mil.

Spousal Scholarships and Loans

If negotiating any educational benefits for the spouse in order for that person to become more marketable in the job market or to limit spousal support, then consider applying for a scholarship or loan available from the Service relief societies. The Army Emergency Relief provides such financial support, as do the Air Force Air Society and Navy-Marine Corps Relief Society. Benefits are often available for those stationed overseas as well. For example, the Air Force Aid Society distributes about $1.5 million each year in scholarships to spouses overseas. Do not overlook this excellent source.

Leaving the Service with Educational Debts

When the service pays for education, the beneficiary may be obligated to remain on active duty for a specified period. If military service is terminated before the obligatory period, then the government will recoup the money. If leaving under one of the special programs where a bonus is offered to leave, then it is necessary to apply for a waiver on repayment of any educational debts. Deductions may be made from any bonus payments made as a condition of leaving active duty.

EMPLOYMENT BENEFITS

Service members and spouses should avail themselves of the education centers that are located on many military installations. Within them are employment resource centers to help the spouses find employment. Workshops, which are usually free, are offered in job interviewing and resume writing. Representatives from The Retired Officers Association (TROA) travel from installation to installation giving transition briefings for separating and retired officers.

Active Duty and Reserve Components

Military members who are retiring or separating are eligible for various employment counseling and assistance benefits. (See "TRANSITION BENEFITS" elsewhere in this chapter.)

Spousal Employment

Spouses, while married to the service member, are also eligible for employment counseling and assistance under the Transition Assistance Program. (See "TRANSITION BENEFITS" elsewhere in this chapter.)

In addition, spouses are eligible for preferential civil service hiring within the Department of Defense, grades GS-1 through GS-15 levels. There are also special hiring policies (non-competitive appointments) for spouses who are relocating from overseas to stateside with their sponsor (service member).

EXCHANGE SHOPPING PRIVILEGES

Both active duty and Reserve Component personnel have unlimited shopping privileges at all Army and Air Force Exchange Service facilities in the continental United States. Reservists and Guard members do not have to be on active duty or training status to shop at CONUS AAFES facilities (exchanges, clothing sales, food facilities, barber and beauty shops, laundry and dry cleaning, florists, auto repair, video rental, movie theaters, and the exchange mail-order catalog). When deployed however Reserve Component personnel need a copy of their orders and their I.D. card to shop in AAFES facilities overseas. Family members of Reserve Component personnel who are on active duty are entitled to the same privileges as family members of active duty personnel.

Exchange shopping privileges are available to 20/20/20 former spouses.

FEDERAL TAX ADVANTAGES

Certain allowances and pay are currently not subject to

federal tax: BAS, BAH, overseas housing allowances, FSA, combat zone (restrictions for officers), hostile fire pay, among others. The service member's basic pay is, however, subject to Social Security Tax withholding, all federal taxes, and applicable state income taxes. Tax laws change frequently; readers should verify the current tax status for any benefit cited in this chapter.

FINANCIAL RESOURCES— RETIREMENT FUNDS

Civil Service Retirement

If either spouse has worked for the Federal Government, then you should obtain a copy of Pamphlet #5, Retirement Facts: Survivor Benefits Under the Civil Service Retirement System. The Office of Personnel Management (OPM) has other titles in its Retirement Facts Series. The nearest federal installation's personnel office should be consulted.

Private Retirement Benefits

If either spouse has worked for a private company, be aware of the marital asset represented by the company's 401(k) plan. Unlike the company's defined plan, these plans have tremendous flexibility. The employee can raise or lower his or her contribution, borrow from the plan, and move assets from one investment to another. In addition, the employee can make, with restrictions, withdrawals for "hardships." Lastly, the money can be withdrawn after the age of 59 1/2. (Before that age, there is the 10 percent penalty.) *The important point to note is that there is no law that requires the spouse to notify the other spouse of any of these actions.* There are efforts underway in Congress (led by Sen. Carol Moseley-Braun, D-IL) to prevent either spouse from draining the account and taking off with the proceeds. Companies are upset about the law because of its voluminous administrative and paperwork requirements, and retirees are upset because they would have to wait for a long time to get access to their own money (over a period of 5 to 9 years). Readers are advised to write their elected representatives to learn where they stand on this issue.

HARDSHIP DUTY PAY

This pay, up to $300 a month, with a target implementation date of mid 1999, is planned to replace Certain Places Pay (also known as foreign duty pay) for service members who are deployed to arduous duty locations or for long or frequent deployments. The pay may vary according to location, grade, years of service, and other factors to recognize the levels, frequency, and duration of hardships at different location. The only glitch is that Congress has not provided any funding for this new compensation.

However, the latest changes to the monthly stipend would be based on duties, not the location, and would expand to stateside as well as overseas assignments.

HAZARDOUS DUTY
AND HOSTILE FIRE PAY

Hostile fire pay also known as imminent danger pay, is $150 a month.

Enlisted Flight Crews

As of 19 June 1998, legislation had been approved by the Senate to increase the hazardous duty pay for enlisted flight crew members. Readers are advised to check on the currency and applicability of any pending legislation.

Active Duty

Active duty members may receive 100 percent of monthly hostile fire pay for any exposure to a hostile environment (one day or event equals 100 percent monthly pay).

Reserve Components

Hostile fire pay for reservists is paid on a pro-rata basis; that is, a reservist, completing the same one-day event, would qualify for only 1/30th of the same entitlement, despite facing the same dangers.

HEALTH BENEFITS

The previous medical benefits provided under the CHAMPUS program have now been replaced by the TRICARE program, which is a 3-tier program requiring various enrollment fees and an annual deductible. The old CHAMPUS healthcare program was a fee-for-service plan. TRICARE has replaced that program and is a health maintenance organization, or HMO. It is not the intent in this book to explain these programs in any detail, as they are quite complex, and the various levels of health care differ for active duty and retirees. Medical benefits are available to former unremarried spouses in a 20/20/20 marriage. Former 20/20/15 spouses divorced before 1 April 1985 have permanent military medical care. TRICARE does not cover marital or family counseling (e.g., for members going through a divorce). Because of the erosion in military medical benefits, ARA recommends that both parties have supplemental health insurance, preferably through a civilian employer (for the non-military spouse).

Under the CHAMPUS program, former spouses who are unremarried and who do not have an employer-sponsored health plan receive indefinite eligibility when the former spouse and service member were married for at least 20 years during which the member also had 20 years of creditable service which overlapped with the 20 years of marriage. Prior to 31 December 1988 there were several transitional eligibility programs. Dependents of reservists called to active duty for 31 or more consecutive days are also covered. Former spouses who are eligible for military health care lose their eligibility permanently if they remarry, unless they remarry a military member.

Military members who retire and work for the federal government may opt for health benefits under the Federal Employees Health Benefits (FEHB) program, which is administered by OPM. The OPM publishes the FEHB Enrollment Information Guide and Plan Comparison Chart for former spouses (RI 70-5). A former spouse who is enrolled in the FEHB program and who cancels his or her enrollment, cannot reenroll as a former spouse. However, if enrollment is terminated because other FEHB coverage is acquired, the right to FEHB coverage under spouse equity continues.

When corresponding with the TRICARE Support office, Aurora, Colorado 80045-6900, ARA recommends that mail be sent via Certified–Return Receipt Requested. Both parties should evaluate all their health care options and determine their continuing financial obligations vis-a-vis the benefits for health care coverage under all programs available to either or both parties.

HOMEOWNER ASSISTANCE

Home Loans—Selected Reserve

Public Law 102-547 extended eligibility on a 7 year test basis (that expires 27 October 1999) for home loan guarantees for certain members and former members of the Selected Reserve who have completed six or more years of honorable service in the Selected Reserve and are not otherwise eligible for such guarantees (such as prior active duty service). This particular benefit, as of July 1998, could be permanently opened to National Guard members and reservists under a proposal approved by a House subcommittee.

Home-Sale Tax Break

Military members on active duty should look to Congress to obtain relief from the 1997 Taxpayer Relief Act that excludes up to $500,000 of profit on the sale of their principal residence if they lived there for at least 24 months during the previous five years. Many military members would not be eligible for the exclusion because of the residency requirement under the law as it was originally passed. (Legislation was pending at publication).

Homeowner's Assistance Program (HAP)

This program helps military homeowners whose property value has gone down because a base is closing or the base population is shrinking. The Government pays the difference between the home's appraised value at the time of the sale and 95 percent of its value before the closure announcement was made. If the home cannot be sold, the Government will buy it.

To be eligible for HAP, the service member must be on active duty in a military service or in the Coast Guard, or a current federal civilian or non-appropriated fund employee. The home, which must be owned and lived in on the day that the closure or realignment is announced, must be near a base that has been approved for HAP. Not all bases undergoing realignment necessarily qualify homeowners for HAP.

HAP eligibility has also been extended to owner-occupants who were transferred, retired, or separated from active duty within six months before the closure announcement; those who left because of an unaccompanied overseas assignment within 15 months of the announcement; and those who were ordered into military housing within six months of the announcement. HAP payments are taxable.

INCENTIVE AND SPECIAL PAY

Nomenclature in the uniformed services is constantly changing, and the term incentive can also refer to other special pays such as bonus pay and special-duty assignment pay as well. The most common of these is flight pay, for those on flying status, and sea pay for naval personnel on sea and submarine duty. Others include flight deck and proficiency pay. The maximum flight pay is $650 a month (in addition to annual bonuses up to $22,000 being offered, e.g., by the Air Force). Sea pay maximums are $380 a month for officers, and $520 for enlisted members. Enlisted personnel on submarine duty receive an additional $355 a month up to $540. Submarine officers who are nuclear trained can receive extra bonuses up to

$15,000. Parachute-duty pay ranges from $150 to $225 a month for both officer and enlisted personnel. All these pays are taxed. When the member leaves such a status, the incentive pay does not always stop so long as the individual is required to maintain currency in that specialty. For example, field grade officers may move into a "desk" job and still be required to maintain flying proficiency and, thus, continue to receive flight pay.

Look for constant changes in the incentive and special pay arena. For example, the Air Force is proposing to eliminate special-duty assignment pay for AWACS operators as part of a larger plan to standardize special pays for all career enlisted aviators. The new pay would be known as "career enlisted flight-incentive pay." The issue of military aviation compensation is currently being studies by Congress. Some on flying status also receive hazardous-duty pay, which would be eliminated under the proposal. Assignment pay was implemented as a temporary retention measure and is being phased out (and could be reinstituted at any time). Like all other benefits, and particularly those peculiar to each Service, it is important to note that the adage "here today, gone tomorrow" is very much alive regarding incentive pays.

LEAVE

Active Duty

Military members can be compensated for unused leave to a total of 60 days in a lifetime.

Reserve Components

Most reservists cannot be compensated for leave that they earn and are unable to use while serving on active duty tours even if operational requirements of their tours prevent them from taking leave they accrue.

Leave Sell-back for Combat-Zone Duty

Reservists who receive compensation for the use or sale of leave earned while in a combat zone or qualified hazardous-duty area may exclude such compensation from their gross income taxation. The rules for how much is exempt or excluded are complicated, as well as the recoupment of taxes previously paid on such compensation. The IRS has agreed to an alternative recoupment proposal. Reservists should call their Reserve Pay Office for more information.

LIFE INSURANCE

General

Determining whether to purchase SBP or regular life insurance requires extensive research and knowing exactly what your financial needs will be. (For information on SBP, see Chapter 11). If you are considering SBP with your children as beneficiaries, you may want to consider regular life insurance, since the premiums would be based on the life expectancy of the child. (The premiums for life insurance are based on mortality statistics.) Life insurance can help with college costs if it builds up cash equity. The SBP premiums will rise and increase with retired pay increases, since a straight percentage is taken off the top before taxes. An important thing to remember is to keep sight of insurance objectives, whether commercial insurance or SBP. There may be other financial vehicles that better fit your objectives.

SGLI & VGLI *(Term Life Insurance Plans)*

Regardless of what the divorce decree says, the service member (policy owner) has complete control of this insurance according to the insurance companies) and may change the beneficiary or drop the policy at any time. Enrollment must take place while on active duty. A retiree has 120 days after retirement to convert SGLI to one of several options.

Servicemen's Group Life Insurance, or SGLI, is an insurance program for active duty members and reservists for which premiums are deducted from their pay. The top coverage was increased from $100,000 to $200,000 in January, 1993. Unless they ask for less, members are automatically enrolled for the maximum insurance coverage, at the rate of $8.00 per $100,000 of coverage. This insurance *does not continue* after retirement or separation from the military. SGLI is available for active reservists assigned to units as part of the Ready Reserve and "gray area" reserve retirees.

At retirement, active duty members who are eligible for Veteran's Group Life Insurance (VGLI) may buy a five-year policy. The premiums are only guaranteed for each five-year increment and will increase as the retiree ages. The VGLI is not available to most reservists.

PCS RELOCATION REIMBURSEMENTS

Active duty members and their families enjoy a number of reimbursements in connection with a "permanent change of station" (PCS) move. These include per diem for the member and dependents when traveling between duty stations by privately owned vehicle (or a monetary allowance in lieu of transportation), temporary lodging allowance (overseas) or temporary lodging expense (in

CONUS), dislocation allowance, and house-hunting travel. There is a limitation, based on pay grade and number of dependents, on the amount of household goods (weight) that can be shipped at government expense.

Military members are not always adequately reimbursed for all the expenses incurred on PCS moves, and should be prepared to pay some out-of-pocket costs.

PROMOTIONS

Active Duty

Be aware that some states consider any post-divorce promotions a part of future retired pay that can be awarded to the ex-spouse, even though the service member would consider them his or her own separate property. When a specific formula is used in the divorce decree that is not based on the years of marriage at the time of divorce, post-divorce promotions and their subsequent monetary increases will be divided accordingly.

Moreover, unless the final divorce decree states that payments of retired pay will be made to the former spouse on the basis of the pay grade extant at the time of divorce, the former spouse may realize a "windfall benefit" by being paid at a rate commensurate with the member's pay grade at the date of retirement. This payment could be detrimental to current or future children borne to the service member, and ignore the contributions of the spouse who is actually married to the member longer than the first spouse.

For example, assume the member is divorced at the 8- or 10-year point, remarries and is married for another 20 years, and retires with 28 or 30 years of total military service. The former spouse, if awarded 50 percent of the retired pay, will receive an amount based on 28 or 30 years of service, not 8 or 10 at the time of the divorce. More and more courts are dividing retired pay on the basis of the rank at the time of the divorce, just as other assets such as stocks to be divided. Assets are most often valued on the date of separation or divorce, with the exception of a house that will be sold, with the expenses and profits being shared.

Reserve and Guard

Timing is everything, and the length of time needed to hold a promotion that results in a higher retired pay or even eligible retired pay for a rank is no exception. Under the new reserve promotion programs, there are minimum periods that reservists and guard personnel must hold a rank if they want to retire at that rank. These range from no minimum for certain enlisted ranks to three years for certain officer ranks, and these vary by service. Entering the picture is the requirement that the rank held be based on "satisfactory" service. If the member does not hold a rank long enough, then the service is not "satisfactory," and the retired pay will be based on the next lower rank.

RETIRED PAY

Active Duty

Service members become eligible for retired pay after completing 20 years of satisfactory service. There are three formulas used to compute retired pay. Dependence on the pay charts that appear yearly in various publications is not recommended, and such charts should only be used as broad guides. The military finance center has the final word on the exact retired pay that the service member will receive.

Retired pay is computed under three separate formulas,[1] depending on when the service member joined. The most favorable system covers those who first entered the military before 8 September 1980. Retired pay is based on the highest pay grade in which they served satisfactorily and the pay scale in effect when the service member starts drawing retired pay (see 10 U.S.C. §1406). Members who entered the military on or after 8 September 1980, have their monthly retired pay computed on the average of the base monthly pay in effect for the three years just before they retired (10 U.S.C. §1407).

The third formula is called the "redux" system, for those entering after 31 July 1986. Instead of the service members receiving 50 percent of what was earned on active duty at the high point, the service member who joined after the above date averages 40 percent in retired pay.

One last caveat about retired pay that many are unaware of: You may think that retired pay is a vested right, but it is not, as written in 10 U.S.C §12732. *There is no vested or contractual right to retired pay with respect to service in armed forces and such is dependent upon statutory right by law rather than common law rules governing private contracts.* This is another way retired pay is wholly within the control of and subject to congressional fiat. Only contributory pensions confer vested rights and, since military members make no such contributions, they do not receive a pension as such. They receive "retainer pay" because they are in an "on call" status, making them available for military service on a standby basis. Many states are ordering active duty members to begin paying the share of retired pay immediately upon divorce. These states consider the military retired pay "vested." Since the member is not retired, he or she is not receiving any retainer pay.

Reserve Components

For those entering before 8 September 1980, the calculation is made as follows: Divide the Total Retirement Points by 360 to determine Years of Service. Then, multiply the Years of Service by 2.5 percent; this equals the percentage of base monthly pay that can be drawn for retirement. Multiply that percentage by the monthly base pay in effect when the member retires, and you have the final monthly pre-tax retired pay.

An easier way is to multiply the number of points by the factor established by DoD to arrive at a dollar figure.

The retired pay formulas presented above do not apply to everyone in the Reserve or Guards. There are several ways to compute retired pay depending on numerous factors. It is important that members of a Reserve Component keep up to date on their point credit and accounting, and ensure that their yearly summary is accurate.

In preparation for discovery during a divorce, the service member needs to prepare, or have prepared, a spreadsheet showing the number of points earned prior to the marriage, during the marriage, and those earned after separation and divorce. Reserve Component members need to be aware of the same disturbing trend in divorce cases as active duty members face. Some courts consider military retired pay as "vested." A military member cannot be ordered to retire in order to commence payments under the USFSPA. Another problem reservists face are awards that include "bad years," years in which the minimum points were not earned. Points that are earned in "bad years" are still counted when dividing retired pay.

SEPARATION PAY AND BONUSES

SSB and VSI

When the separation is voluntary, the lump-sum pay is an early-out bonus known as a Special Separation Benefit (SSB).

The Special Separation Benefit (SSB) is computed as follows: a lump sum payment to the member of 15 percent of annual base pay times the number of years of service. This sum is taxable.

The Voluntary Separation Incentive (VSI) is computed as follows: 2.5 percent of the member's monthly base pay times 12 months times years of service. This amount is paid on a *yearly* basis for twice the number of years the member was on active duty. This pay is taxable.

Separation Bonuses—General

While bonuses have been paid for early retirement and voluntary separations to trim the military, there is no assurance that such bonuses will continue in the future. Not all career fields at any given time are eligible for exit bonuses. Senate aides expect that requests from the Pentagon to extend such retirement and exit incentives for both active and Reserve Forces through FY2003 will be approved in the FY99 Defense Authorization Bill. The incentives are needed to prevent the services from involuntarily separating personnel with fewer than 20 years of active service. Currently, the Navy has an abundance of petty officers in some skills and would like incentives to reduce their numbers.

Former service members who took separation pay or a bonus as an incentive to leave active duty must repay that money, including the amount withheld in taxes, if they receive a Department of Veterans Affairs disability rating and qualify for disability compensation.

Reserve Components

Separation pay is paid to reservists and Guard personnel who are involuntary separated. They must have at least 6 but less than 15 years of service. It is a one-time payment and must be repaid if recipients rejoin the military.

Reserve special separation pay may be offered to those younger than 60 who are involuntarily separated with 20 or more years or service, the last six of which must be in the Selected Reserve.

SOCIAL SECURITY BENEFITS FOR DIVORCED SPOUSES

Former spouses are entitled to Social Security checks calculated according to his/her ex-spouse's work history if the following four tests are met: (1) One-half of the ex-spouse's age-65 benefit is larger than the benefit which would be received based on the service member's own work history. (2) Married for at least 10 years. (3) Divorced for at least two years. (4) Must not be married to someone else at the time payment of benefits starts. The former spouse can begin receiving checks as soon as both parties are at least 62, even if neither is retired. If remarried after payments begin, the former spouse will see his or her benefits terminate. The ARA recommends that if a divorce is planned, and the marriage is close to passing the 10-year mark, your attorney or accountant should calculate the financial implications of delaying the divorce until after the 10-year mark has passed.

SPACE-AVAILABLE TRAVEL

Once a lucrative perk, this benefit is fast disappearing as the number of bases and posts close and services are consolidated. Departure sites for Space-A travel, as it is called, are pretty much limited to either coast, which means getting there is a must. When considering where to retire, don't forget about this benefit. It could ease the financial burden of visiting dependent children.

TEMPORARY DISABILITY
RETIREMENT LIST (TDRL)

Active duty and reserve personnel ordered to active duty for more than 30 days may be placed on the TDRL, receiving a minimum of 50 percent of their basic pay and not more than 75 percent. The exact amount is determined by a formula. Personnel who are placed on this list are, basically, military retirees. However, once on this list, the military member can be discharged if doctors decide he or she will not recover sufficiently to resume military duties; or, the service member could be ordered back into uniform. There is a five-year deadline.

The amount received can be computed by two methods. Those who joined the service before 8 September 1980, use the last monthly basic pay received, which is then multiplied by 2.5 percent for each year on active duty. Or, it can be multiplied by the percentage figure assigned as the veteran's disability. Those who joined after that date must use the average basic pay for their top 36 months of military income. This income is taxable for anyone who joined the military after 24 September 1975. An exemption from federal taxes remains for those receiving disability compensation related to combat, hazardous duty or conditions simulating war.

Those on the TDRL may obtain a waiver that allows the service member to stay in uniform and perform limited duties.

TEMPORARY DUTY

Service members on duty away from their home stations receive a per diem allowance, which varies based on whether quarters and government dining facilities are available, and the location of the duty.

TRANSITION BENEFITS

Transition benefits began in 1990 (in 1993 for reservists) and have undergone many changes since then. Members and their families should check with their local military installation to determine whether there are any special programs available at the time. An example would be programs to help departing members become teachers or law enforcement workers.

Active Duty—
Voluntary Separation and Retirement

Military Services are required to grant certain benefits to separating members who retire or separate (with a minimum of at least six years on active duty) under honorable conditions. Transition Assistance Programs (TAP) are held regularly at military installations to provide the information needed to smoothly transition from active duty to civilian status.

Benefits include pre-separation counseling for the member and spouse, employment and relocation assistance for the member and spouse, options on health insurance, and transportation of household goods (including storage).

Other benefits include the Special Separation Benefit (SSB) and the Voluntary Separation Incentive (VSI) (for those not eligible for retired pay), given under specific conditions.

Active Duty—Involuntary Separation

There are additional benefits for service members who are involuntarily separated or separated under the SSB or VSI programs. These include extended medical care, GI Bill benefits, extended commissary and exchange privileges, extended stay in government quarters, shipment and storage of household goods, federal employment hiring preference, additional leave or permissive temporary duty for job and house hunting, and priority placement in a Reserve Component or the National Guard. Active duty members residing overseas at the time they are to be involuntarily separated are authorized to keep a dependent in high school if the child is completing the senior year.

Service members who have between six (five years for officers) but less than 20 years of service who are involuntarily separated under honorable conditions, are eligible for separation pay equal to 10 percent of monthly base pay times 12 months times the number of years of service. This is a single taxable payment at the time of separation.

Reserve and Guard

Transition assistance is available for members of Reserve Components with between six and 15 "good" years. These benefits vary, but generally include separation pay, reduced retired pay for fewer than 20 years of service (retired pay still does not begin until age 60), and special separation pay.

Reservists who lost their position due to downsizing

receive priority placement in other units, assuming the individual meets the qualifications for which he or she has applied. If a reservist accepts separation pay and subsequently joins another Selected Reserve unit, the reservist will have to repay the separation bonus. Educational benefits, and commissary and exchange privileges are also extended to certain separating reservists.

Transition Benefits and Divorce Planning

Both the member and spouse should take advantage of this assistance while still married, as such employment counseling and other transition benefits will not usually be available to the spouse once the couple is divorced. Further, there is no cost to the member and spouse for these services. Comparable services, such as employment counseling and job hunting assistance, or re-training programs on the "outside," could run into several thousand dollars.

BOTTOM LINE

As should be obvious from the extensive list provided in this chapter, federal benefits *must* be considered in any military divorce. The time for this is during the discovery and interrogatory processes at the outset of the proceedings. No two situations will be alike, therefore, no "canned" solutions can be offered. The best solution will evolve from a situation in which both parties can agree to an amicable discussion of options which will serve the discrete needs of both parties. Each must reconcile themselves to accepting that some things are unlikely ever to be as good as they were while married. The challenge is to reduce the possibility that life as divorcees will not be as bad as it could be if federal benefits are not fully, honestly, and objectively considered during the divorce proceedings.

CHAPTER ENDNOTES

1. See Endnote #1 in Chapter 8.

10

FINANCIAL MANAGEMENT BEFORE AND AFTER YOUR DIVORCE

There is no getting around it—divorce can be and is, for many people, devastating both emotionally and financially. Whatever emotional turmoil attaches to a divorce, the end of a marriage usually also involves financial considerations that can be overwhelming and may create new long-term complications for both parties. In most cases, both parties will experience a decrease in their living standards, if for no other reason than it costs money to get a divorce and then to maintain separate households. Making decisions in a divorce while under emotional stress is difficult enough, but it is the financial decisions made during this period that will have the greatest impact on the futures of both parties. The decision process can be materially handicapped if both parties have not been actively involved in the management of household finances. Professional assistance may be needed to assure the fair and equitable treatment of both parties to the divorce.

The best advice we can give you, if it is at all possible, make a clean break when dividing the property and allocating your debts. When you stay obligated or connected to each other financially, you are both at risk.

The financial decision process starts by applying a monetary value to assets, something that most couples find difficult, if not distasteful. In the course of doing so, neither should forget that marital debts, even if incurred by one spouse, are considered to have benefited both parties during the marriage. And while a court may divide the marital debt, liability for that debt if incurred in both names remains with each party.

Your attorney may tell you that a divorce is really just another business relationship gone awry. But what happens when a business must dissolve? The assets are valued and divided—no different than in a divorce. Many accountants will reduce everything to present value (some states require the valuation as of the separation date, others as of the actual divorce date; still others let you choose). However, you need to look also at future needs. The information in this chapter was obtained from public data which is readily available. However, it would be prudent to consult a tax attorney, accountant, or other professional specifically conversant with such matters.

You need to start with some basic questions and steps as you consider the factors cited below.

1. Which parties work?
2. How close is either party to retirement?
3. What is the job market like, right now and projected, for the soon-to-be retired service member or soon-to-be ex-spouse?
4. Have both parties considered career counseling?
5. What other possible financial sources does each party have? (Potential inheritances, professional degrees, postgraduate education?)

6. What are the minimum acceptable life-style standards of both parties? Are they attainable? If not, what are the alternatives?

7. Are you being realistic about your family's financial situation?

8. What are the earning potentials of both parties, short- and long-term?

9. Consider what usual post-divorce actions will be affected or may need to be taken before the divorce is final: Change beneficiaries on insurance policies, retirement plans, employment income, bank accounts, investment accounts; close joint credit-card accounts; redo your will and update any powers-of-attorney.

The ARA recommends that any payments military members must make as a result of divorce be in the form of an allotment from active duty or retired pay. The advantages are obvious. Both parties know that payments will be made on schedule, and the emotional stress (if anger is still there) is mitigated because neither party has to write or mail a check or ask for what is due. The FY97 Defense Authorization Act allows retirees up to six allotments from their retired pay.

As you value your assets for the discovery process or for financial planning, it is best to value on the low side for your personal property. As one lawyer says, how much would you get for it at a garage sale? Start with that figure. Readers are directed to Appendix O for state criteria covering various divorce issues.

ALIMONY

If you are the party awarded alimony, consider funding your IRA for that year with the money. Your tax savings, both federal and state, could be significant if the amount is deductible.

ALLOWANCES

Regulations normally permit only one member of a dual-service couple to receive the housing or other family allowances for dependents. However, military members married to each other may receive, in some circumstances, dependents' housing benefits simultaneously, even though only one parent has custody. The parent without custody is expected to use the extra money to make court-ordered child-support payments to the ex-spouse. Check with your personnel office for details.

Relocation allowances continue to be excludable from gross income for tax purposes. However, this is one area Congress has gone after in the past (to have service members include the reimbursements in their gross income) and will continue to target in the future.

AUTOMOBILE INSURANCE

1. Who continues paying the insurance?
2. Are the vehicles registered in both names?
3. If separated, the parties need to notify the insurance company that the vehicles are no longer jointly garaged.
4. One spouse may have to apply for insurance in his or her own name.

If the insurance company is USAA (headquartered in San Antonio, TX), ex-spouses may be eligible for insurance with subsidiaries for ex-dependents. Former spouses interested in talking to USAA about insurance can call 800-531-8080 (in San Antonio, 210-498-8080).

BANK AND OTHER FINANCIAL ACCOUNTS

No matter what the height of anger or depth of emotional upheaval attributable to the divorce, do not empty or raid any bank accounts. If the income usually received is no longer coming in, take only what you need to live on. If an allotment is being made to a bank account, then continue it until told otherwise by an attorney or both parties agree as to how the money will be divided. Courts see through vengeful tactics; such tactics are dangerous and could come back to haunt the offending party later in the divorce.

BONUSES

Government-Owed Debts Recouped from Bonuses

Any government-owed debts, such as recoupment for civilian schooling, may be deducted from any bonuses the service member may receive. Depending on your state's divorce law, such debts may be considered separate, owed by the service member only, or joint, by both the member and spouse. A reduction in the bonus monies, nonetheless, must be taken into consideration.

VSI Continues Even When Not Promoted

A reservist who is receiving annual VSI payments and fails to get promoted will continue to receive VSI. (VSI is the exit bonus that is paid annually to some people leaving active duty for twice as long as they were on active duty.)

VSI/SSB Recouped from Drill and Retired Pay

Active duty members who accept the VSI bonus and join the Reserve/Guard and subsequently retire, must repay the government for their VSI at the time they begin to receive retired pay. VSI and SSB recipients must repay the government for the money withheld for taxes. If recipients earn drill pay have that money withheld to repay their VSI and SSB, that money is subtracted from the amount they are obligated to pay. The rules are complicated; consult the military pay office.

CHILDREN

Claiming the Children on Your Income Tax Form

A child's exemption is claimed by the parent who provides more than half of the child's support. The parent who has custody of the child for the greater part of the year is generally treated as the parent who provided more than half the child's support. If neither the divorce decree nor agreement establishes custody, the parent with physical custody for the greater part of the year is considered to have custody of the child. The custodial parent can release the exemption to the non-custodial parent by signing a written declaration, IRS Tax Form 8332, "Release of Claim to Exemption for Child of Divorced or Separated Parents," or similar statement.

Consider for each year who will derive the most tax benefit by claiming exemptions for the children. It may not be the same spouse each year. Transferring the exemption to the higher-bracket parent may produce net tax savings. See IRS Tax Form 8332. Be sure this item is included in your divorce decree.

Child Support

Child support payments are not eligible for the earned income credit under IRS Code Section 32 (see also IRS

Publication 596). Further, child support payments cannot be deducted for tax purposes. Neither does the spouse receiving child support payments report them as income.

Child support is not limited to monthly payments until the child reaches 18. It means discussing with each other all the other implications that raising children involve—who pays for the extras, such as summer camp, private schools or tutoring, travel between the two parents and even grandparents.

Reaching age 18 does not always mean the end of support, either. Some courts may order the wealthier spouse to pay for college expenses. One couple we know solved the college education problem quite simply. Each spouse promised to pay one-third of the college education of their children (one helps with tuition, the other with room and board—with expenses about equal, assuming both parties can afford it), and dividing the expenses three ways—mother, father, and child. The children not only had to apply for financial aid or win a scholarship, but they were told by the parents they had to work part-time jobs in the summer and during vacations. If they did not do their part applying for loans to help pay for college expenses or working, then both parents were under no obligation to pay anything. The problem with many expenses is that people see them in black and white—when there are many shades of gray.

Visit a domestic court before a child-support hearing so that you will know what to expect and what you will need to do to prepare for it. One source to help you prepare is the book *Child Support: How to Get What Your Child Needs and Deserves*, by Carole A. Chambers (Summit Books, 1230 Avenue of the Americas, NY 10020, $19.50).

CREDIT CARDS

Credit cards can be a major source of trouble in a divorce proceeding. The ultimate protection is, of course, the spending limit, but even that may be beyond the financial resources (singly or joint) of the parties concerned. Both parties should cooperate in determining what cards exist and who has transactional authority. Outstanding balances should be determined and agreement should be reached on payment plans.

Your divorce decree does not change your legal obligations to creditors. Even if one spouse agrees to pay the bills, the other spouse is not off the hook legally. If one spouse refuses to pay, loses his or her job, or files for bankruptcy, the other spouse will be stuck paying, and your credit could be damaged.

All joint cards should be surrendered and new credit card accounts should be reopened in the names of the individual parties. Both parties should agree on spending patterns and ceilings which are to prevail until the divorce is final. Any evidence of malicious buildup of credit card debt is likely to be viewed, by the court, with prejudice against the offender. So long as the cards are joint, all debts incurred will be considered joint. Credit cards stand with bank accounts at the leading edge of the financial arena where the switch from joint to unilateral money management must be made.

EDUCATION

Service members who separate before completing a service obligation required for government-paid civilian schooling may have to pay back the cost of that education. Recoupments may also be made from any bonus (VSI/SSB) or other separation pay the member might receive.

EMPLOYMENT WITH THE
FEDERAL GOVERNMENT

Reservists or others with military time who work for the federal government will have to make a payment into the civil service retirement system if they wish their military time to be counted toward their civil service retirement. If they do not do this, their civil service annuity will be reduced at the time they become eligible for Social Security at age 62. If the individual was hired on or after 1 October 1982, he or she will have to make a deposit of seven percent of basic military pay, plus interest, accrued since 1985, for military time to be counted in their civil service retirement. If hired on or after 1 January 1984, the deposit is three percent, plus interest.

HEALTH INSURANCE

The divorce decree needs to address health insurance to cover the military member, the former spouse and, if necessary, the children.

If the marriage is not a 20/20/20 one (married 20 years to a military member who had 20 years of service creditable to retirement, with a 20-year overlap of marriage and military service), and, for example, the military member is working and is eligible for health insurance, then you need to look into the employer's health insurance coverage to review any coverage that would be available under the Consolidated Omnibus Budget Reconciliation Act (COBRA)[1] that allows a divorced spouse to purchase health insurance coverage provided by the other spouse's employer at group rates up to a certain period after the divorce. There are time limits for signing up.

Unremarried former spouses who qualify under the 20/20/20 rule qualify for a Dependent's I.D. card which entitles them to full military base privileges. Unremarried former spouses with less than 20/20/20 but at least 20/20/15 are eligible for medical care for one year from the date of divorce, followed by the right to convert to the Continued Health Care Benefit Program (CHCBP). The program provides care similar to the former CHAMPUS program. If a former spouse is no longer eligible for a DoD I.D. card, the retiree sponsor must notify the Defense Enrollment Eligibility Reporting System (DEERS) at 1-800-334-4162 (California only), 1-800-527-5602 (Alaska and Hawaii), or 1-800-538-9552 (all other states); fax: (408) 655-8317; or e-mail: addrinfo@osd.pentagon.mil. *Failure to notify DEERS that a former spouse is no longer eligible for care may render the retiree liable for the former spouse's medical care costs.*

Medical benefits for an unremarried former spouse whose marriage covered at least 20 years of military service will be granted regardless of the date of divorce, provided the spouse is not covered by employer-sponsored medical insurance. Commissary, theater, and exchange privileges may be reinstated to a 20/20/20 former spouse whose remarriage ends in death, divorce or annulment. Medical benefits are NOT restored. Questions in this area should be directed to the nearest military base facility issuing DoD I.D. cards.

Recipients of SSB or regular separation pay are eligible for government-paid health coverage, but it only lasts 60 days after the date of discharge for those who served less than six years on active duty, and 120 days for those who served longer.

Other options for health insurance include group plans through associations, alumni, union, and similar groups.

Retiree health care under TRICARE stops at age 65, when the retiree becomes eligible for Medicare. Supplemental insurance will most likely be needed.

HOUSE

Next to child support needs, the marital home may be the next most important concern. The house is usually considered a source of financial security, but often the parties do not think through what keeping a house entails and they let emotions, rather than economics, rule. As the saying goes, when you own a Pinto, you have $200 repair problems; if you own a Mercedes, you get $2,000 repair problems. Some of the questions you need to discuss are:

1.   Who will get the house?

2.   Should it be sold? (What is the seller's climate in your city right now? Can you agree on a selling price? If the house cannot be sold immediately, can you come to an agreement?)

3.   Will keeping the house by one spouse be a financial burden (mortgage, taxes, insurance, utilities, maintenance, etc.)?

4.   Who will get the tax deduction on the interest payments? (The loss of that deduction could seriously damage a spouse's tax status.)

5.   Is it feasible to buy one spouse's equity out of the house? If you negotiate to buy out your spouse's share, negotiate a rate that reflects your additional costs for any capital gains liability and other sales costs. Most certainly one will agree to only a share of the equity value (fair market minus the mortgage) versus the financial value (fair market value minus mortgage, taxes and sales costs).

In the majority of cases, keeping the house, unless there are other independent means to keep it, is not a palatable option. One creative method, where minor children are involved (and the market for selling is not right), is where both spouses keep the house and you both take a small apartment. (You would own the home as tenants in common—see your tax advisor.) The children remain in the marital home and are not uprooted weekly or monthly or whatever to go spend time with the other spouse, and the parents are the ones who spend time in the house on a rotating basis.

Regardless of what decision is made, divorcing spouses should examine the tax consequences of both selling and keeping the home.

LEGAL FEES

Whatever you think your divorce might cost, multiply it by 10, and you might come pretty close to what it ends up costing you. Attorneys' fees can range from $125 to more than $300 an hour. If one party has no visible source of income, the other will most likely be required to pay for the attorney. An uncontested divorce might cost less than $1000, but when there is a pension involved, this is not usually considered something that can be done quickly and without negotiating. Uncontested divorces are practically unheard of when there is military retired pay involved.

Both spouses can help keep legal fees down in a number of ways. The first is by cooperating with each other for data requests, and maintaining a civil behavior to each other. By obtaining checklists[2] ahead of time that both can go through, you can lessen the amount of time you need to spend in your respective attorney's office; otherwise, your bill will be higher. The best advice is to settle as many issues as possible before even seeing an attorney. This is quite easy, given the number of divorce self-help books on the market.

Second, in some cases where the parties are not on good speaking terms, they might consider mediation, which is less costly than having attorneys hammer out everything. Keep in mind, however, that some attorneys do not favor mediation and may not suggest it. If you obtain and complete checklists found in the self-help books, then you might derive some benefit in meeting with a mediator. (There is a move underway by states to make public-sponsored mediation mandatory.) Your mutual objectives should be to avoid an adversarial environment.

Third, regardless of the other two ways to keep legal fees down, keep good financial records and stay involved about your family finances. If your attorney has to hire an accountant to analyze your tax returns, evaluate your property, study pension plans and other benefit packages, you will pay for those services.

LIFE INSURANCE

The primary reason why people buy life insurance is to protect the family's financial security upon the death of the breadwinner. You must first determine the nature of your financial picture:

1. Review your policies to see who is named as beneficiaries.

2. Determine whether the need for a certain policy exists—would you be better off replacing your existing policy, and with what?

3. If there is a cash buildup, what will be done with it? Particularly if the insurance is no longer needed, this could be a source of cash during or after the divorce.

4. Does your employer furnish life insurance that you may have initially waived but could use now?

5. If life insurance is awarded in the divorce, are the beneficiaries irrevocable?

6. How insurable is either spouse? Just because you apply for life insurance does not mean that the company will insure you. Do you participate in high-risk activities (e.g., flying, scuba diving)? Have you had a serious health

problem? Attorneys will usually advise that any requirement for life insurance in a divorce settlement be applied for before the divorce is final so that you find out whether the party is insurable and whether you have to adjust your negotiating plans because one of the parties is uninsurable and unable to pass a medical exam.

7. Do not give up any present policies until the replacement policies, if any, are in force.

If the service member anticipates receiving a disability retirement from the VA, he or she may be eligible for a Service-Disabled Veterans National Service Life Insurance (SDVI) policy. Application must be filed within one year of the VA rating. Veterans who already have $10,000 of National Service Life Insurance or the U.S. Government Life Insurance are not eligible for the SDVI. For further information, call your regional VA office at 800-827-1000.

As a source of income, don't forget the cash value in your government (VA) life insurance policies.

MOVING EXPENSES

You must budget and save money for moving expenses if one spouse's move will not be covered by the military. (If there were ever a time to get rid of stuff, now is the time to do it. Remember, if you don't have it, you don't have to move it, clean it, store it, maintain it, or pay insurance on it!)

If the military member is stationed overseas on an accompanied tour, you will need to consult with the JAG's office for details on moving your household goods back to the states to a different location other than your PCS assignment or your home of record. If the member is on an unaccompanied tour and has property in the marital home, then the spouse will need a power of attorney to handle the moving of the member's personal belongings if the member will not be there.

PROPERTY TRANSFERS

Congress passed the Deficit Reduction Act of 1984 that states for transfers of property between spouses or former spouses after 18 July 1984, no gain or loss is recognized against the transferor if the transfer occurs during the marriage or is incident to a divorce. (This law applies only if the transferee is a U.S. citizen or a resident alien.) Such transfers of property (including cash) pursuant to a divorce are treated as gifts between the spouses. No gift taxes are paid because of the unlimited marital deduction and a carry-over basis applies. For example, the wife buys out half the equity in their home for $80,000 and continues to live in the home. The wife has made a "gift" of $80,000 to the ex-husband and he has made a "gift" to the wife of his one-half interest in the home.

A word of caution must be given, however. Assume that instead of transferring the house to the wife now, the parties agree that they will obtain a divorce decree, and sell the house at a future date. The wife will get all the proceeds. The now-divorcing parties own the property as "tenants in common," rather than tenants by the entirety. If the divorce decree was entered into after 18 July 1984, it could be argued that the transfer is "incident to the divorce." According to IRS Code Section 1041, a transfer of property is incident to the divorce if such a transfer occurs within one year after the date on which the marriage ceases and is related to the cessation of the marriage. The IRS has taken the position that if the transfer is required in the divorce decree or separation agreement, it is incident to the divorce if the transfer occurs within six years after the date on which the marriage ends. If the transfer is not made under a divorce decree or separation agreement, or does not occur within six years after the marriage ends, it is presumed not to be related to the ending of the divorce. In the above example, the wife would be subject to any gains.

Consider, however, if the two parties agree to split the proceeds. The husband has not lived in the property for two years, and could be subject to gains tax. (The Tax Court has ruled in favor of the party paying the mortgage, taxes, etc., even though not residing in the house.) It is ARA's position that as many assets of the marriage be divided as equitably and cleanly as possible, so as to prevent any negative consequences, tax or otherwise, down the road.

Disposing of other property, such as a boat or car, means that both parties must agree as to what the selling price will be and how the proceeds will be divided. Some spouses would be better off opting for a lump-sum cash property settlement rather than taking hard assets. Reality must sink in at some point, and sometimes it takes a third party to make it sink in. (For example, do you really want to keep the boat because you like sailing? Or is it the status symbol that you believe your friends might think less of you if you don't have it? No one cares!)

RETIRED PAY—CONDITIONS UNDER WHICH YOU COULD LOSE IT

We take for granted that retired pay continues no matter what. Some of the conditions under which military retired pay would stop or be suspended include: commission of a felony, garnishment for debts owed the federal government or for court-ordered garnishment orders, serving in a foreign military. The divorce decree should include a provision or contingency for such a loss.

SEPARATION DATE—MARITAL

Planning your separation date may be one of the more fiscally responsible steps you both take. In some states, assets are valued and divided as of the date of separation, not the date of divorce. To consider with this date would be other events, such as distributions from investments, contributions to retirement plans and bonuses (if either party is employed by a private company).

SEPARATION DATE—MILITARY

If the service member is close to retiring with 20 years of service and the marriage will be a 20/20/20, staying together "on paper" may be a move both the member and the spouse should discuss, so that the spouse will be eligible for various military benefits (commissary, medical, exchange, etc.)

SEPARATION PAY
AND SSB/VSI BONUSES—
RESERVE AND GUARD

If the service member has any plans to join a reserve or guard unit, he or she should think twice before spending any separation bonus—it is not theirs to spend. Congress declared that reservists will have to repay the government for their exit bonus. For example, assume the member leaves active duty after 12 years and serves another eight years in the Reserves. The reservist will qualify for 20 years of service and a reserve retirement at the age of 60. Since 60 percent (12/20) of the total military time was on active duty, then 60 percent of each monthly retirement check will be withheld until the entire SSB, VSI, or other separation pay is repaid.

SOCIAL SECURITY

For marriages which last(ed) for at least 10 years, a former spouse qualifies for Social Security payments amounting to 50 percent of the former military member's entitlement, commencing at age 62, provided the former spouse has been divorced two years or more. A surviving (widowed), divorced former spouse qualifies for Social Security benefits at age 60—and if disabled, at age 50.[3] Additional entitlements derive from the custody of dependent children. Former spouses would be well advised to check, as early as practicable during the divorce process, with an office of the Social Security Administration to ascertain the amount of any Social Security benefits for which they may be eligible and the date they will be available. Military members should encourage this inasmuch as Social Security payments to an ex-spouse have no impact on the member's financial status and the monies involved might be a factor influencing the determination of the amount and length of time for financial support which the member must pay.

SPOUSE PREFERENCE

In the Military Family Act of 1985, Congress authorized DoD officials to give all military spouses preference in filling Civil Service jobs. Before that, only spouses who were overseas received preference. Be sure to examine this source for employment before the divorce is final.

SUPPORT PAYMENTS

Support payments come in two forms: alimony and child support. Whether support is awarded is largely dependent on the status of the union at the time of divorce.

If the marriage has lasted only a year or two, there are no children and both parties are gainfully employed, there will likely be no award of support payments.

If the marriage has lasted for some time (e.g., at least 10 years) and one of the parties has no marketable skills, then it is reasonable to expect an award of alimony—payable until the payee remarries or during a finite period of 'rehabilitation.'

If either party has some physical ailment which precludes gainful employment or reduces the chances of remarriage, alimony for life is a distinct possibility.

In any case where minor children are involved, child support payments will very likely be awarded in addition to alimony.

State laws governing alimony and child support vary widely. As a general rule, alimony stops upon the remarriage of the benefiting ex-spouse. Some states limit the period for the payment of alimony, irrespective of the remarriage consideration. Some states allow the termination of child support payments upon the remarriage of the ex-spouse having custody; some do not. Formulas for computing the size of alimony and child support payments vary widely but, in most cases, are negotiable. It is reasonable to seek trade-offs between immediate property concessions and long-term support payments.

Alimony is tax-deductible for the party paying it and taxable to the party receiving it. Child support is not tax deductible for the party paying it, however, it is tax-free to the party receiving it. The party paying child support should be alert for any strategy which maximizes child support payments and minimizes alimony.

It is important to remember that, while alimony is tax deductible, lump-sum property or cash settlements, voluntary (i.e., not under a court order) payments of an ex-spouse's debts, payments of premiums on life insurance on which the ex-spouse is the beneficiary (but not the policy owner), are *not* tax deductible.

Some courts may order that the party making support payments take out some form of life insurance for the period over which payments must be made. This is most simply accomplished by contracting for some form of term life insurance. An offer of insurance might also be a negotiation tool during the determination of the size of support payments. Properly entered in the divorce decree, the premiums for such insurance could be tax deductible.

TAX CONSIDERATIONS

The simplest financial concerns related to a military divorce concern the tax implications. One of the best sources we have found for tax information is *The Retired Officer Magazine's* (published by TROA) annual Income Tax insert, with information applicable to military. The following is a primer on some basics.

Alimony

Alimony is usually deductible by the person paying it and included as income by the receiver, when there is a decree of divorce or separate maintenance, or when payment is made under a written separation agreement or temporary support order [as described in IRS Code Sec. 71 (b)(2)]. Keep in mind that alimony is not deductible if the two parties are still residing in the same household [(IRS Code Section 71(b)(1)(C)]. Alimony payments are not eligible for the earned income credit under IRS Code Section 32. See IRS Publication 596. However, alimony is considered earned income for purposes of the IRA deduction. You do not have to itemize to claim alimony payments. Consult a tax adviser if you are unaware of the IRS's "recapture rules." This is an area of tax law, designed to prevent couples from front-loading alimony payments in the first years after a divorce, that has tripped up many divorced couples. Consider whether receiving alimony may place the recipient into a higher marginal tax bracket. If this is the case, consider offsets with child support or other property divisions.

Disability Retired Pay

Disability retired pay may or may not be taxed, based on where the military member retires.

VA Disability Compensation

VA disability compensation paid by the VA to retirees with service-connected disabilities is exempt from income tax. Retirees must waive an equal amount of military retired pay. [Legislation continues to be proposed to end the dollar-for-dollar offset for disability retired pay. However, efforts to date have not succeeded. One of the latest proposals (11 March 1998) is contained in HR 3434, sponsored by Rep. Lane Evans (D-IL), whereby retirees would lose only 50 cents of their retired pay for every dollar received in disability compensation once the retiree reaches age 65, and the offset would be eliminated after reaching age 70. Like the other bills, this one has almost no chance of passing Congress.]

SBP/RSFPP Annuities

SBP/RSFPP annuities may or may not be taxed by each state. The federal estate tax treatment of SBP depends on the member's specific SBP election.

Social Security

Social Security income may or may not be taxable, subject to income restrictions. If you are thinking about remarriage, keep in mind that the IRS is not a true believer in some family values, at least if you are younger than age 60. The rule is that if you expect to receive your deceased spouse's Social Security benefits, you forfeit all rights to his or her Social Security account if you remarry before age 60. If you remarry after age 60, the government allows you to claim Social Security benefits as either a spousal or survivor benefit. Usually, you will get a lot more if you receive it as a widow or widower, and a lot sooner, age 60 versus 62.

State Income Tax

All military retired pay is tax exempt in the following states: AL, HI, IL, KY, LA, MI, MT, NY, OR, and PA. USPHS and NOAA retired pay is not, however, exempt in MI. Disability retired pay is exempt in a number of states. State income tax can be withheld from retired pay. Consider whether receiving alimony may place the recipient into a higher tax bracket. If this is the case, consider offsets with child support or other property division.

Legal Fees and Court Costs Incurred in a Divorce

The costs of obtaining a divorce are generally not deductible. However, you may be able to deduct legal fees paid for tax advice in connection with your divorce and deduct legal fees to collect alimony that you must include in gross income. You may also be able to deduct fees paid to such professionals as appraisers and accountants, for services in determining the correct amount of tax or in helping to obtain alimony. Always obtain an itemized statement from such people.

Tax Filing Status

Your marital status as of the end of the tax year (usually 31 December) determines your filing status. Those able to file as "head of household" enjoy a more favorable tax status. Couples not divorced by the end of the year generally have the option to file either a joint or a separate return (married filing separately). Figure your tax both ways to make sure you are using the method that will result in the lower tax. If either spouse suspects that the other is hiding income, then filing a separate return is advisable. Consult your tax adviser.

Unpaid Taxes

Since March 1996, the IRS has notified divorced and separated spouses when it takes action to collect jointly owed taxes from the other spouse. Complaints from divorced spouses caused this change, as the IRS was going after the most readily accessible spouse—often the woman who stayed in the family home—rather than the spouse who was most responsible for back taxes.

Signing a Joint Return

While joint filing usually offers the lowest tax rates, ARA must issue a word of caution to couples who are separated and still filing joint tax returns. Your signature guarantees that a joint return is correct and that you guarantee payment of all the tax, plus all interest and civil penalties that arise from any error or finagling. Divorce decree clauses that commit one former spouse to paying joint deficiencies does not bar the IRS from going after both ex-spouses. Sometimes you can rescue yourself by proving you were an "innocent spouse," but to do so you must "jump through hoops" (go through a maze of tests in the IRS Code) to prove you are truly "innocent." Remember, the IRS is under no obligation to help you prove your case as the innocent spouse. The simplest way to avoid such problems is to file separate returns, even though this may mean paying more to Uncle Sam.

Be sure to check with a tax adviser if you live in a community property state and you are separated. Generally, each must report one-half of the community income, regardless of who earned it. However, one spouse may be able to avoid reporting income earned by the other if they live apart and do not file a joint return. At the very least, consider reading one of the tax preparation guides, such as J.K. Lasser's, and also call the IRS.

IRS Publications

The IRS offers a free publication of particular interest to military taxpayers, entitled, IRS Publication 3, "Tax Information for Military Personnel." At various times, the IRS may also publish publications to cover specific situations, as it did with Publication 945, "Tax Information for Those Affected by Operation Desert Storm."

WILLS

1. Do you have a current one? If not, go to your JAG office or a competent attorney to execute one.
2. In some states, you may not be able to write your spouse out of the will until you are actually divorced.
3. Once you divorce, rewrite your will. Consider who your new heirs will be.

POST-DIVORCE FINANCIAL MANAGEMENT

Review Your Withholding Allowances

Be sure to review your withholding allowances (Form W-4, "Employee's Withholding Allowance Certificate") with your employer when you become divorced (as well as when you separate). For example, if you receive alimony that is not subject to withholding, you may have to ask for additional withholdings from your salary or make estimated tax payments in order to avoid interest and penalties for underpayment of your taxes.

Obtain IRS Publication 504, "Divorced or Separated Individuals," for further information. It is free by calling 1-800-829-3676.

Put Yourself on a Budget

You are no longer receiving the tax advantages for being a one-earner couple. Or, if you both worked, you must face the fact that you will lose one income. Cut up credit cards if necessary. Notify (if you did not do so during the divorce) all creditors where you were both jointly liable. You remain so until you make a change with the credit card company.

Educate Yourself About Family Finances

If you did not maintain the books during your marriage, you cannot afford to not learn how to do so now. Learn your financial picture.

IN SUMMARY

Try to keep your financial aspects separate from your

emotional aspects. Get a grip on reality—neither party can live the way you used to. Expect some sacrifice in your lifestyle and a financial recovery period of at least three years, and usually longer.

Get rid of your attitude of "I have to win." Those who have it frequently end up losing in the long run. You do not have to be ashamed that you must now put yourself on a budget and tighten your belt—besides, it's the "in" thing right now, 'simplifying one's life' and 'downsizing.' Consider your divorce settlement a starting point for a new investment plan.

If you were not savvy in managing your household finances, you need to be now. Many of the financial problems that occur in divorce could be eliminated if each party had a full understanding of what goes into managing a household and providing for a family. Work with each other to negotiate a fair division of assets that will provide the basis to rebuild your lives and provide for your children as well. Seek advice from your attorney on how to prevent your spouse from erasing any obligations to pay debts through bankruptcy.

Thus, careful financial planning must start before the divorce so that getting the divorce does not spell financial ruin for either party.

CHAPTER ENDNOTES

1. The U.S. Department of Labor publishes the brochure "Health Benefits under COBRA."

2. See Appendix P for books with checklists.

3. At age 62, the surviving former spouse can switch to your own Social Security account if it pays more.

11

Survivor Benefit Plan*

The Survivor Benefit Plan (SBP) is a voluntary program in which a military retiree may elect to receive a reduced amount of retired (or retainer) pay to provide an annuity to eligible survivor(s). (This reduction is referred to as a "premium.") SBP is available to retired members of the Uniformed Services, including the U.S. Coast Guard, Public Health Service, and the National Oceanic and Atmospheric Administration. Service members who retire under the 15-year temporary early retirement authority (TERA) are eligible to enroll in SBP. The same rules, regulations and laws apply to the 15-year as does the 20-plus year retirement. Survivors of SBP participants receive annuities up to 55 percent of the participant's retired pay.

Retirement-eligible (20 years of active service) members of the above services who are serving on active duty

*The American Retirees Association wishes to thank the Uniformed Services Almanac, Inc., for permission to reprint this excerpt on SBP. USA publishes several excellent books covering active duty, Reserve/Guard, and retired personnel. See Appendix P for ordering information.

are covered by SBP at the maximum level as long as they remain on active duty. Upon retirement, enrollment in SBP with the maximum level of coverage is automatic unless a member elects to decline participation or to participate with a reduced "base amount" prior to the date on which the member becomes entitled to retired pay. Written concurrence of the member's spouse is required to decline participation or to elect a reduced level of coverage for spouse only, spouse and child(ren) or child(ren) only options.

A member's "base amount" is a dollar amount selected by a member at the time of enrollment on which the member's monthly premium and the survivor's monthly annuity will be computed. A base amount may be any amount between a $300.00 minimum and the member's full gross retired pay.

NOTE: The FY98 Defense Authorization Act also provides an opportunity to discontinue participation in the SBP. Enrolled members will have a one-year period commencing on the second anniversary of the receipt of retired pay to withdraw from the SBP. Written spousal concurrence will be required. This provision became effective 17 May 1998. Retirees who have passed their second anniversary of receipt of retired pay when the law is implemented will have one year from implementation in which to withdraw.[1]

Members of the Reserve Forces, including the Army and Air National Guard, are eligible to participate in the Reserve Component-Survivor Benefit Plan (RC-SBP) upon completion of 20 years of qualifying service or upon early retirement (15-19 years). Under the provisions of Public Law 95-397, enacted 30 September 1978, reservists may: (A) decline to make an election until attaining age 60 when they become eligible to receive retired pay and participate in SBP; (B) elect coverage for annuities to begin upon the reservist's death or upon the date the reservist would become age 60, whichever is later; or (C) elect coverage for annuities to begin upon the reservist's death, regardless of the reservist's age when death occurs. Reservists who elect either options B or C at less than the maximum level of spouse coverage or for children only must provide the written concurrence of their spouses.

COVERAGES AVAILABLE

There are six categories of beneficiaries that may be elected to receive survivor protection under SBP. The category elected determines the amount of a member's premium and the survivor's annuity. The categories are: Spouse Only, Spouse and Children, Children Only, Former Spouse, Former Spouse and Children, and Persons with Insurable Interest (e.g., a close relative). See table 11-1 for SBP spouse-only premium costs.

We have included the information that relates to Former Spouse and Former Spouse and Children coverage.

Former Spouse. The Uniformed Services Former Spouses' Protection Act of 1982, enacted 8 September 1982 (P.L. 97-252), amended the SBP program to permit retiring service members to voluntarily elect SBP coverage for former spouses.

Public Law 98-525, enacted 9 October 1984, permitted the enforcement of court orders in which members agree to voluntarily provide continued SBP coverage to former spouses. In order for such a court order to be enforced, the former spouse or the attorney serving as agent for the former spouse must request the election be deemed on

TABLE 11-1

COST (Premiums)

SURVIVOR BENEFIT PLAN SPOUSE ONLY MONTHLY AMOUNTS

Base Amount of Retired Pay $	Monthly Payment for Surviving Spouse* $		SBP Premium** $	
	55%	35%	2.5% of $446 plus 10% of remaining amount	6.5%
300.00	165.00	105.00	7.50	19.50
446.00	245.30	151.90	11.15	28.99
500.00	275.00	175.00	16.55	32.50
600.00	330.00	210.00	26.55	39.00
700.00	385.00	245.00	36.55	45.50
800.00	440.00	280.00	46.55	52.00
900.00	495.00	315.00	56.55	58.50
955.00	525.25	334.25	62.05	62.08
***956.00	525.80	334.60	62.15	62.14
1,000.00	550.00	350.00		65.00
1,200.00	660.00	420.00		78.00
1,400.00	770.00	490.00		91.00
1,600.00	880.00	560.00		104.00
1,800.00	990.00	630.00		117.00
2,000.00	1,100.00	700.00		130.00
2,500.00	1,375.00	875.00		162.50
3,000.00	1,650.00	1,050.00		195.00
3,500.00	1,925.00	1,225.00		227.50
4,000.00	2,200.00	1,400.00		260.00
4,500.00	2,475.00	1,575.00		292.50
5,000.00	2,750.00	1,750.00		325.00
5,500.00	3,025.00	1,925.00		357.50
6,000.00	3,300.00	2,100.00		390.00
6,500.00	3,575.00	2,275.00		422.50
7,000.00	3,850.00	2,450.00		455.00

*	Amount in left column is amount of annuity for beneficiaries under age 62; amount on right is amount for beneficiaries over age 62. Amount in right column applies to survivors of members who retired or were retirement eligible after 1 October 1985. Survivors of members who retired before 1 October 1985 will also usually receive this amount, but a small number of survivors may receive slightly greater amounts under the old Social Security offset method. Service finance centers will compute the annuity both ways and pay the larger amount.

**	Amount in left column applies to members who entered service before 1 March 1990.

***	Premiums for members with base amounts of $956 or greater retiring in 1998 are the same regardless of when they entered service.

the member's behalf within one year of the date of the court order.[2]

Public Law 99-661, enacted 14 November 1986, permitted state courts to order members to elect former spouse coverage (applies only to court orders issued on or after 14 November 1986).

Former spouses are ineligible to receive SBP annuities if they remarry before age 55, and their annuities are subject to the same reduction at age 62 as spouse annuities.

A former spouse who was not a member's former spouse on the date a member became eligible to participate in SBP must have been married to the member for at least one year in order to be named as an SBP former spouse beneficiary. (In other words, a former spouse acquired after retirement must have been an eligible spouse beneficiary.)

Former spouse elections are permanent and irrevocable, except as follows: members who voluntarily elect coverage on behalf of a former spouse may only change their elections to spouse coverage after remarrying; members who elect former spouse coverage in compliance with a written agreement, which has not been incorporated into a court order, may change their elections to spouse coverage after remarrying only with the written concurrence of the former spouse; members who elect former spouse coverage in compliance with a court order which orders them to provide such coverage, or which incorporates an agreement to voluntarily provide such coverage, may change their elections to spouse coverage after remarrying only if they obtain a court order which relieves them of the requirement imposed by the prior court order. The following exception applies: A member who had a court ordered (elected or deemed) FS-SBP and later remarries and does not change coverage to the new spouse, may cover the new spouse if the former spouse dies. (COMPGEN Ruling B-249740, dated 4 June 1993 states that the death of the former spouse terminates the legal contract to provide/enforce FS-SBP coverage.)

NOTE: The time limit to change from former spouse to spouse coverage under SBP will be waived for remarriages occurring on, before or after the date of enactment of the FY98 Defense Authorization Act (18 November 1997). The former spouse coverage continues to be protected in current law.[3]

Former Spouse and Child(ren). Public Law 99-145, enacted 8 November 1985, with an effective date of 1 March 1986, provided for the cost and annuity amounts to be computed at the same rate as coverage for spouses and permitted children (from the marriage to the former spouse) to be included with the election.

PREMIUMS

Spouse/Former Spouse Coverage. Coverage for spouses and former spouses is the same. Public Law 101-189, enacted 29 November 1989, and effective 1 March 1990, reduced the cost of SBP coverage for the majority of participants. Premiums for members who entered service on or after 1 March 1990 are computed at 6.5 percent of the member's base amount. Premiums for members who entered service before 1 March 1990 are computed at either 6.5 percent of the member's base amount or 2.5 percent of the first $446* of the base amount, plus 10 percent of the remaining base amount, whichever method results in a lower premium. For members retiring in 1997 who entered service before 1 March 1990, the 6.5 percent calculation method results in a lower premium for base amounts of $956 or greater. Members who retired before 1 March 1990 had their premiums recalculated as of that date and reduced to 6.5 percent of their base amounts if they had been paying more than that amount under the old formula.

---

*This amount increases at the same time and by the same rate as cost-of-living adjustments to active duty military pay. The rate is $446, effective 1 January 1998.

Participants' retired pay is reduced by the amount of SBP premium only during periods in which the participant has an eligible beneficiary.

If a member elects to provide coverage on behalf of a former spouse, regardless of whether the election is voluntary or court-ordered, SBP premium reductions in retired pay begin the first day of the month following the month in which the member requests the election change. If a former spouse requests an election change be deemed on a member's behalf on the first of the month following the date of a court order which requires that a member elect former spouse coverage, and the member fails to voluntarily change his or her election during the one-year period, SBP premium reductions in retired pay are applied retroactively to the date of the court order.

Spouse/Former Spouse and Child(ren) Coverage. A member's premium for spouse and child(ren) coverage or former spouse and child(ren) coverage is calculated at the same rate as spouse or former spouse coverage, plus a small additional charge for the child(ren) portion of the coverage. Typical premiums are about one-half of one percent of the base amount on average, but could be higher or lower depending on the difference in the age span between the parents and the youngest child.

If a participant with this election loses a spouse or former spouse beneficiary, the participant's premium will be recalculated using the actuarial factor that applies to the ages of the member and the youngest child at the time.

REMARRIAGE—ITS EFFECT ON THE SURVIVOR BENEFIT PLAN

A retiree initially participating in SBP with either spouse or spouse and child(ren) coverage has several options when that marriage ends in death, divorce, or annulment, and the retiree remarries.

Upon notification to the Defense Finance and Accounting Service of the retiree's change in marital status, his or her SBP participation and costs will be suspended, not terminated. If coverage was not converted to cover the former spouse, then, under the law, upon remarriage, the new spouse is automatically covered under SBP one year after the retiree's remarriage with the same level of coverage as the prior spouse. (An earlier date applies if a child is born of that marriage, or if the service member remarries the former spouse.)

The retiree's options upon remarriage are: (1) resume spouse coverage at the same level and cost as you had for your first spouse (under the "automatic" provisions of the law); (2) elect not to resume spouse coverage, provided your election to do so is received by the finance center within one year after your remarriage; (3) increase your SBP base amount, if you previously were under reduced coverage (you must pay any difference plus interest prior to the first year anniversary of the remarriage); and (4) add supplemental SBP coverage for your new spouse.

The important thing to remember is that the retiree must notify the finance center when he or she remarries. If notification is not done, the new spouse will be automatically covered under SBP, and the retiree will be responsible for SBP costs retroactive to one year after the remarriage.

OFFSETS

Social Security Offset

SBP guarantees that surviving spouses of SBP participants are able to receive an income from government sources equal to at least 55 percent of a participant's base amount. Under age 62, this benefit is generally provided solely through SBP; after age 62 it is a combination of SBP and the Social Security survivor's benefits.

Because the federal government pays part of the cost for both SBP and Social Security, SBP payments to a surviving spouse will be offset by the amount of Social Security survivor's benefit which would be paid if based solely on the member's military service. There is no offset if the annuitant is still employed and has earnings too high for Social Security benefits to be paid only until age 70. To gain exemption from the SBP offset, a working widow(er) must obtain a statement from the Social Security Administration stating that she or he is not eligible for benefits because of excess earnings. This statement must then be sent to the finance center that pays the SBP annuity. Once a working widow(er) stops working and begins receiving Social Security benefits, the offset is applied or is automatically applied at age 70.

Increases in Social Security benefits during the 1970s resulted in much larger offsets to SBP annuities than originally intended. As a result, Congress enacted Public Law 96-401 on 9 October 1980, which placed a limit on the Social Security offset to 40 percent of the SBP annuity. In order to increase benefits and reduce the administrative burden involved with computing the offsets, Congress eliminated the Social Security offset effective 1 March 1986, and replaced it with a "two-tier" method of calculating annuities after age 62. Under this method, annuities are reduced at age 62 from 55 percent of the member's base amount to 35 percent of the member's base amount. The two-tier method is used automatically for survivors of members who become eligible for retirement on or after 1 October 1985. Survivors of members who retired or were eligible for retirement before 1 October

1985 are grandfathered under the original Social Security offset method. Finance centers calculate annuities using both methods when an annuitant attains age 62 and pay the higher amount. In most cases, survivors receive higher annuities under the two-tier method than under the original method. Social Security offsets to SBP are seldom more than the actual amount of the Social Security benefit received unless the member had no Social Security wage credits other than the military and the spouse takes early benefits (before age 62).

Understanding how the SBP program is funded may help in understanding why the reduction in SBP annuities at age 62 must occur, even though a surviving spouse may receive Social Security benefits based upon his or her own earnings record rather than the member's. SBP was designed to operate with a 40 percent subsidy from the Federal Government, with participants paying the remaining 60 percent through monthly reductions in their retired pay. The rate of members' premiums was determined by calculating the amount of benefits surviving spouses are expected to receive during their lifetimes, which naturally includes benefits received both before and after age 62. In other words, the reduced benefit level after age 62, as well as the full 55 percent benefit level before age 62, were both factored into the formula which was used to determine the rate of participants' premiums. If the integration of the two government subsidized programs at 62 did not occur, members' premiums would be significantly higher than 6.5 percent.

Government Pension Offset

Social Security spouse's benefits provide income to spouses who have limited or no Social Security benefits of their own. Since the beginning of the Social Security program, spouse's benefits were intended for women and men who were financially dependent on their husbands or wives who worked at jobs covered by Social Security.

Spouse's benefits are normally offset by the amount of any benefits that a spouse may receive based on his or her own earnings *covered* by Social Security. Under the government pension offset, the spouse's benefit is offset by a government pension based on earnings *not covered* by Social Security.

COLA ADJUSTMENTS

SBP premiums and survivor annuities are adjusted at the same time and by the same percentage as military retired pay. Military retired pay is usually adjusted annually at the same rate as the annual increase in the Consumer Price Index (CPI). This is a significant advantage of SBP that is generally not offered by alternative life insurance programs.

TAX TREATMENT

Since SBP premiums are paid in the form of reductions in participants' retired pay, they are not counted as taxable income. This tax break is especially important when comparing SBP to life insurance alternatives. For example, if a member's SBP premium is $100 a month and the member is in the 28 percent tax bracket, the member's actual out-of-pocket cost for SBP coverage is only $72; i.e., if the member elected to decline SBP participation and receive the $100 instead, the member would only get to keep $72 after paying taxes on the $100. Therefore, $72 is the amount that one would use in comparing the cost of SBP to the cost of a comparable amount of life insurance. Studies show that, except in unusually rare circumstances, no life insurance policy can guarantee equal or greater protection for equal or less cost than SBP.

SBP annuities are considered taxable income for federal income tax purposes. Many states exempt SBP annuities in whole or in part from taxable income for state income tax purposes.

CHAPTER ENDNOTES

1. This applies to military retirees who are paying premiums for SBP coverage to a former spouse.

2. Forms to initiate SBP coverage can be obtained online through DFAS. (See Appendix P).

3. Changes to former spouse SBP coverage in the FY99 Defense Authorization Bill are quoted as follows:

   Under section 1448(b)(3), a member who is a participant of the Plan and providing coverage for a spouse and has a former spouse who was not the member's former spouse when the member became eligible to participate in the Plan may elect to provide an annuity to that former spouse. This describes a member who is divorced after retiring.

12

51 FLAVORS AND COUNTING*

State-by-State Analysis of the Divisibility Of Military Retired Pay[1]

On 30 May 1989, the United States Supreme Court announced its decision in *Mansell v. Mansell*.[2] In *Mansell*, the Court ruled that states cannot divide the value of Department of Veterans Affairs (VA) disability benefits that are received in lieu of military retired pay.[3] The Court's decision clarifies that states are limited to dividing disposable retired pay, as defined in 10 U.S.C. §1408(a)(4).[4] When using the following materials, remember that *Mansell* effectively overrules some of the listed case law

*ARA expresses its gratitude for this reprint of the state-by-state analysis obtained from the Department of the Army Judge Advocate General's School, Administrative and Civil Law Department, Charlottesville, Virginia 22903-1781.

predating the decision, at least to the extent a case suggests state courts have the authority to divide more than disposable retired pay. Since *Mansell*, courts have generally recognized the limitations of the disposable retired pay definition found in Title 10. For example, in *Torwich v. Torwich*, a New Jersey appellate court wrestled with the impact that waiver of military retired pay associated with receipt of VA benefits has on disposable retired pay.[5] Also, in *Knoop v. Knoop*,[6] the North Dakota Supreme Court addressed a situation involving the impact of the Dual Compensation Act[7] on disposable retired pay.[8]

Alabama

Divisible as of August 1993 when the Alabama Supreme Court held that disposable military retirement benefits accumulated during the course of the marriage are divisible as marital property, *Vaughn v. Vaughn*, 634 So.2d 533 (Ala. 1993). *Kabaci v. Kabaci*, 373 So. 2d 1144 (Ala. Civ. App. 1979) and cases relying on it that are inconsistent with *Vaughn* are expressly overruled. Note that Alabama has previously awarded alimony from military retired pay, *Underwood v. Underwood,* 491 So. 2d 242 (Ala. Civ. App. 1986) (wife awarded alimony from husband's military disability retired pay); *Phillips v. Phillips*, 489 So. 2d 592 (Ala. Civ. App. 1986) (wife awarded 50% of husband's gross military pay as alimony).

Alaska

Divisible. *Chase v. Chase*, 662 P.2d 944 (Alaska 1983), overruling *Cose v. Cose*, 592 P.2d 1230 (Alaska 1979), *cert. denied*, 453 U.S. 922 (1982). Non-vested retirement benefits are divisible. *Lang v. Lang*, 741 P.2d 649 (Alaska 1987). Note also *Morlan v. Morlan*, 720 P.2d 497 (Alaska 1986) (the trial court ordered a civilian employee to retire in order to ensure the spouse received her share of a pension—the pension would be suspended if the employee continued working; on appeal, the court held that the employee should have been given the option of continuing to work and periodically paying the spouse the sums she would have received from the retired pay; in reaching this result, the court cited the California *Gillmore* decision). Also see *Clausen v. Clausen*, 831 P.2d 1257 (Alaska 1992) which held that while *Mansell* precludes division of disability benefits received in lieu of retired pay, it does not preclude *consideration* of these payments when making an equitable division of marital assets.

Arizona

Divisible. *DeGryse v. DeGryse*, 135 Ariz. 335, 661 P.2d 185 (1983); *Edsall v. Superior Court of Arizona*, 143 Ariz. 240, 693 P.2d 895 (1984); *Van Loan v. Van Loan*, 116 Ariz. 272, 569 P.2d 214 (1977) (a nonvested military pension is community property). A civilian retirement plan case (*Koelsch v. Koelsch*, 148 Ariz. 176, 713 P.2d 1234 (1986)) held that if the employee is not eligible to retire at the time of the dissolution, the court *must* order that the spouse begin receiving the awarded share of retired pay when the employee becomes *eligible* to retire, whether or not he or she does retire at that point.

Arkansas

Divisible, but watch for vesting requirements. *Young v. Young*, 288 Ark. 33, 701 S.W.2d 369 (1986); *but see Durham v. Durham*, 289 Ark. 3, 708 S.W.2d 618 (1986) (military retired pay not divisible where the member had not served 20 years at the time of the divorce, and therefore the military pension had not "vested"). *Also see Burns v. Burns*, 31 Ark. 61, 847 S.W.2d 23 (1993) (In accord with *Durham*, but strong dissent favors rejecting 20 years of service as a prerequisite to "vesting" of a military pension).

California

Divisible. *In re Fithian*, 10 Cal. 3d 592, 517 P.2d 449, 111 Cal. Rptr. 369 (1974); *In re Hopkins*, 142 Cal. App. 3d 350, 191 Cal. Rptr. 70 (1983). A non-resident service member did not waive his right under the USFSPA to object to California's jurisdiction over his military pension by consenting to the court's jurisdiction over other marital and property issues, *Tucker v. Tucker*, 226 Cal. App. 3d 1249 (1991) and *Hattis v. Hattis*, 242 Cal. Rptr. 410 (Ct. App. 1987). Nonvested pensions are divisible; *In re Brown*, 15 Cal. 3d 838, 544 P.2d 561, 126 Cal. Rptr. 633 (1976). *In re Mansell*, 265 Cal. Rptr. 227 (Cal. App. 1989) (on remand from *Mansell v. Mansell*, 490 U.S. 581 (1989), the court held that gross retired pay was divisible since it was based on a stipulated property settlement to which *res judicata* had attached). State law has held that military disability retired pay is divisible to the extent it replaces what the retiree would have received as longevity retired pay (*In re Mastropaolo*, 166 Cal. App. 3d 953, 213 Cal. Rptr. 26 (1985); *In re Mueller*, 70 Cal. App. 3d 66, 137 Cal. Rptr. 129 (1977), but the *Mansell* case raises doubt about the continued validity of this proposition. If the member is not retired at the time of the dissolution, the spouse can elect to begin receiving the award share of "retired pay" when the member becomes *eligible* to retire, or anytime thereafter, even if the member remains on active duty. *In re Luciano*, 104 Cal. App. 3d 956, 164 Cal. Rptr. 93 (1980); *see also In re Gillmore*, 29 Cal. 3d 418, 629 P.2d 1, 174 Cal. Rptr. 493 (1981) (same principle applied to a civilian pension plan).

Colorado

Divisible. *In re Marriage Of Beckman and Holm,* 800 P.2d 1376 (Colo. 1990) (nonvested military retirement benefits constitute marital property subject to division pursuant to §14-10-113, C.R.S. (1987 Repl.Vol. 6B)). *See also In re Hunt*, 909 P.2d 525, (Colo. 1996), reversing a previous decision of its own, the Colorado Supreme Court holds that post-divorce increases in pay resulting from promotions are marital property subject to division and approves use of a formula to define the marital share. In the formula discussed, final pay of the member at retirement is a percentage defined by 50% of a fraction wherein the numerator equals the number of years of overlap between marriage and service, and the denominator equals the number of years of total service of the member.

Connecticut

Probably divisible. Conn. Gen. Stat. 46b-81 (1986) gives courts broad power to divide property. Note *Thompson v. Thompson*, 183 Conn. 96, 438 A.2d 839 (1981) (nonvested civilian pension is divisible).

Delaware

Divisible. *Smith v. Smith*, 458 A.2d 711 (Del. Fam. Ct. 1983). Nonvested pensions are divisible; *Donald R.R. v. Barbara S.R.*, 454 A.2d 1295 (Del. Sup. Ct. 1982).

District of Columbia

Divisible. See *Barbour v. Barbour*, 464 A.2d 915 (D.C. 1983) (vested but unmatured civil service pension held divisible; dicta suggests that nonvested pensions also are divisible).

Florida

Divisible. As of 1 October 1988, all vested and nonvested pension plans are treated as marital property to the extent that they are accrued during the marriage. Fla. Stat. §61.075(3)(a)4 (1988); see also §3(1) of 1988 Fla. Sess. Law Serv. 342. These legislative changes appear to overrule the prior limitation in *Pastore v. Pastore*, 497 So. 2d 635 (Fla. 1986) (only vested military retired pay can be divided). This interpretation was recently adopted by the court in *Deloach v. Deloach*, 590 So.2d 956 (Fla. Dist. Ct. App. 1991).

Georgia

Probably divisible. *Cf. Courtney v. Courtney*, 256 Ga. 97, 344 S.E.2d 421 (1986) (nonvested civilian pensions are divisible); *Stumpf v. Stumpf*, 249 Ga. 759, 294 S.E.2d 488 (1982) (military retired pay may be considered in establishing alimony obligations) *see also Hall v. Hall*, 51 B.R. 1002 (1985) (Georgia divorce judgment awarding debtor's wife 38% of debtor's military retirement, payable directly from the United States to the wife, granted the wife a non-dischargeable property interest in 38% of the husband's military retirement); *Holler v. Holler*, 257 Ga. 27, 354 S.E.2d 140 (1987) (the court "[a]ssum[ed] that vested and nonvested military retirement benefits acquired during the marriage are now marital property subject to equitable division," citing *Stumpf and Courtney*, but then decided that military retired pay could not be divided retroactively if it was not subject to division at the time of the divorce).

Hawaii

Divisible. *Linson v. Linson*, 1 Haw. App. 272, 618 P.2d 748 (1981); *Cassiday v. Cassiday*, 716 P.2d 1133 (Haw. 1986). In *Wallace v. Wallace*, 5 Haw. App. 55, 677 P.2d 966 (1984), the court ordered a Public Health Service employee (who is covered by the USFSPA) to pay a share of retired pay upon reaching retirement age whether or not he retires at that point. He argued that this amounted to an order to retire, violating 10 U.S.C. §1408(c)(3), but the court affirmed the order. In *Jones v. Jones*, 780 P.2d

581 (Haw. Ct. App. 1989), the court ruled that *Mansell's* limitation on dividing VA benefits cannot be circumvented by awarding an offsetting interest in other property. It also held that *Mansell* applies to military disability retired pay as well as VA benefits.

Idaho

Divisible. *Ramsey v. Ramsey,* 96 Idaho 672, 535 P.2d 53 (1975) (reinstated by *Griggs v. Griggs,* 197 Idaho 123, 686 P.2d 68 (1984)). Courts cannot circumvent *Mansell's* limitation on dividing VA benefits by using an offset against other property. *Bewley v. Bewley,* 780 P.2d 596 (Idaho Ct. App. 1989). See *Leatherman v. Leatherman,* 122 Idaho 247, 833 P.2d 105 (1992). A portion of husband's civil service annuity attributable to years of military service during marriage was divisible military service benefit and thus subject to statute relating to modification of divorce decrees to include division of military retirement benefits. *Also see Balderson v. Balderson,* 896 P.2d 956 (Idaho Sup. Ct. 1995)(cert. denied by the U.S. Supreme Court, 116 S.Ct. 179 (mem.) (affirming a lower court decision ordering a service member to pay spouse her community share of the military pension, even though he had decided to put off retirement), *Mosier v. Mosier,* 122 Idaho 37, 830 P.2d 1175 (1992), and *Walborn v. Walborn,* 120 Idaho 494, 817 P.2d 160 (1991).

Illinois

Divisible. *In re Brown,* 225 Ill. App. 3d 733, 587 N.E.2d 648 (1992); the Court cites Congress' enactment of the Uniformed Services Former Spouses' Protection Act (Pub.L. No. 97-252, 96 Stat, 730-38 (1982) as the basis to permit the courts to treat pay of military personnel in accordance with the law of the jurisdiction of the court (*In re Dooley,* 137 Ill. App. 3d 407, 484 N.E.2d 894

(1985)). The court in *Brown* held that a military pension may be treated as marital property under Illinois law and is subject to the division provisions of 5/503 of the Illinois Marriage and Dissolution of Marriage Act (Dissolution Act). See *In re Korper*, 131 Ill. App. 3d 753, 475 N.E.2d 1333 (1985). *Korper* points out that under Illinois law a pension is marital property even if it is not vested. *In Korper*, the member had not yet retired, and he objected to the spouse getting the cash-out value of her interest in retired pay. He argued that the USFSPA allowed division only of "disposable retired pay," and state courts therefore are preempted from awarding the spouse anything before retirement. The court rejected this argument, thus raising the (unaddressed) question whether a spouse could be awarded a share of "retired" pay at the time the member becomes *eligible* for retirement (even if he or she does not retire at that point); see *In re Luciano*, 104 Cal. App. 3d 956, 164 Cal. Rptr. 93 (1980) for an application of such a rule. Note also Ill. Stat. Ann. ch. 40, para. 510.1 (Smith-Hurd Supp. 1988) (allows modification of agreements and judgments that became final between 25 June 1981 and 1 February 1983 unless the party opposing modification shows that the original disposition of military retired pay was appropriate).

Indiana

Divisible, but watch for vesting requirements. Indiana Code §31-1-11.5-2(d)(3) (1987) (amended in 1985 to provide that "property" for marital dissolution purposes includes, *inter alia*, "[t]he right to receive disposable retired pay, as defined in 10 U.S.C. §1408(a), acquired during the marriage, that is or may be payable after the dissolution of the marriage"). The right to receive retired pay must be vested as of the date the divorce petition in order for the spouse to be entitled to a share (*Kirkman v. Kirkman*, 555 N.E.2d 1293 (Ind. 1990)), but courts should consider the nonvested military retired benefits in adjudging a just and reasonable division of property. *In re Bickel*, 533 N.E.2d 593 (Ind. Ct. App. 1989). *See also Arthur v. Arthur*, 519 N.E.2d 230 (Ind. Ct. App. 1988) (Second District ruled that §31-1-11.5-2(d)(3) cannot be applied retroactively to allow division of military retired pay in a case filed before the law's effective date, which was 1 September 1985). *But see Sable v. Sable*, 506 N.E.2d 495 (Ind. Ct. App. 1987) (Third District ruled that §31-1-11.5-2(d)(3) can be applied retroactively).

Iowa

Divisible. *See especially In re Howell*, 434 N.W.2d 629 (Iowa 1989). In *Howell*, the member had already retired in this case, but the decision may be broad enough to encompass nonvested retired pay as well. The court also ruled that disability payments from the Veterans Administration, paid in lieu of a portion of military retired pay, are not marital property. Finally, it appears the court intended to award the spouse a percentage of gross military retired pay, but it actually "direct[ed] that 30.5% of [the husband's] *disposable retired pay*, except disability benefits, be assigned to [the wife] in accordance with section 1408 of Title 10 of the United States Code..." (emphasis added). The U.S. Supreme Court's *Mansell* decision may have overruled state court decisions holding courts have authority to divide gross retired pay.

(Note: A disabled veteran may be required to pay alimony and/or child support in divorce actions, even where his only income is veterans' disability and supplemental security income. *See In re Marriage of Anderson*, 522 N.W.2d 99 (Iowa App. 1994), applying *Rose v. Rose*, 481 U.S. 619, 107 S.Ct. 2029, 95 L.Ed.2d 599 (1987). The

Iowa Court of Appeals ruled: "It is clear veteran's benefits are not solely for the benefit of the veteran, but for his family as well.")

Kansas

Divisible. Kan. Stat. Ann. §23-201(b) (1987), effective 1 July 1987 (vested and nonvested military pensions are now marital property); *In re Harrison,* 13 Kan. App. 2d 313, 769 P.2d 678 (1989) (applies the statute and holds that it overruled the previous case law that prohibited division of military retired pay).

Kentucky

Divisible. *Jones v. Jones,* 680 S.W.2d 921 (Ky. 1984); *Poe v. Poe,* 711 S.W.2d 849 (Ky. Ct. App. 1986) (military retirement benefits are marital property even before they "vest"); Ky. Rev. Stat. Ann. §403.190 (1994), expressly defines marital property to include retirement benefits.

Louisiana

Divisible. *Swope v. Mitchell,* 324 So. 2d 461 (La. 1975); *Little v. Little,* 513 So. 2d 464 (La. Ct. App. 1987) (nonvested and unmatured military retired pay is marital property); *Warner v. Warner,* 651 So. 2d 1339 (La. 1995) (confirming that 10-year test found in 10 U.S.C. § 1408(d)(2) is a prerequisite to direct payment, but not to award of a share of retired pay to a former spouse); *Gowins v. Gowins,* 466 So. 2d 32 (La. Sup. Ct. 1985) (soldier's participation in divorce proceedings constituted implied consent for the court to exercise jurisdiction and divide the soldier's military retired pay as marital property); *Jett v. Jett,* 449 So. 2d 557 (La. Ct. App. 1984); *Rohring v. Rohring,* 441 So. 2d 485 (La. Ct. App. 1983). *See also Campbell v. Campbell,* 474 So.2d 1339 (Ct. App. La. 1985) (a court can award a spouse a share of disposable retired pay, not gross retired pay, and a court cannot divide VA disability benefits paid in lieu of military retired pay; this approach conforms to the dicta in the *Mansell* concerning divisibility of gross retired pay).

Maine

Divisible. *Lunt v. Lunt,* 522 A.2d 1317 (Me. 1987). *See also* Me. Rev. Stat. Ann. tit. 19, §722-A(6) (1989) (provides that the parties become tenants-in-common regarding property a court fails to divide or to set apart).

Maryland

Divisible. *Nisos v. Nisos,* 60 Md. App. 368, 483 A.2d 97 (1984) (applies Md. Fam. Law Code Ann. §8-203(b), which provides that military pensions are to be treated the same as other pension benefits; such benefits are marital property under Maryland law; *see Deering v. Deering,* 292 Md. 115, 437 A.2d 883 (1981)). *See also Ohm v. Ohm,* 49 Md. App. 392, 431 A.2d 1371 (1981) (nonvested pensions are divisible). "Window decrees" that are silent on division of retired pay cannot be reopened simply on the basis that Congress subsequently enacted the USFSPA. *Andresen v. Andresen,* 317 Md. 380, 564 A.2d 399 (1989).

Massachusetts

Divisible. *Andrews v. Andrews,* 27 Mass. App. 759, 543 N.E.2d 31 (1989). Here, the spouse was awarded alimony from military retired pay; she appealed, seeking a property interest in the pension. The trial court's ruling was upheld, but the appellate court noted that "the judge could have assigned a portion of the pension to the wife [as property]."

Michigan

Divisible. *Keen v. Keen*, 160 Mich. App. 314, 407 N.W.2d 643 (1987); *Giesen v. Giesen*, 140 Mich. App. 335, 364 N.W.2d 327 (1985); *McGinn v. McGinn*, 126 Mich. App. 689, 337 N.W.2d 632 (1983); *Chisnell v. Chisnell*, 82 Mich. App. 699, 267 N.W.2d 155 (1978). Note also *Boyd v. Boyd*, 116 Mich. App. 774, 323 N.W.2d 553 (1982) (only vested pensions are divisible, but what is a vested right is discussed broadly and discretion over what is marital property left to the trial court).

Minnesota

Divisible. Military retired pay not specifically addressed in statute. Case law has treated it as any other marital asset, subject to equitable division. *Deliduka v. Deliduka*, 347 N.W.2d 52 (Minn. Ct. App. 1984). This case also holds that a court may award a spouse a share of gross retired pay, but *Mansell* may have overruled state court decisions that they have the authority to divide gross retired pay. Note also *Janssen v. Janssen*, 331 N.W.2d 752 (Minn. 1983) (nonvested pensions are divisible).

Mississippi

Divisible. *Powers v. Powers*, 465 So. 2d 1036 (Miss. 1985). In July, 1994, a deeply divided Mississippi Supreme Court formally adopted the equitable distribution method of division of marital assets. *Ferguson v. Ferguson*, 639 So. 2d 921 (Miss. 1994), and *Hemsley v. Hemsley* 639 So. 2d 909 (Miss. 1994). Marital property for the purpose of a divorce is defined as being "any and all property acquired or accumulated during the marriage." This includes military pensions which are viewed as personal property and while USFSPA does not vest any rights in a spouse, a military pension is subject to being divided in a divorce. *Pierce v. Pierce,* 648 So. 2d 523 (Miss. 1995). In *Pierce,* the Court expressly held that a claim for division of property can only be viewed as separate and distinct from a claim for alimony. Since property division is made irrespective of fault or misconduct, military pensions may be divided even where the spouse has committed adultery, assuming that the facts otherwise justify an equitable division of property.

Missouri

Divisible. Only disposable retired pay is divisible. *Moon v. Moon,* 795 S.W.2d 511 (Mo. Ct. App. 1990). *Fairchild v. Fairchild,* 747 S.W.2d 641 (Mo. Ct. App. 1988) (nonvested and nonmatured military retired pay are marital property); *Coates v. Coates,* 650 S.W.2d 307 (Mo. Ct. App. 1983).

Montana

Divisible. *In re Marriage of Kecskes*, 210 Mont. 479, 683 P.2d 478 (1984); *In re Miller*, 37 Mont. 556, 609 P.2d 1185 (1980), *vacated and remanded sub. nom. Miller v. Miller,* 453 U.S. 918 (1981).

Nebraska

Divisible. *Ray v. Ray*, 222 Neb. 324, 383 N.W.2d 756 (1986); Neb. Rev. Stat. §42366(8) (1993) (military pensions are part of the marital estate whether vested or not and may be divided as property or alimony).

Nevada

Probably divisible. *Tomlinson v. Tomlinson*, 729 P.2d 1303 (Nev. 1986) (the court speaks approvingly of the USFSPA in dicta but declines to divide retired pay in this case involving a final decree from another state).

Tomlinson was legislatively reversed by the Nevada Former Military Spouses Protection Act (NFMSPA), Nev. Rev. Stat. §125.161 (1987) (military retired pay can be partitioned even if the decree is silent on division and even if it is foreign). The NFMSPA has been repealed, however, effective 20 March 1989; see Senate Bill 11, 1989 Nev. Stat. 34. The Nevada Supreme Court subsequently has ruled that the doctrine of *res judicata* bars partitioning military retired pay where "the property settlement has become a judgment of the court"; *see Taylor v. Taylor,* 775 P.2d 703 (Nev. 1989). Nonvested pensions are community property. *Gemma v. Gemma,* 778 P.2d 429 (Nev. 1989). The spouse has the right to elect to receive his or her share when the employee spouse becomes retirement eligible, whether or not retirement occurs at that point. *Id.*

New Hampshire

Divisible. "Property shall include all tangible and intangible property and assets . . . belonging to either or both parties, whether title to the property is held in the name of either or both parties. Intangible property includes . . . employment benefits, [and] vested and nonvested pensions or other retirement plans . . . [T]he court may order an equitable division of property between the parties. The court shall presume that an equal division is an equitable distribution . . ." N.H. Rev. Stat. Ann. §458:16-a (1987) (effective 1 January 1988). This provision was relied on by the New Hampshire Supreme Court in *Blanchard v. Blanchard*, 578 A.2d 339 (N.H. 1990), when it overruled *Baker v. Baker*, 120 N.H. 645, 421 A.2d 998 (1980) (military retired pay not divisible as marital property, but it may be considered "as a relevant factor in making equitable support orders and property distributions").

New Jersey

Divisible. *Castiglioni v. Castiglioni*, 192 N.J. Super. 594, 471 A.2d 809 (N.J. 1984); *Whitfield v. Whitfield*, 222 N.J. Super. 36, 535 A.2d 986 (N.J. Super. Ct. App. Div. 1987) (nonvested military retired pay is marital property); *Kruger v. Kruger,* 139 N.J. Super. 413, 354 A.2d 340 (N.J. Super. Ct. App. Div. 1976), *aff'd,* 73 N.J. 464, 375 A.2d 659 (1977). Post-divorce cost-of-living raises are divisible; *Moore v. Moore,* 553 A.2d 20 (N.J. 1989) (police pension).

New Mexico

Divisible. *Walentowski v. Walentowski*, 100 N.M. 484, 672 P.2d 657 (N.M. 1983)(USFSPA applied); *Stroshine v. Stroshine*, 98 N.M. 742, 652 P.2d 1193 (1982); *LeClert v. LeClert,* 80 N.M. 235, 453 P.2d 755 (1969). See also *White v. White*, 105 N.M. 800, 734 P.2d 1283 (Ct. App. 1987) (court can award share of gross retired pay; however, *Mansell* may have overruled state court decisions holding courts have authority to divide gross retired pay). In *Mattox v. Mattox,* 105 N.M. 479, 734 P.2d 259 (1987), in dicta the court cited the California *Gillmore* case with approval, suggesting that a court can order a member to begin paying the spouse his or her share when the member becomes eligible to retire—even if the member elects to remain in active duty.

New York

Divisible. Pensions in general are divisible; *Majauskas v. Majauskas,* 61 N.Y.2d 481, 463 N.E.2d 15, 474 N.Y.S.2d 699 (1984). Most lower courts hold that nonvested pensions are divisible; *see, e.g., Damiano v. Damiano*, 94 A.D.2d 132, 463 N.Y.S.2d 477 (N.Y. App. Div. 1983). Case law seems to treat military retired pay as subject to division; *e.g., Lydick v. Lydick*, 130 A.D.2d 915, 516 N.Y.S.2d 326 (N.Y. App. Div. 1987); *Gannon v.*

Gannon, 116 A.D.2d 1030, 498 N.Y.S.2d 647 (N.Y. App. Div. 1986). Disability payments are separate property as a matter of law, but a disability pension is marital property to the extent it reflects deferred compensation; *West v. West*, 101 A.D.2d 834, 475 N.Y.S.2d 493 (N.Y. pp. Div. 1984).

North Carolina

Divisible. The vesting requirement contained in the old N.C. Gen. Stat. §50-20(b) (1988) which expressly declared *vested* military pensions to be marital property; **was changed by new legislation. For all equitable distribution cases filed after 1 October 1997, there is *no vesting requirement to divide military pensions*.** For cases filed prior to 1 October 1997 old vesting rules apply. Those old rules require the pension be vested as of the date the parties separate from each other. In *Milam v. Milam*, 373 S.E.2d 459 (N.C.App. 1988), the court ruled that a warrant officer's retired pay had "vested" when he reached the 18-year "lock-in" point. In *George v. George*, 444 S.E.2d 449 (N.C.App. 1994), the court held that an enlisted member's right to retirement benefits vests when he/she has completed 20 years of service. In *Lewis v. Lewis*, 350 S.E.2d 587 (N.C.App. 1986) the court held that a divorce court can award a spouse a share of *gross* retired pay, but, because of the wording (at that time) of the state statute, the amount cannot exceed 50% of the retiree's *disposable* retired pay; *Mansell*, 490 U.S. at 589, may have overruled the court's decision in part as to dividing gross pay. The parties are not, however, barred from a consensual division of military retired pay, even though it is "nonvested" separate property, and an agreement or court order by consent that divides such pension rights will be upheld. *Hoolapa v. Hoolapa*, 412 S.E.2d 112 (N.C.App. 1992). Attorneys considering valuation issues should also review *Bishop v. Bishop,* 440 S.E.2d 591 (N.C.App. 1994), which held that valuation must be determined as of the date of separation and must be based on a present value of pension payments that the retiree would be entitled to receive if he or she retired on the date of marital separation, or when first eligible to retire, if later. Subsequent pay increases attributable to length of service or promotions are not included.

North Dakota

Divisible. *Delorey v. Delorey,* 357 N.W.2d 488 (N.D. 1984). *See also Morales v. Morales,* 402 N.W.2d 322 (N.D. 1987) (equitable factors can be considered in dividing military retired pay, so 17.5% award to 17-year spouse is affirmed), and *Knoop v. Knoop,* 542 N.W.2d 114 (N.D. 1996) (confirms that definition of "disposable retired pay" as defined in 10 U.S.C. §1408 provides a limit on what states are authorized to divide as marital property, but holds that the USFSPA does not require the term "retired pay" to be interpreted as "disposable retired pay." *Knoop* is also of interest because it addresses a waiver of retired pay associated with the Dual Compensation Act, and the court acknowledges that once 50% of "disposable retired pay" is paid out in satisfaction of one or more orders dividing military retired pay as property, the orders are deemed satisfied by federal law (referencing 1990 amendment to 10 U.S.C. §1408(e)(1)).

Ohio

Divisible. See *Lemon v. Lemon,* 42 Ohio App. 3d 142, 537 N.E.2d 246 (1988) (nonvested pensions are divisible as marital property where some evidence of value demonstrated). *But also see, King v. King,* 78 Ohio App. 3d

599, 605 N.E.2d 970 (1992) (Trial court abused its discretion by retaining jurisdiction to divide a military pension that would not vest for nine years where no evidence of value demonstrated); *Cherry v. Figart*, 86 Ohio App. 3d 123, 620 N.E.2d 174 (1993) (distinguishing *King* by affirming division of nonvested pension where parties had agreed to divide the retirement benefits and suit was brought for enforcement only—the initial judgment incorporating the agreement had not been appealed); and *Ingalls v. Ingalls*, 624 N.E.2d 368 (Ohio 1993) (affirming division of nonvested military retirement benefits consistent with agreement of the parties expressed at trial).

Oklahoma

Divisible. *Stokes v. Stokes*, 738 P.2d 1346 (Okla. 1987) (based on a statute that became effective on 1 June 1987). The State Attorney General had earlier opined that military retired pay was divisible, based on the prior law. Only a pension vested at the time of the divorce, however, is divisible, *Messinger v. Messinger*, 827 P.2d 865 (Okla. 1992). A former spouse is entitled to retroactive division of retiree's military pension pursuant to their property settlement agreement that provided that the property settlement was subject to modification if the law in effect at the time of their divorce changed to allow such a division at a later date.

Oregon

Divisible. *In re Manners*, 68 Or. App. 896, 683 P.2d 134 (1984); *In re Vinson*, 48 Or. App. 283, 616 P.2d 1180 (1980). *See also In re Richardson*, 307 Or. 370, 769 P.2d 179 (1989) (nonvested pension plans are marital property). The date of separation is the date used for classification as marital property.

Pennsylvania

Divisible. *Major v. Major*, 359 Pa. Super. 344, 518 A.2d 1267 (1986) (nonvested military retired pay is marital property).

Puerto Rico

Not divisible as marital property. *Delucca v. Colon*, 119 P.R. Dec. 720 (1987) (the original Spanish version; English translation can be found at 119 P.R.Dec. 765), overruling *Torres v. Robles,* 115 P.R. Dec. 765 (1984), which held that military retired pay is divisible. In overruling *Torres*, the court in *Delucca* reestablished retirement pensions as separate property of the spouses consistent with its earlier decision in *Maldonado v. Superior Court*, 100 P.R.R. 369 (1972). *Also see Carrero v. Santiago*, 93 JTS 103 (1993) (the original Spanish version; English translation not yet available), which cites *Delucca v. Colon* with approval. Note that pensions may be considered in setting child support and alimony obligations.

Rhode Island

Divisible. R.I. Pub. Laws §15-5-16.1 (1988) gives courts very broad powers over the parties' property to effect an equitable distribution. Implied consent by the soldier cannot be used, however, to satisfy the jurisdictional requirements of 10 U.S.C. §1408(c)(4). *Flora v. Flora*, 603 A.2d 723 (R.I. 1992).

South Carolina

Divisible. *Tiffault v. Tiffault*, 401 S.E.2d 157 (S.C.1991), holds that vested military retirement benefits constitute an earned property right which, if accrued during the marriage, is subject to equitable distribution. Nonvested military retirement benefits are also subject to equitable division, *Ball v. Ball*, 430 S.E.2d 533 (S.C. Ct. App. 1993)

(NCO acquired a vested right to *participate* in a military pension plan when he enlisted in the army; this right, which is more than an expectancy, constitutes property subject to division). *But see Walker v. Walker*, 368 S.E.2d 89 (S.C. Ct. App. 1988) (wife lived with parents during entire period of husband's naval service; since she made no homemaker contributions, she was not entitled to any portion of the military retired pay).

South Dakota

Divisible. *Gibson v. Gibson*, 437 N.W.2d 170 (S.D. 1989) (the court states that military retired pay is divisible—in this case, it was reserve component retired pay where the member had served 20 years but had not yet reached age 60); *Radigan v. Radigan,* 17 Fam. L. Rep. (BNA) 1202 (S.D. Sup. Ct. Jan. 23, 1991) (husband must share with ex-wife any increase in his retired benefits that results from his own, post divorce efforts); *Hautala v. Hautala,* 417 N.W.2d 879 (S.D. 1987) (trial court awarded spouse 42% of military retired pay, and this award was not challenged on appeal); *Moller v. Moller*, 356 N.W.2d 909 (S.D. 1984) (the court commented approvingly on cases from other states that recognize divisibility but declined to divide retired pay here because a 1977 divorce decree was not appealed until 1983). *See generally Caughron v. Caughron*, 418 N.W.2d 791 (S.D. 1988) (the present cash value of a nonvested retirement benefit is marital property); *Hansen v. Hansen*, 273 N.W.2d 749 (S.D. 1979) (vested civilian pension is divisible); *Stubbe v. Stubbe*, 376 N.W.2d 807 (S.D. 1985) (civilian pension divisible; the court observed that "this pension plan is vested in the sense that it cannot be unilaterally terminated by [the] employer, though actual receipt of benefits is contingent upon [the worker's] survival and no benefits will accrue to the estate prior to retirement").

Tennessee

Divisible. Tenn. Code Ann. §36-4-121(b)(1) (1988) specifically defines all vested pensions as marital property. In 1993, the Tennessee Supreme Court affirmed a trial court's approval of a separation agreement after determining that the agreement divided a non-vested pension as marital property. *Towner v. Towner*, 858 S.W.2d 888 (Tenn. 1993). In 1994, the Tennessee Court of Appeals held that the Tennessee code's reference to vested pensions was illustrative and not exclusive. As a result, the court determined that *non-vested* military pensions can properly be characterized as marital property. *Kendrick v. Kendrick*, 902 S.W.2d 918 (Tenn. Ct. App. 1994).

(Note: A disabled veteran may be required to pay alimony and/or child support in divorce actions, even where his only income is veterans' disability and supplemental security income. *See Rose v. Rose*, 481 U.S. 619, 107 S.Ct. 2029, 95 L.Ed.2d 599 (1987)(Supreme Court upheld exercise of contempt authority by Tennessee court over veteran who would not pay child support, finding that VA benefits were intended to take care of not just the veteran. Justice White in dissent argued unsuccessfully that the state's authority was preempted by the bar to garnishing VA disability payments, and federal discretion to divert some of the VA benefits to family members in certain cases.))

Texas

Divisible. *Cameron v. Cameron*, 641 S.W.2d 210 (Tex. 1982). *See also Grier v. Grier*, 731 S.W.2d 936 (Tex. 1987) (a court can award a spouse a share of gross retired pay, but post-divorce pay increases constitute separate property; *Mansell* may have overruled *Grier* in part). Pensions need not be vested to be divisible. *Ex Parte Burson*, 615

S.W.2d 192 (Tex. 1981), held that a court cannot divide VA disability benefits paid in lieu of military retired pay; this ruling is in accord with *Mansell.*

Utah

Divisible. *Greene v. Greene*, 751 P.2d 827 (Utah Ct. App. 1988). The case clarifies that non-vested pensions can be divided under Utah law, and in dicta it suggests that only disposable retired pay is divisible, not gross retired pay. *But see Maxwell v. Maxwell*, 796 P.2d 403 (Utah App. 1990) (because of a stipulation between the parties, the court ordered a military retiree to pay his ex-wife one-half the amount he had over-withheld from his retired pay for taxes).

Vermont

Probably divisible. Vt. Stat. Ann. tit. 15, §751 (1988) provides that "The court shall settle the rights of the parties to their property by...equit[able] divi[sion]. All property owed by either or both parties, however and whenever acquired, shall be subject to the jurisdiction of the court. Title to the property . . . shall be immaterial, except where equitable distribution can be made without disturbing separate property." The Connecticut Supreme Court recently held in *Krafik v. Krafik*, 21 Fam. Law Rep. 1536 (1995), that vested pension benefits are divisible as marital property in divorce. Although the issue was not raised in *Krafik*, the court noted that the legislative and logical basis for dividing vested pension benefits would apply to unvested pension benefits as well.

Virginia

Divisible. Va. Ann. Code §20-107.3 (1988) defines marital property to include all pensions, whether or not vested. *See also Mitchell v. Mitchell*, 4 Va. App. 113,

355 S.E.2d 18 (1987); *Sawyer v. Sawyer*, 1 Va. App. 75, 335 S.E.2d 277 (Va. Ct. App. 1985) (these cases hold that military retired pay is subject to equitable division). Also see *Owen v. Owen*, 419 S.E.2d 267 (Va. Ct. App. 1992) (settlement agreement's guarantee/indemnification clause requires the retiree to pay the same amount of support to the spouse despite the retiree's collection of VA disability pay—held not to violate *Mansell*).

Washington

Divisible. *Konzen v. Konzen*, 103 Wash. 2d 470, 693 P.2d 97, *cert. denied,* 473 U.S. 906 (1985); *Wilder v. Wilder*, 85 Wash. 2d 364, 534 P.2d 1355 (1975) (nonvested pension held to be divisible); *Payne v. Payne,* 82 Wash. 2d 573, 512 P.2d 736 (1973); *In re Smith*, 98 Wash. 2d 772, 657 P.2d 1383 (1983).

West Virginia

Divisible. *Butcher v. Butcher*, 357 S.E.2d 226 (W.Va. 1987) (vested and nonvested military retired pay is marital property subject to equitable distribution, and a court can award a spouse a share of gross retired pay; however, *Mansell* may have overruled state court decisions holding courts have authority to divide gross retired pay).

Wisconsin

Divisible. *Thorpe v. Thorpe*, 123 Wis. 2d 424, 367 N.W.2d 233 (Wis. Ct. App. 1985); *Pfeil v. Pfeil*, 115 Wis. 2d 502, 341 N.W.2d 699 (Wis. Ct. App. 1983). *See also Leighton v. Leighton*, 81 Wis. 2d 620, 261 N.W.2d 457 (1978) (nonvested pension held to be divisible) and *Rodak v. Rodak*, 150 Wis. 2d 624, 442 N.W.2d 489, (Wis. Ct. App. 1989) (portion of civilian pension that was earned *before* marriage is included in marital property and subject to division).

Wyoming

Divisible. *Parker v. Parker*, 750 P.2d 1313 (Wyo. 1988) (nonvested military retired pay is marital property; 10-year test is a prerequisite to direct payment of military retired pay as property, but not to division of military retired pay as property). *See also Forney v. Minard*, 849 P.2d 724 (Wyo. 1993) (Affirms award of 100% of "disposable retired pay" to former spouse as property, but acknowledges that only 50% of this award can be paid directly. Note that this holding is inconsistent with 1990 amendment to USFSPA at 10 U.S.C. §1408(e)(1) which deems all orders dividing military retired pay as property satisfied once a threshold of 50% of the "disposable retired pay" is reached —*see* the discussion in *Knoop v. Knoop* referenced under the North Dakota section of this guide.)

Canal Zone

Divisible. *Bodenhorn v. Bodenhorn*, 567 F.2d 629 (5th Cir. 1978).

CHAPTER ENDNOTES

1. This note updates the Note, "State-by-State Analysis of the Divisibility of Military Retired Pay," ARMY LAW., July 1994, at 41. It was developed with the assistance of military attorneys, active and reserve, and civilian practitioners located throughout the country. In a continuing effort to foster accuracy and timeliness, updates and suggested revisions from all jurisdictions are solicited. Please send your submissions to the Administrative and Civil Law Department, The Judge Advocate General's School, ATTN: JAGS-ADA-LA, Charlottesville, Virginia 22903-1781.

2. 490 U.S. 581 (1989).

3.   *Id.* at §594.

4.   *Id.* at §589.

5.   660 A.2d 1214 (N.J. Super. 1995). *See also* TJAGSA Practice Note, *Reductions in Disposable Retired Pay Triggered by Receipt of VA Disability Pay: A Basis for Reopening a Judgment of Divorce*, *Army Law.*, Oct. 1995, at 28.

6.   542 N.W.2d 114 (N.D. 1996).

7.   5 U.S.C.A. § §5531-5404.

8.   *See also*, TJAGSA Practice Note, *Reductions in Disposable Retired Pay Triggered by the Dual Compensation Act, Army Law.*, Mar. 1996, at 133.

13

THE DIVORCE PROCESS

What You Need to Know If You Plan to Divorce

This book is not meant to be a procedural guide for divorce, but you do need to know what some of the "military" implications and complications are for some of the routine steps in the initial phases of the divorce process. Both the military member and spouse may want to go to your local base or post legal office to obtain *general* information on the following for your state: general filing and residency requirements, service, grounds, support (spousal and child), property division, and appeal rights. Keep in mind, however, that your local military legal office[1] may not be able to answer any specific questions, particularly if the military lawyer is not a domestic relations expert licensed in your state. If you do not have a military legal office nearby, then you should educate yourself regarding the following points so that you can maximize your discussions with your chosen attorney (and minimize your legal fees).

General Filing and Residency Requirements

As mentioned in Chapter 8, the issue of jurisdiction in a divorce can be very complicated, since meeting residence requirements and notifying the other spouse may present severe problems, particularly when one is out of the country or serving in combat. Frequent moves may mean that not enough time has passed to be considered a resident. The usual proof for establishing residency may be lacking with a military couple, such as owning a home, paying taxes in the state, voting, etc. Some states may, however, have special requirements that allow service members to get divorces even though they are not legal residents.

Some of the questions that can be raised, then, concerning meeting the general requirements, are: Do you file in the county in which you are a resident or in which your spouse resides? In other words, if you claim one state and your spouse claims another, what are your state's venue requirements? One state might require you to file in the county in which the defendant (e.g., your spouse) resides, another in which grounds accrue; or, if the defendant is a nonresident, you might be able to file in any county in the state. Some states require that you be a resident for six months prior to filing for divorce; others require one year.

If you think you may be eligible to file in more than one state, you may wish to select the state which has the simpler procedures. Exercise caution, however, if you are currently living in one location and choose to have your divorce processed in another state. What may start out to be a "no fault" or amicable divorce may end up in litigation. Long-distance calls to and from your attorney will add up fast, not to mention fax charges and overnight mail. You could even be required to attend more than one hearing or deposition or have to travel to that state for unforeseen court-related requirements. And, you could be ordered to pay such costs for your spouse. Obviously, in some cases, you will not have a choice as to where the divorce is processed.

If you are still on active duty, claiming residency is further complicated by the fact that you continually move around. The military member should not get lulled into thinking that just because you claim a certain state on your "Leave and Earnings Statement" (LES), that state will be the one to retain jurisdiction over you for divorce purposes. Although some states are obviously more liberal when it comes to what you need to "prove" that you live there, others are not so lenient. A driver's license alone, the claiming of a state on your LES, or the fact you were previously stationed in a state, will usually not be enough.

One last comment about filing—if divorce is your final decision, it does not matter whether the husband or the wife files for divorce.[2] The courts do not presume that one is at fault more than another, or that the plaintiff (the one who files first) is "not guilty."

Service—Having Divorce Papers Served

The law states that the other party has the right to be notified of any divorce action and to be given sufficient time to respond. This process is called "service of process," and the other party is said to be "served" or "served papers." These papers are the legal notice of the divorce, and neither party should ignore such service. Each state has its own rules for service, such as how it may be done (e.g., personal delivery by the sheriff, publication, certified mail with return receipt requested), and how many days ahead the service must take place prior to a hearing. In addition, if the nonmilitary spouse serves the member with papers while the member is on active duty, then there must also be a statement called (the title varies) a Soldiers and Sailors Affidavit.[3,4] This form is a safeguard for the military defendant who does not answer the complaint (e.g., divorce petition) or appear at a hearing. The form is a sworn statement and often has to be signed in the presence of a notary public.

Grounds for Divorce

The choices here are usually no-fault and fault. Within these two categories, there are various other requirements. For example, one state may allow a divorce under no-fault and call it irreconcilable differences, either 90 days after filing the complaint with mutual consent, or after a three-year separation without mutual consent, for example. Another state might also allow no-fault, and require only one year of living apart as part of a separation decree. In still others, the time periods may depend on whether there are minor children.

Be advised here that the wording for the grounds is usually standard (i.e., your state has particular wording to use). You might find the wording in your divorce petition rather old-fashioned or even outrageous or insulting, perhaps stronger than what you would use to describe marital conflict which cannot be resolved. Although you might try asking your attorney to use different wording, do not be surprised to hear that is what is always used.

In addition to no-fault grounds, there are fault grounds. Fault grounds include adultery, extreme cruelty, desertion, habitual drunkenness, felony conviction, permanent insanity, and other situations. Some states have completely abolished fault grounds. Others require an extensive set of rules and procedures to prove the grounds.

If you wish to proceed on the basis of a fault divorce, then you should question your attorney as to his or her experience with that type of divorce. Keep in mind that there will be a lot more paperwork to prove the ground, more court appearances, more delays, and in general, the whole matter will likely take more time than a no-fault divorce.

We need not tell you that your attorney fees will accrue rapidly in a fault-grounds divorce. Indeed, some lawyers charge a flat fee to appear in court for you, whether it takes one hour or one day. And you are usually billed for the time the attorney sits around waiting for a courtroom or a judge, as they have blocked that time for you.

Although it was the intent of the no-fault grounds to remove much of the adversarial nature of divorce, this is not always the case. By its very nature, a divorce is an adversary action. And, while your divorce may end up being uncontested (there is no full-blown trial), it will probably involve a lot of unpleasant meetings, with parties on all sides very angry that the whole process is not moving faster (or that it is moving too fast).

We cannot stress enough how important it is that you and your spouse try to resolve all issues out of court. Try formulating a separation agreement before you go to court. There are various books (See Appendix P, "Resources") that can assist you with checklists. (Nolo Press in California is known for its legal self-help books, which can be found in most bookstores.)

Spousal Support

Support is often called maintenance or alimony. It can be temporary or permanent, or be "reserved" (the party may request it later). In some states, fault is considered in the award of support, in others, it is not. A state may even disallow court-ordered permanent alimony (if that is the case, the parties may be able to agree to periodic payments). Maintenance may also be nonmonetary. Usually, support ends automatically at remarriage or sometimes ends with cohabitation. Or, there may be no statutory provisions for termination upon remarriage.

If your state can award permanent alimony, the court will also award a portion of military retired pay. It is in the member's best interests to inform his or her attorney of both parties' situation relative to support. The factors the court will consider (as will you and your spouse's attorney) are age and health, potential for supplementary income (in addition to retired pay) as well as future earning ability, educational level, standard of living during the marriage, and the length of the marriage, among other considerations. Do not overlook the fact that the spouse may qualify for various military benefits, such as medical and commissary. If you both cannot agree on the amount or type of support, then be prepared for the courts to decide for you. Like child support, some courts have schedules that the judges can use, based on income.

Child Support

Child support varies from state to state. Most states now have charts or schedules where the courts do not even have to "think" this issue through—the charts state how much support will be awarded based on number of children and income. (You can usually get a sample child support schedule from the court clerk, or look up the schedule in the "Family" or "Domestic Relations" portion of your state's code.) A state may require that a bond be posted. In some states mandatory wage assignment is made. Generally, the award of child support can be modified based on changed circumstances (although other provisions of the divorce decree cannot).

Keep in mind here that the award of either maintenance or child support or both can be *in addition* to the award of retired pay. Although the military finance center will not pay out more than 65 percent (50 percent for division of property, plus 15 percent for child support) of the retiree's pay *directly* to the former spouse, this does not mean that the court cannot award more than that amount. The difference will have to come directly from the pocket of the military member.

For some service members, their retired pay is their only source of income. But keep in mind that the duty to support children is paramount in the court's view, as well as society's, and it is your responsibility and legal duty to provide support. It is also your responsibility, as mentioned earlier, to keep your attorney informed. This means providing your attorney with a listing of your monthly living expenses, an inventory of your property, and some kind of forecast as to your current and future financial requirements.

If the noncustodial parent paying child support later takes physical custody, be sure your decree provides for a cease payment to the previous custodial parent.

For those members still on active duty, it is important to educate your attorney on those financial benefits you may currently be receiving, and which can change at any time. (See Chapter 9 on "Federal Benefits.") Your child support or spousal support should be based on your base pay, as all other special pays are temporary.

Property Division

Property can be tangible (e.g., a house) and intangible (e.g., professional license), and is distributed in one of three ways—equitable distribution, community property, and common law title. Sometimes fault is considered in the award of property. Many states now recognize the contribution of the nonworking spouse and include the economic value of the homemaker's contribution as a marital asset.

Although most states recognize the homemaker's non-monetary contribution, keep in mind that the USFSPA does not require a showing of the military spouse's contributions in order for the court to award a share of the retired pay. In other words, unlike civilian divorces where property division is often based on financial and economic need and a host of other considerations, the military spouse need not prove anything other than the length of the marriage in order to receive a portion of the military retired pay. (Congressional testimony during the time that USFSPA was being considered does contain comments relative to the "plight" of the military spouse.)

It can be argued that in the 1990s, the original intent of USFSPA has changed. Indeed, the general trend in state courts is to not award alimony when both spouses are able to support themselves; or if awarded, it is temporary. This has little or nothing to do with a USFSPA award.

Property also includes pensions and retirement benefits, vested and nonvested. Most states determine the right to such property by dividing the number of years the employed spouse was both a member of a retirement plan and married, by the number of years of work required before the pension payments will be made. Despite the USFSPA's lack of a provision that computes the award based on number of years of marriage, more and more states are making the division using such a formula. (ARA's legislative agenda includes equity in this regard.) Keep in mind that the USFSPA requires the marriage to have lasted 10 years (during 10 years of military duty) in order for the former spouse to receive direct payment from the finance center. The marriage can last less time and still qualify for a division of the retired pay.

If you were divorced before 5 February 1991, then the portion of military retired pay going to a former spouse is based on a net disposable figure (versus the gross amount), i.e., disposable pay is figured after the amounts withheld for income tax, and the member can deduct payments to the former spouse as if they were alimony on his or her federal income tax return. Caution: Disposable pay for divorces on and after 5 February 1991 is figured pretax.

Appeal Rights

A divorce is usually not "final" until an appeal period has passed. Most states allow a party to appeal a divorce judgment within 30 days of the entry of the judgment. What this means is that if either party plans to remarry, he or she must wait until the appeal period has ended. Appeals rarely occur in uncontested divorces. If either party contested the divorce and felt that some action was taken in error, then he or she would may have the right to appeal. (If you have selected a competent and thorough attorney, such actions should be unnecessary.)

Do not confuse appeal rights, however, with the fact that you might be dissatisfied with your divorce judgment. If you failed to raise an issue in your original complaint (petition) or hearing, then your action (failure to do so) will be construed as a waiver of your right to raise the same issue on appeal. For example, consider the military member who is notified that he or she is being retired early involuntarily (e.g., a SERB action). Perhaps the individual feels he is now being forced to accept a lower standard of living because of not being able to stay in the military longer to earn more money and, hence, a higher retired paycheck. He might overlook telling this to his lawyer. The military member cannot now raise the issue of the SERB action on appeal and how that action has cut short his plans to save more for his retirement years. Keep in mind that disobeying or ignoring court orders can constitute waivers, also.

Careful planning and the selection of a competent lawyer could minimize, if not eliminate, any need for you to appeal. This does not mean that the other party cannot appeal. What it does mean is that you ask your attorney what the appeal waiting period is, and you do not go out and remarry immediately until that time has passed.

Your Base Legal Office

You may be wondering whether to seek advice through your local judge advocate general's office. Most large military installations will have a legal office with one or more "JAGs" and a (senior) staff judge advocate, including civilian lawyers. Although the military attorneys can provide some help with personal legal matters (e.g., they can prepare a will for you free of charge, or review a lease, etc.), the military member and the spouse are responsible for seeking a civilian attorney in divorce matters.

The military attorneys can advise both parties of their rights and benefits, provide checklists and forms for accomplishing a separation agreement, and assist in helping the spouse obtain family support. This assistance will be done only in person and not over the phone. The legal offices will often have literature available pertinent to the state where you are serving in, along with fact sheets on the USFSPA and SBP.

Occasionally you may meet a reservist who is performing an annual two-week active duty tour in the base legal office. And, you may be lucky to learn that the reservist is a practicing attorney (you are really lucky if the attorney/reservist is a domestic relations lawyer) in the local area (or in the state) who knows the state rules and procedures. Such a resource can be invaluable to you as you begin the process. But, keep in mind that the reservist is there for only a short period, and that it is still your responsibility to retain a civilian attorney.

The Other Part of the Divorce Process

The legal aspects of your divorce may well be over-shadowed by the emotional toll a divorce can take on you, whether or not you are the one who initiates the divorce. Various studies have analyzed the stages of bad marriages, with one researcher identifying three stages to a dying marriage: initial disappointment; a middle phase of intense hurt and anger; and disaffection, marked by anger, apathy, and hopelessness.

ARA is not qualified to provide professional counseling to the service member or the spouse. However, we feel it important enough to mention that you will most likely experience a period, as you go through your divorce, when you may think you are not normal. We want to assure you that you are, and that many couples have gone before you and will go after, who survive the divorce process and go on with their lives.

During the next year, more than 11 million people will be afflicted with depression, and many of them are going through a divorce. Most of the depression will go undiagnosed and those suffering will go untreated. You need to know what symptoms to look for and to acknowledge to yourself that you are not going insane—you are going through a divorce. What you are feeling is not uncommon.

If you are experiencing any of the following symptoms (noted by the American Psychiatric Association) and they are severely impairing your everyday functioning, you should see your family doctor:

1. Change in appetite with a weight gain or loss not attributable to dieting.
2. Feelings of worthlessness (e.g., "I'll never be able to find another man [woman]").
3. Feelings of inappropriate guilt (e.g., "I am not a good wife [husband], if I had been, this would not be happening").
4. Change in sleeping habits (e.g., sleeping more, or insomnia).
5. Persistent feeling of hopelessness.
6. Difficulty concentrating, focusing, thinking, or making decisions.
7. Overwhelming feelings of grief and sadness.
8. Irritability or anxiety.
9. Disturbed thinking, such as unrealistic beliefs.
10. Decreased energy, fatigue, or feeling "slowed down."
11. Recurring thoughts of death or suicide, wishing to die, or attempting suicide.
12. Physical symptoms, such as headaches, backaches, stomach aches or chronic pain that do not respond to treatment.

The important thing to remember is that you will most likely experience one or more of the above symptoms and that is normal when going through a divorce.

CHAPTER ENDNOTES

1. Some military legal offices actually do help couples process their divorce. However, in one instance we know of, the civilian lawyer working in the military legal office draws up the property settlement for both parties. We, as well as all lawyers we have dealt with, strongly encourage each party to retain his or her own attorney. The reasons are obvious.

2. In general, in two-thirds of cases it is the wife, not the husband, who files. For further research on this, see: "Who Divorced Whom: Methodological and Theoretical Issues." *Journal of Divorce & Remarriage*, Vol. 20 (1/2), 1993, by Sanford L. Braver, Marnie Whitley, and Christine Ng. Dr. Braver can be contacted at the Department of Psychology, Arizona State University, Tempe, AZ 85287-1104, Tel. (602) 965-5405.

3. Because the duties of military personnel may prevent them from defending themselves against a civil action (which includes divorce), the Soldiers' and Sailors' Civil Relief Act of 1940 (50 U.S.C. §§501-591) was enacted. This act protects active duty military from the entry of a default judgment or order against them. The Act requires that the plaintiff file an affidavit stating that the defendant is not in the armed services before a default order can be entered. If the plaintiff does not provide such a statement, then the court cannot enter a default judgment against the military member without appointing an attorney to represent the member. Failure to adhere to the requirements of the Soldiers' and Sailors' Civil Relief Act allows an active duty member to petition to set aside the judgment up to six months following discharge from the military. See the book, *Servicemember's Legal Guide,* (listed in Appendix P of this book), for a more detailed explanation of this Act, along with a sample letter to request a delay in a lawsuit.

4. One publicized case where the U.S. Supreme Court has applied the Soldiers' and Sailors' Civil Relief Act is that of Army Colonel Thomas Conroy. On 31 March 1993, the justices unanimously ruled that the Act provides blanket protection to service members on active duty and that in the case of Colonel Conroy, the property of active duty members may not be seized for unpaid taxes, no matter why they did not pay. In an article in the 19 April 1993 issue of the *Air Force Times* (page 9), the opposing side was quoted: "The legitimate state, social and economic goals would be absolutely frustrated if a career serviceman is permitted to use (the act) to protect him from economic responsibilities he has voluntarily taken on." The Supreme Court did not agree with that reasoning, saying "it would

not read an exception into the law where Congress has not put one." *Editorial comment:* In some respects, the *McCarty* decision elicited the same response from the Supreme Court— it would not read a connotation of community property into the meaning of retired pay and if Congress wanted to change the intent, then it would have to pass new legislation (which it did).

14

SELECTING AN ATTORNEY

The Most Critical Step in Your Divorce

The most critical step you will take in your divorce, besides educating yourself on the USFSPA and the general legal requirements for divorce, will be your selection of an attorney. While retaining an attorney is not absolutely necessary in a divorce, it is the rare couple, indeed, who can agree to the division of all property and who know what tax or other legal implications may result from such a division. Notwithstanding the legal process involved in a divorce, there is the emotional trauma of one of the most stressful events in our lives (others being the death of a spouse or a child). Based on the personal stories we have heard, as well as reading on the subject, people in the process of divorce, men and women alike, are rarely able to tend to all the legal steps that must be followed. Maintaining your mental health becomes a number one priority. (See Appendix P for some suggested reading to help you cope with the emotional impact of divorce.)

You Are Still Responsible

Leaving the legal responsibilities to a competent attorney does not mean that you turn your life over to the attorney. The divorce is still your responsibility and it is you who must obtain and organize the information that the attorney will need.

We recommend that you find an attorney who specializes in domestic relations law, preferably divorce. It does not matter whether the attorney is male or female. What counts is what they know about military divorces, for it is rare, indeed, that the typical military person has any knowledge of the law in this area. (From the calls it gets, ARA is convinced that many lawyers are not knowledgeable on this subject, either.)

Don't Go to a Lawyer Who Does Not Specialize in Domestic Relations Law

You wouldn't go to a dentist to have your broken leg set in a cast, would you? The same advice follows for selecting a lawyer. There are many types of lawyers—some practice corporate law, others specialize in bankruptcy, and others specialize in domestic relations law, and even in the more specialized area of divorce.

Retain the services of an attorney who is absolutely knowledgeable and experienced in "military" divorces. Knowledge of domestic or family law is not enough; the attorney must be intimately familiar with military marriages, benefits, and military retirement and divorce law. Do not assume that just because the attorney is a former JAG (military lawyer, judge advocate general), that he or she knows about divorce law, let alone military divorce. They may not know the particular family law in the state where you will be obtaining a divorce, either.

Interviewing Attorneys

You will obviously have come up with some questions specific to your situation and should make a list of these before you interview your first attorney. Appendix M is a basic list of questions you will need to have answered on the first interview to determine whether you and your attorney will make a good "fit."

In general, your questions will deal with the following: the attorney's experience in handling military divorces, the attorney's general qualifications, the fee arrangements and administrative matters (how the attorney likes to work with the client).

Do not choose an attorney strictly because he is a family friend or has had a close relationship with both you and your spouse. If upon mentioning phrases such as "SBP" and "combining your military retirement with a Civil Service retirement" you get a questioning look on the attorney's face, do not hesitate to terminate the interview. You are not there to train the lawyer.

One last point—if *you* feel uncomfortable with the attorney (i.e., you feel the attorney appears inexperienced, too young to comprehend the issues in a long-term marriage, not appreciative of a military career and retirement, or whatever the reason), and more particularly, if the attorney has not been able to answer your questions so you can understand them, *do not hire that attorney*. It is very important that you feel comfortable with the attorney. Although firing an attorney is the choice of last resort, you do need to realize when to cut your losses. Such situations only get worse if you decide later that you want to switch attorneys.

If you remember only one thing from this chapter, let it be that the attorney charges just as much for talking to you as for listening to you. Please keep in mind that you are entering a business arrangement with the attorney—the attorney is not your therapist or best friend. What you perceive as a lack of empathy may be, for the most part, an objective approach to your case for your sake. This is not to say that the attorney should not acknowledge your situation; but that your emotional investment is, by far, your investment, and not your attorney's. The attorney's job is to obtain the best and fairest settlement that will allow both you and your spouse to continue on with your lives in a manner as close as possible to what you enjoyed during the marriage, and to do it in the shortest possible time. Be advised that more and more attorneys are charging their regular fee for initial consultation. We feel that there should be no charge for a 15 minute consultation (assuming you are organized, that may be all the time you need). However, if you do have to pay, the money will be well spent if all you learn is whether this attorney is the right one for you. Sometimes you can determine whether an attorney can handle your case by simply calling the attorney's office and asking.

Preparation—What You Need to Take to the Attorney's Office

In Appendix N you will find a checklist for the things you will need to provide an attorney. The checklist is also excellent in helping you to prepare for an interview with an attorney. Following is a summary of the information you will need.

Basic Information

Be prepared to provide general information (for the first interview) such as: how long you have been married, number of children and their ages, you and your spouse's status relative to income, health, education, work experience, contribution to the marriage (monetary and nonmonetary). In short—the attorney needs to know what standard of living you have established and what is expected to happen to it once you are divorced. The attorney will also want to know the circumstances contributing to the divorce so that the grounds can be established.

Personal and Real Property

If you have never inventoried your assets (all of them— marital and nonmarital), you will need to in preparation for the divorce. You will also have to assess the fair market value of all your property. Some attorneys will advise you to assess what you think you could get for the property at a yard sale. If you have access to software such as "Managing Your Money" or "Quicken," you will find this task much easier.

Financial Status

The attorney will need to know your specific financial status, including your monthly joint and separate budgets. You can often obtain such forms from your local bank or credit union, or a realtor. Your attorney will also provide you the forms. The service member will have to provide, at least, a current copy of his or her Leave and Earnings Statement. If the member is already retired, provide a copy of the monthly retiree's account statement. If you are a reservist, provide one of your weekend drill statements, as well as your most recent point accounting statement. Income tax returns for the last three to five years will also be needed. Besides your monthly budget, you will have to list all your financial assets—savings accounts, bonds, IRAs, etc.

Summary of Military Service

The opposing attorney will no doubt require, under the process for obtaining information known as "discovery," a listing of the military assignments (when, where, how long), and whether the spouse accompanied the member. So, now is a good time to compile such a list. Also indicate whether the spouse worked, and the approximate yearly income, for each assignment period. It is also important to know the relative situation of each spouse. Did the spouse take a traditional role in the family, while the service member's career was the priority? If so, your attorney will be better able to advise you of the local court's treatment of such marriages. Does the member anticipate receiving a disability retirement? Is he or she still capable of working (and relatively young)? Will the spouse be eligible for military medical care, and commissary and exchange privileges? Such questions need to be addressed.

Preparation Is Necessary

All of this information will provide a better representation of the marital fiscal picture. The fact is that some attorneys are not experienced enough, or will not take on cases that have peculiar aspects. Thus, it is important that you not hold back information when discussing your case with an attorney. One attorney we know refuses to accept cases where the spouse has committed adultery. Other attorneys do not handle divorces where child support is involved. Still others may need to refer you to another lawyer if domestic violence is involved.

Each case is different, and the lawyer you interview should be able to tell you, from your information and questions, whether he or she can handle your case with the least number of complications.

A Word About Attorney Fees and Other Divorce Costs

We are often asked how much the divorce will cost. There are no averages—each one is different. An uncontested divorce can cost $2,000 or more. More complex cases, even without contentious parties, will run to $10,000 or more. If the divorce is long distance, you will have the added costs of phone bills (both yours and your attorney's) and postage (all certified with return receipts). We hope your divorce bills do not even come close to those of Stanley and Dorothy Diller (See Chapter 19).

The least expensive lawyer may not always be able to handle your divorce as expeditiously as the more expensive and experienced lawyer. Thus, it pays to investigate your attorney's experience in light of the fees that are charged.

We do know that there are some factors that will help you to control your costs:

1. Become and remain organized.
2. Respond quickly to requests for information.
3. Stay in control of your emotions.
4. Get support from family and friends and experts.
5. Get rid of your "someone must win and someone must lose" mentality.
6. Stay fair and honest in all your dealings with each other.

Using Appendix M—Checklist for Interviewing an Attorney

As you prepare your own list of questions and after you have read this book, assess your interview with the objective of selecting the most knowledgeable attorney you can find on military divorce. If you have done your homework, you will not choose an attorney who is more likely to make one of the most common mistakes ARA has found that divorce lawyers make in handling military divorces. First and foremost is the fact that they just do not understand the USFSPA and have never really studied it or its related regulations.

Second, all but a few attorneys just are unwilling to research jurisdictional requirements, which can be cumbersome. If you and your spouse can agree ahead of time on which state you will file and accept jurisdiction in, then you can proceed without worrying about jurisdiction. However, a competent attorney will provide you options and consequences regarding which state you can or should file in.

The last mistake attorneys often make is that they have not provided a clear description in your divorce decree as to the division of retired pay, nor does the decree contain the elements that DFAS must have in order to pay a share of the retired pay to the former spouse. Such a lack of detail results in clarification or modification orders, not to mention the possibility of an appeal. In short, both parties end up back in court, paying legal fees for what should have been already done by the attorneys.

A Final Word on You and Your Attorney

There is a saying that an incompetent attorney can delay a case for months, but the competent attorney can delay it even longer. Numerous studies abound about the ethics and professionalism of lawyers. While some attorneys (and some people, like the Marines, are still looking for a few good ones) are highly critical of their peers in their rush for money, you should be aware that your being naive and not overseeing your own case in a zealous manner could hurt you financially.

Attorneys are often pressured to snare clients and bring money to their firms. Professors who study the business of law say that outright fibbing exists in attorneys' eagerness to log time even if the expense is not worthwhile to the clients. Heightened competition is causing some of the changes, and others are caused by pure greed.

Your attorney is a business—and to stay in business he or she must earn a profit. In a national survey of attorneys, judges and law students, one-third of those responding said attorneys are more likely to lie today than in earlier eras; three-quarters said attorneys are more money-conscious; and nearly one-half said they are less civil. We tell you this so that you do not become an unhappy client or the victim of an incompetent or unscrupulous attorney.

Do not ever forget that you are entitled to certain rights in your contract with your attorney.[1] First and foremost of these is that you are entitled to an attorney capable of handling your military divorce competently and diligently, and who provides you his or her undivided loyalty. You are entitled to a clear explanation of how the attorney charges and to itemized bills for the services you are paying. You are entitled to prompt and clear responses to your telephone calls, questions, and correspondence, as well as copies of papers your attorney prepares or files on your behalf. In return, you need to comply with your attorney's requests for data and to do so in a timely manner. You need to give your attention to your divorce and to not expect the attorney to read your mind. Your mutual goal is to complete the divorce in the most equitable manner possible and to move on with your life.

You may not be "happy" with the results of your case, but you need to keep in mind that when you hire an attorney, you are paying for someone to provide you an objective, less emotional point of view than your own. To that end, attorneys must look at all sides of the case so that they can anticipate problems and be prepared. Just because you did not, in your own mind, "win," does not mean that you had a bad lawyer. Equitable does not mean equal.

One final note for those with access to the Internet, you may now browse the Martindale-Hubbell Law Directory online to find an attorney at: www.lawyers.com. It has state-by-state listings of more than 420,000 attorneys.

CHAPTER ENDNOTES

1.   Complaining to the State Bar about an attorney should be carefully considered. In many states, complaints filed against attorneys are not public information. Further, the process of complaining is a difficult one, and the consumer is often the victim in that process, even if he or she has grounds for a valid complaint. Consider consumers in California. In 1998, callers to the California State Bar's 800 number heard a taped message announcing its shutdown. Worse, written complaints were returned to the sender! If you follow the advice in this book, then you should not have to complain.

15

STRATEGIES

Many military members and spouses have asked for a step-by-step guide to the USFSPA and their divorce. Every situation is different and no one publication will be able to answer all your questions or even apply in every instance to your particular case. No book or attorney can make your decisions for you—you will have to do that. As you both consider the ramifications of a divorce in light of military service and obligations to your family, there are some strategies you can essay. As you review them, keep in mind that ARA does not endorse a win-lose situation (unless it is couched in the facetious terms that the only winners in a divorce are the lawyers), although we realize that many divorces end up in such a battle. The ARA's position is that these matters should be based on merit, need, and the ability to pay.

Further, the ARA believes in the fair and equitable treatment of *both* members of a military marriage that ends in divorce.

Legal and Moral Obligations in a Divorce

As we have pointed out several times, the military member and spouse have both moral and legal obligations when it comes to the family. The most important *legal* matters that a divorce will resolve will be the division of your property; decisions on where your children will live, who will care for them, and how they will be cared for; and the distribution of income between the spouses. While it would be nice for you to discuss all the terms of your divorce settlement with each other in an amicable manner, we realize that is not always possible.

Considerations and Approaches

Just as discussions regarding the divorce settlement may not always be pleasant, neither will the negotiation sessions go so well when either side is ill informed about the law as it relates to divorce involving a military member. If the decision to divorce has been made, then there are some steps you can take to make it as simple as possible.

Suggested Strategies

1. GET AN EDUCATED ATTORNEY

This is advised earlier in this book; but it is repeated because it is important. It is imperative that each of you retain the services of an attorney who is absolutely knowledgeable on this subject. Knowledge of domestic or family law is not enough; the attorney must be intimately familiar with military marriages, military benefits, and military retirement and divorce law.

Finding an attorney who is knowledgeable on military divorces may not be easy. If you cannot find such a person, you will have to educate your attorney on the USFSPA before you go to court. *That* can be an expensive endeavor.

Also, while you may get references from other people, keep in mind that the facts of your case may not be the same as those of your friend or reference. You may have details that complicate your case beyond the experience of that attorney. Moreover, there is a thing called "lawyer-client chemistry."

Some people advocate finding the best lawyer possible, despite the fact that such a person may also be the most expensive. A very experienced lawyer could save you money by not having to research everything to "get educated." A good lawyer can cut the time it takes to bring your divorce to closure because he or she has a reputation for "cutting to the chase."

You may want to sit in on some cases in the courtroom, or find out whether there are any retired men or women in your area who conduct courtroom observations.

The final choice of an attorney is yours. If you are comfortable with the lawyer you have interviewed and selected (i.e., the attorney's knowledge of military divorce, a grasp of your situation particulars, and sufficient experience to proceed in an expeditious manner), then it probably may not matter that the attorney you have chosen is not the "best" in the region.

2. THE USFSPA IS A PERMISSIVE LAW

While some state courts have automatically been awarding 50 percent of the military member's retired pay to the former spouse, be aware that the USFSPA states that they *may* treat the retired pay as property and award a portion to the former spouse, up to 50 percent (65 percent with child support). Unlike civilian divorces where property division is often based on a number of factors, including financial and economic need, the USFSPA does not require the military spouse to prove either in order to receive a portion of the military retired pay. If either attorney automatically says 50 percent, with no attempt to negotiate a more reasonable settlement for the service member who must serve at least 20 years to be eligible for retired pay, when the marriage has not lasted 20 years, then the service member should ask why, since the law is permissive.

3. KNOW THE LAW REGARDING COURT RULINGS ON RETIRED PAY WHILE ON ACTIVE DUTY

Federal law (the USFSPA) provides that the service member cannot be ordered to retire involuntarily so that payments to a former spouse can begin. Nor does the USFSPA allow a court to order the military member to begin payments (i.e., distributions from active duty pay) while the member is still on active duty.[1] USFSPA payments are not authorized after recall of retired military members to active duty. The member cannot collect retired pay, or pay it out, unless he or she is retired. Either party could, of course, be ordered to pay alimony or child support, with the source not specified.

4. DO NOT FORGET THE DENOMINATOR

The computation that many states are now using to determine the pro rata share that will go to the spouse is based on the number of years the spouse was married while the service member was in the military (creditable time, the numerator), divided by the member's total current military time *at the time of the divorce* (the denominator). The longer the member stays in the military before retiring, the more favorable the formula under which the retired pay will be divided.

An illustration of this type of calculation would work like this (and is the case in many courts):

At the time of divorce, a couple was married for 12 years concurrently with military service; the military member had served 20 years at time of retirement, and the award was for 50 percent. The calculation would be:

12/20 x .50 = 30% to spouse

If, on the other hand, the military member stays in for 30 years, the calculation would be 12/30 x .50 = 20% to spouse.

This might, of course, be offset by promotions after divorce if the final divorce decree did not specify that the ex-spouse's share was to be calculated at the pay grade extant at the time of divorce.

5. KNOW THE LAW REGARDING DISABILITY PAY—USFSPA DOES NOT AWARD IT

As affirmed by the U.S. Supreme Court decision in *Mansell v. Mansell* (1989), the USFSPA does not authorize a court to include disability pay in the definition of "disposable pay" if it is being received from the VA under Title 38 of the U. S. Code, or from DoD under Chapter 61 of Title 10 of the U. S. Code. However, some states have ignored the law in this area.

If the court does award the disability pay, the member may have an appealable case. Consult an attorney.

6. CONSIDER INCOME TAX IMPLICATIONS

The bottom line (for both the member and spouse) is affected by the effective date of your divorce, not the military member's retirement date. If the divorce occurred before 3 February 1991, then the amount of the share to the spouse was based on all the tax liability (both of you) being taken from the member's check prior to dividing it with the spouse. The spouse still has to pay tax on his or her share.[2] If the divorce occurred on or after 3 February 1991 (Public Law 101-510, §555), then each of you will be responsible for your own taxes. See Chapter 10 on "Financial Management" for other tax considerations.

7. IF YOU WERE DIVORCED ON OR PRIOR TO 25 JUNE 1981

If you were divorced on or prior to 25 June 1981 *and* your final decree did not make an award of military retired pay *or* reserve the option of the court to later make an award, the ex-spouse cannot exploit the USFSPA to force the member into ex-post facto payments.

Unfortunately, some courts are still ignoring Public Law 101-510 §555 which provides this protection. If the court ignores this amendment to the USFSPA, the member may have an appealable case.[3] The point of law is federal supremacy. Under the supremacy clause of the U.S. Constitution, federal law prevails over state law when the two are in direct conflict.

The member and his or her attorney may wish to remove the case to a federal court, since an appeal to a higher state court may well result in an affirmation of a lower court's erroneous ruling. Your counsel should check your state courts' record in this regard vis-a-vis USFSPA matters.

8. AVOID WINDFALL BENEFITS

If you are divorcing while the service member is still on active duty, the member should make sure the decree states that payments after the member retires will be based on the member's pay grade at the time of divorce, the only fair way to calculate it. The COLAs are usually included, and will be when payment is made directly by the finance center. This method is better than payments based on the pay grade at which the service member finally retires, which is unfair to the service member (because it awards windfall benefits to the ex-spouse).

If the divorce decree was silent as to how the calculation was to be made, any clarification should clearly indicate the rank/pay grade in effect on the date of the divorce.

9. CONSIDER A SEPARATION AGREEMENT

If you have the time and the relationship permits, it may be possible to execute a separation agreement which addresses all the issues (e.g., division of property, alimony, child support, etc.) before going into court. This permits a rational approach to problems in the presence of counsel (separate counsel for each recommended) in a more relaxed environment than a courtroom.

Moreover, it can result in settlements based on full discussion and negotiation, rather than the (snap) decisions of a judge who may be given an incomplete picture of the circumstances and issues of the divorce. Most courts will accept a properly executed separation agreement as the basis for a final divorce settlement. A separation agreement can reduce costs, save time, and minimize the possibility of misunderstandings later on.

10. DON'T FORGET SBP, LIFE INSURANCE, AND OTHER SURVIVOR BENEFITS

The spouse may be entitled to coverage under the

Survivor Benefit Plan. If she or he is awarded SBP, the member is allowed to deduct the amount of the SBP premiums from USFSPA payments (and they come "off the top," before tax liability is computed). The member will not be able to deduct (for income tax purposes) the premiums on any commercial life insurance for which the ex-spouse is the beneficiary *unless* she or he is the legal owner of the policies. Survivor benefits are very important to post-divorce financial planning and may be important negotiating points in any pre-divorce negotiations.

Consider also any Social Security benefits the spouse will receive, based on either the military retiree's employment or the spouse's own work record.

11. KEEP YOURSELF INFORMED

Your divorce strategy is inextricably tied to the law as it exists at the time of your divorce. Changes to the USFSPA are under constant consideration. Many attorneys for the spouses are including in the divorce decree language that allows the spouse to return to court to receive additional benefits, should the law change.[4]

While such changes might not necessarily change the net due the service member,[5] both of you could find yourself facing additional expenses as the attorneys work out the appropriate wording, or one of the parties causes additional work that incurs legal fees. To protect yourself, you may want to include language that states that whatever additional changes are incurred, the party filing same also pays the legal fees and related costs.

One of the ways you can keep yourself informed is by becoming a member of the ARA. Its Web page and newsletter can keep you informed of upcoming legislative events that could work to both of your advantages in a divorce.

Another way is to spend an afternoon in your local law

library reading the section on divorce code and reviewing representative cases. If you need help on where to go or what to search, see Appendix P, "Resources."

You can also consult with local groups about divorce procedures in your area. Men's as well as women's groups, including women's centers (often open to men), and county agencies provide free information and often seminars on divorce procedural requirements. A call to your county court offices can also yield information.

12. GET ORGANIZED AND KNOW WHEN TO CUT YOUR LOSSES

While we would like to think this is not true, no one has stepped forward to refute the following rule:

> *"Whatever it is, it will always take longer than you had expected, cost more than you had expected, and produce results you had not expected." And its close relative: "When you need it, you won't be able to find it."*

One of the interpretations of this is that "time is money"— most often, yours. A divorce creates an extremely stressful situation. Matters are further compounded by all the factors affecting military couples that are discussed in this book. Approaching your divorce with due regard to the emotional and mental health aspects of the situation in an organized manner will help you immensely. Many people have told us that it was not until some time after their divorce that they realized that during the process they had acted quite irrationally. Be aware that this can happen and keep a constant check on your emotions and thought processes. Appendix P lists some books that may be of help in this regard.

The following are some basic steps you should take to become and stay organized. Doing so can save you money and aggravation.

A. Keep a Log Book

Organize it by date—enter all major actions in your case *as they happen*. Include the times (beginning and ending) and dates you talk with your attorney, when your attorney says he or she has talked or written something to your spouse's attorney, and when your attorney has gone to court on your behalf. Sometimes the only way you will become aware of such information is through telephone conversations or other oral communications. Log it while it is still clear in your mind.

B. Establish a File Box

Get an empty box or plastic file container (preferably one with handles) and a bunch of file folders. The following are the *minimum* number of categories you should have. Label them as follows:

SUSPENSE FILE
Keep a record of any tasks assigned to you by your attorney and a record of what you do about them. Also note any special dates (e.g., hearings, meetings with your spouse's attorney). If your attorney (or opposing attorney) has said he or she will do something (you might find this in a piece of correspondence), note it in this file. Deadlines are critical in legal actions. Missing deadlines can be catastrophic.

CORRESPONDENCE TO/FROM ATTORNEY

This file also includes copies of correspondence the opposing attorney sends to your attorney. Note the receipt dates in your log book.

COURT DOCUMENTS

This file holds the papers that your attorney and opposing attorney have filed with the court, e.g., petition, motions, temporary orders.

NOTES/LETTERS FROM YOUR SPOUSE

If you are both on speaking terms (even if hostile), include here any letters, notes of phone conversations, etc. Do this even if you are under restraining orders not to communicate or if your attorney has instructed you not to do so. Those restraints may not apply to your spouse and what you receive may be useful.

FINANCIAL DATA (see Appendix N)

Subdivide this folder into several folders that contain income statement (monthly budget—what you receive and spend, your living expenses), copies of income tax records for last three years, complete financial disclosure, etc.

BILLINGS (FROM ATTORNEY)
(other labels: Invoices, Statements)

Put the statements you receive from your attorney into this file. Also include the retainer letter or statement you initially executed regarding the fee arrangement. If you don't have one, be sure to confirm in writing with your attorney the arrangements you have agreed to (and put that letter in this file). If there is any misunderstanding later on, you want to get it cleared up as quickly as possible. When you receive a statement, cross check it with your log and the correspondence (including court papers) you have received in the last 30 days.

Attorneys can and do make billing mistakes—careful checking can result in significant savings. Do not hesitate to query your attorney about billing inconsistencies. Generally, they are more than willing to correct a mistake in your favor. Put your inquiry in writing and include a copy of the bill. Your attorney should be billing you monthly in detail, by listing the date, description of activity, and time involved. If you are not receiving monthly bills, then be sure to bring this to your attorney's attention. DO NOT LET GRASS GROW when it comes to legal bills.

For more complicated divorce cases, you should consider designing (or having someone design) an automated database to track information, particularly if you or your attorney expects protracted litigation.

A file plan such as this will keep you organized and on track with your divorce actions. Such a structure and methodology will also signal when there is something awry with the legal representation you are receiving and the course your divorce is taking. By educating yourself and listening to your instincts, you will usually know when you need to pull in the reins and, as a last resort if necessary, switch attorneys.

People, in our experience, frequently forget that the attorney is working for them and that attorneys can be dismissed and replaced when the representation is not getting the job done or the lawyer-client chemistry is not right . . . BUT, make sure your problem is with the attorney and not your misconceptions of what he or she should be able to do for you.[6]

Never forget that *you* are responsible for your divorce.

Your attorney's duty is to counsel and advise you and then represent you in decisions which remain *your* responsibility to make.

If you are unsure of what is happening (and the fact that things not going your way is not necessarily a reason for firing your attorney), the ARA can help you.

One Final Note About Records

Our advice on how long the file on your divorce should be kept is **FOREVER**. Some attorneys do shift law firms and areas of the law in which they work. Many people have told us that the principal reason they prevailed when their divorce case was reopened unexpectedly was that *their* files contained the information they needed.

Remember—currently there is *no* statute of limitations on the time allowed for the ex-spouse to petition for the retiree's military retired pay if he or she was not awarded it at the time of divorce. Well-organized files may contain something urgently needed for that reopening.

Summary

There are really only three things you have to do: find yourself a knowledgeable attorney, know the essence of the law yourself, and get organized. Doing these three things will solve the one problem we have found that is pervasive with military divorces, whether it is the military member or the spouse: they found out they had an incompetent lawyer and they did not know about the law until *after* the fact, i.e., when an appeal was taken or the divorce was reopened for clarification, modification, or enforcement.

CHAPTER ENDNOTES

1. This provision of the federal law could be interpreted differently in New Mexico courts. (This statement is made because New Mexico has ignored federal law with respect to military retired pay in divorce cases.) The state now favors "finality" in divorce cases, as ruled in *Ruggles v. Ruggles*, 116 NM 52, 860 P.2d 182 (1993), that where there is a "vested" retirement fund, the attitude is to have the money divided. (Some states have defined the term "vested" to include a retirement where there is no actual monetary investment, such as in the military retired pay system.) This "finality" appears to contradict New Mexico's own reasoning cited in numerous other cases in that, under New Mexico law, there is a "limited reservation of jurisdiction" that is incorporated into every divorce. In other words, the courts are saying it is "OK" to reopen a case at any time for any reason, and that changes in federal law do not preempt or have any authority over New Mexico law. What this could mean to military members is that, at least in New Mexico, the court could order the military member to begin payments of not-yet received retired pay. See Chapter 2, endnote #1. See also Chapter 12, "51 Flavors and Counting."

2. While this is double taxation to the spouse (for pre-February 1991 divorces), it is considered legal by the IRS. (See *Eatinger v. Commissioner of Internal Revenue*, US TC, TC Memo 1990-310, 20 June 1990, 16 FLR 1399.) The IRS does, in reality, collect taxes *twice* on the spouse's share. We do not have any data for cases where the divorce took place *before* February 1991, and the property settlement was not executed until *after* February 1991. We know of one case, however, where the court has been asked to adjudicate the property using the post-February 1991 definition of retired pay (November 1990 amendment to the USFSPA). The particulars of this case, however, are such that the divorce was granted in one state in 1986, with the property settlement begun in another state five years later, and property scattered in three states. The parties reside in different states. Given the legwork that would have to be done to calculate the various years' worth of retired pay for tax purposes, it is no wonder that attorneys for both parties are in agreement that using the February 1991

definition of retired pay is only common sense. It goes without saying that "time is of the essence."

3. As mentioned in endnote #1, New Mexico has ignored the retroactivity amendment as ruled in *Berry v. Meadows*, NMCA No. 14,907, 14 October 1993 (Memorandum Opinion), cert. den. (24 November 1993, the Court of Appeals affirmed the trial court's ruling—unpublished opinion); and in *Gonzales v. Roybal*, Civ. No. 93-1302MV, U.S.D.C.N.M.)

4. We do not mean here the future changes to your income that allow a spouse to reopen a divorce case because "circumstances have changed," as many state courts allow. The changes referred to here are strictly those related to military retired pay and benefits.

5. For example, if the law changed to allow more former spouses to use various military benefits, e.g., the commissary, such a change would not affect the amount of money either of you currently receives from your retirement check.

6. Consult the excellent book, *Using a Lawyer . . . And What To Do If Things Go Wrong* (see Appendix P). Also see Endnote 1 in Chapter 14.

16

LEGISLATIVE ENVIRONMENT: RELUCTANCE AND OBFUSCATION

Despite its unfavorable impact on divorced military veterans, Congress has exhibited, from the outset, an implacable reluctance to amend the USFSPA to cure its most egregious inequities. In 1990, Congressional hearings were first held on USFSPA reform. Even then the results were a *quid pro quo* outcome (i.e., something for both sides) which, for military members, finally codified the expressed (in the Conference report) intent of Congress in 1982, that it did not want the law applied retroactively (for divorces prior to McCarty) and, for the ex-spouses, redefined "disposable pay" as prior to the deduction of federal income taxes withheld by the DFAS. While military members were generally heartened by this outcome, there were many who had been docked for as long as eight years for payments of retired pay to the ex-spouse of a long-buried divorce and many who had been driven into bankruptcy by a court order to pay immense arrearages. None of these payments, which Congress had 'intended' (in its 1982 Conference report) not be paid, was recoverable. Further, all those who had been making payments now deemed to be improper had to continue making them for two more years — until November 1992.

Visible Legislation

The 1990 Congressional hearings were triggered by four bills, three of them (H.R. 572, 2277 and 2300) introduced by Rep. Bob Dornan (R-CA) and one (H.R. 3776) by Rep. Pat Schroeder (D-CO) during the first session of the 101st Congress:

H.R. 572: Terminate the ex-spouse's interest in the military member's retired pay in the event of remarriage subsequent to a USFSPA award.

H.R. 2277: Bar state courts from ordering a military member to retire in order to commence USFSPA payments or to direct the commencement of USFSPA payments prior to retirement.

H.R. 2300: In cases where the military member is divorced while on active duty, provide for the determination of disposable pay based on the actual date of retirement, not the date first eligible to retire.

H.R. 3776: Provide a presumptive entitlement of an ex-spouse to a pro-rata share of a military member's retired pay.

1990 Hearings By the Military Personnel Subcommittee of the House Armed Services Committee

Hearings were held before the House Armed Services Subcommittee on Military Personnel and Compensation on 4 April 1990. Testimony in favor of the spouse was presented by the National Organization for Women (NOW), Ex-Partners of Servicemen (women) for Equality (EX-POSE), the American Bar Association, and the National Military Family Association. Testimony in favor of the military retiree was presented by the American Retirees Association, The American Legion, the Military Coalition (by The Retired Officers Association), and the Non-Commissioned Officers Association.

ARA produced "An Assessment of the Impact of the USFSPA," April 1990. The (then) Deputy Assistant Secretary of Defense for Military Manpower and Personnel Policy testified for the Department of Defense.

Only one provision favorable to the military member was subsequently addressed by Congress, that of prohibiting the reopening of divorce cases completed before 25 June 1981 (and which did not treat or reserve jurisdiction to treat any amount of retired pay as property of the member and spouse).

In favor of the ex-spouse, the House Armed Services Committee changed the definition of disposable retired pay to exclude taxes and other levies from the definition. In some cases, this change was a positive move for the member, as it eliminated paperwork and confusion relative to the payment of taxes between the two parties.

Retroactivity Finally Laid to Rest[1]

The FY91 Defense Authorization Act in the fall of 1990 provided some progress toward equity for the military retiree by ending the discriminatory retroactive treatment of USFSPA provisions. The amendment, passed on 5 November 1990, benefited the military member by doing away with the ability to reopen a divorce case just to decide the military retired pay issue and, thereby, causing unexpected financial disruption and loss.

Section 555 of Public Law 101-510 (National Defense Authorization Act) finally ended the discriminatory retroactive military USFSPA provisions, but not until 5 November 1992.[2]

Disposable Pay Redefined for Divorces Final on or After 3 February 1991

Public Law 101-510 embodied another amendment to the USFSPA which affected military members and their ex-spouses. For divorces that became final after 3 February 1991, the definition of disposable retired pay was significantly changed. Basically, few debts and no income taxes can now be withheld before the former spouse's share is calculated. This change did not affect retirees whose divorces were final before the effective date or for those making USFSPA payments out of pocket.[3]

Perhaps one of the key reasons for such a change has been the tax court case, *Eatinger v. Commissioner of Internal Revenue*, U.S. Tax Court Dkt. No. 16564-89 (1990). Regardless of when the divorce took place, military retirement benefits are included as gross income to the recipient spouse as well as to the military member. The retired income was characterized as deferred compensation to the military member and not a transfer of community property to the spouse. Thus, the spouse who was divorced prior to 3 February 1991, is being penalized twice for taxes.

In cases where the ex-spouse is being paid directly by a

military finance center, this change does simplify the whole issue of tax liability (and subsequent paperwork) for both parties, with neither party having to communicate with the other at tax time. Both parties now receive statements of income from the DFAS, showing what income from the military retired pay was received and the taxes that were withheld. The reporting form, called IRS Form 1099-R, replaces IRS Form W-2P.[4] While this may create the impression that income taxes are being paid on *income*, they are, in fact, being paid on *property*.

Stealth Legislation

Despite a widespread and frequently expressed reluctance by members of Congress to amend the USFSPA—or even to consider shedding some light on its reported inequities—Congress has amended the laws pertaining to military divorce 23 times since the USFSPA was enacted in 1982. Eighteen of these amendments have primarily benefited ex-spouses; one has benefited military members; and four have about equally impacted both sides. All but two of these amendments have been added as sub rosa riders to viable legislation—without public hearings or debate. A summary of this legislative history is provided in Appendix G. Some amendments deserve special mention, as mentioned below.

Ex-spouse Gets First Call on Survivor Benefit Plan

P.L. 98-94, enacted 24 September 1983, permitted military members who divorced before the USFSPA to designate a former spouse as a Survivor Benefit Plan (SBP) beneficiary if the member was a participant at the time of retirement. An open period from 24 September 1983 to 23 September 1984 was established for this purpose.

P.L. 98-525 enacted 19 October 1984 permits the enforcement of court orders in which military members agree voluntarily to provide continued SBP coverage to former spouses. In order for such a court order to be enforced, the former spouse or her/his attorney must request the election be deemed on the member's behalf within one year of the date of the court order.

P.L. 99-661, enacted 14 November 1986, permits state courts to order that the former spouse be designated as the SBP beneficiary. This treatment of the SBP is every bit as unfair as the USFSPA itself. This means that, in the case of a second marriage, the only recourse of the military member to provide life insurance coverage for his or her other second family is from a commercial source while still carrying the "baggage" of the first marriage. The dilemma here is that the costs of commercial insurance in later life are substantially higher than those early in a career, and the member's age and health could work against him or her. The only "benefit" realized by the military member is that the cost of the SBP premium reduces the amount of disposable pay. In the meantime the former spouse and her or his new marital partner enjoy the comforts of SBP coverage for life.

Protection for Abused Military Dependents and Former Spouses

P.L. 102-484, enacted 14 October 1992, provides annuities for former spouses of military members who become disqualified for retired pay due to abuse of a dependent. Known as the Abused Military Dependents Act (AMDA) of 1992, the statute requires the Military Services to pay an annuity, based on the retired pay to which the military member would otherwise have qualified, to eligible spouses and former spouses.[5] Qualified dependents are also eligible for dental and medical care, and commissary, exchange, and other military base privileges.[6]

Although the purpose of this bill is laudatory, it must be noted that it is attached as subsection (h) to 10 U.S.C. 1408, "Benefits for dependents who are victims of abuse by members losing right to retired pay." This means that within the same section of Title 10 of the U.S. Code, there are conflicting provisions for the treatment of ex-spouses of military members. USFSPA benefits for abused ex-spouses terminate upon their remarriage. This is in conflict with USFSPA awards to other ex-spouses which, once made, continue until the death, either of the ex-spouse or the retired military member. Abused ex-spouses are entitled to commissary and exchange store shopping privileges, medical and dental care, and to receive any other benefit that a spouse or former spouse of a retired member of the armed forces is entitled to receive. For all other ex-spouses the 20/20/20 rule applies.

Interestingly, the original draft of this amendment also provided that payments to an abused ex-spouse would be terminated if the spouse resumed cohabitation with his or her military mate. This was dropped during conference. Presumably, then, the retired military member who has been denied retired pay can enjoy de facto access to at least part of it by resuming cohabitation with his or her abused ex-spouse.

Prevention of Circumvention of Court Order by Waiver of (Military) Retired Pay to Enhance Civil Service Retirement Annuity

P.L. 104-201, enacted September 1996, changed the law applicable to retired military members who choose post-military career civil service employment. After 1 January 1997, any military member who waives retired pay who is subject to a court order for which there has been effective service on the Secretary concerned for purposes of 10 U.S.C. §1408, the Military Service on which the retired pay is based may be credited for service ONLY if the employee or member authorizes the Director of the Office of Personnel Management "to deduct and withhold from the annuity payable to the employee or member...an amount equal to the amount, that if the annuity payment was, instead, a payment of the employee's or member's retired pay, would have been deducted and withheld and paid to the former spouse covered by the court order under such Section 1408. The amount deducted and withheld....shall be paid to the former spouse. The period of civil service employment.... shall not be taken into consideration in determining the amount of deductions and withholding or the amount of payments to the former spouse."

Former Spouse Access to Disability Pay

P.L. 104-201, enacted September 1996 provides 'back door' access to disability pay by expanding opportunities to obtain child support and alimony payments through garnishment or similar proceedings. This statute states that the "Federal monies" subject to garnishment are retired pay and VA disability pay. Allowed is the enforcement of any unsatisfied obligation of a member up to a total of 65 percent of the member's retired pay, whether awarded under 10 U.S.C. §1408 or garnished under 42 U.S.C. §659. Any court order which provides for amounts in excess of 65 percent of retired pay available cannot be considered irregular on its face solely for that reason. Military members may be ordered to pay, out-of-pocket, amounts in excess of their retired pay.

Political Flak Vest

P.L. 105-85, enacted October 1997 provided a reasonable(?) excuse for delaying Congressional action on USFSPA reform until at least the fall of 1999. Section 643 directed the Department of Defense to conduct a review of the USFSPA and submit a report to Congress not later than 30 September 1999. This date, on its face, precludes congressional action in 1999, even if the DoD recommended it. Since 2000 is a presidential election year—and election years have always been used as excuses for tabling controversial legislation—Congress set the stage to delay any consideration of USFSPA reform until not earlier than 2001. The DoD could have broken this impasse by completing its work at an earlier date and by recommending some equity amendments. At the date of publication of this book there was no indication that either would happen. Nevertheless, several members of Congress added additional "insurance" by insisting that the military member and ex-spouse communities reach an agreement on legislation satisfactory to both. This adds to the impermeability of the "political flak vest" because the ex-spouse groups are not likely to abandon an advantageous position. Moreover, there is no counterpart (to the ARA) ex-spouse organization which can speak, single voice, for the several ex-spouse groups involved.

On 5 August 1998, hearings were held before the House Veterans Affairs Committee. The text of the hearings, which focused on family obligations of military members vis-a-vis court-ordered support, can be read on-line. For a summary, readers can access the ARA web site. It is hoped that the information presented at the hearings, which also included some other USFSPA inequities, will expedite the DoD's study.

Fairness Amendments

On 2 May 1991, Rep. Dornan introduced H.R. 2200, the "Uniformed Services Former Spouses' Protection Act Fairness Amendments of 1991. This legislation[8] resulted from the hearings held in 1990 by the House Armed Services Subcommittee on Military Personnel and Compensation. Its objectives were to:

1. Terminate payments of retired pay upon the remarriage of former military spouses;
2. Restrict awards under USFSPA to an amount or percentage of the military member's pay at the time of the divorce (not at the time of retirement);
3. Establish a two-year statute of limitations for former spouses to seek a division of retired pay from the time of divorce; and ensure that jurisdiction of a court to hear a subsequent action to divide the retired pay is established independently of the jurisdiction of the court at the time of the original divorce action;[9]
4. Reaffirm the current prohibition on division of veterans' disability pay; and,
5. Prohibit the courts from ordering any payments under USFSPA from active duty pay.

Although the support individual military members and veterans organizations gave to Rep. Dornan was commendable, this legislation lacked the co-sponsors needed for the bill to be enacted. Further, the House Armed Services Committee did not receive very much mail on the subject, thereby giving the impression that enacting this reform legislation was not a high priority.[10]

On 24 September 1997, Rep. Bob Stump (R-AZ), chairman of the House Veterans Affairs Committee, introduced H.R. 2537, the Uniformed Services Former Spouses' Equity Act of 1997.

The purpose of the bill is to restore fairness to the way military retired pay is handled during a divorce. Under the 1982 USFSPA, courts were given the authority to divide military retired pay as *property*. Today, this is standard procedure for virtually all local courts. This means that former spouses continue to receive a share of the retired pay even after one or more remarriages, regardless of the financial status of the former spouse and the military retiree. There are other inequities.

The four provisions to H.R. 2537 would:

1. Terminate payments of retired pay upon the remarriage of a former spouse.
2. Require that a former spouse's share of retired pay be based upon rank and length of service of the military member at the time of divorce, not at the time of retirement.
3. Require that former spouses seek a division of a retiree's retired pay within two years after the date of divorce. Currently, there is *no* limitation on when a former spouse may seek a share of a member's retired pay.
4. Specifically prohibit the payment to former spouses of a retiree's disability pay. Such payments are currently allowed under other statutes, despite a prohibition against them in the USFSPA.

Nothing in H.R. 2537 would preclude the award of military retired pay to a former spouse. Neither would it preclude the contemporaneous award of alimony, child support and other marital assets.

The most contentious issue is the termination of USFSPA payments upon the remarriage of the benefiting ex-spouse. The principal argument for lifetime entitlement is the claim that "spouses serve, just like their military mates." Although there is some question that a former spouse has much influence on the future career of a military member divorced while on active duty, there are ex-spouse advocates who claim that the career impetus provided by a spouse persists for years after. Objections to a statute of limitations are based on lack of widespread knowledge of the USFSPA, particularly among foreign-born spouses of military members. In this area spouses share the lot of military members who are consistently "blindsided" in divorce court because the DoD does not brief its personnel on the USFSPA.

Finally, ex-spouses resent any reduction in their share of military retired pay caused by the exemption of VA disability pay in the calculation of disposable pay. The subject of distribution of disability pay is a particularly contentious one for military members because a growing number of divorce decrees reflect clever and innovative evasions or circumvention of the protection of disability pay embodied in the USFSPA.

H.R. 2537, or something quite similar to it, will remain a principal legislative objective of the American Retirees Association until realized.

On the Legislative Horizon

On 29 April 1995, representatives of the Military Coalition and the American Retirees Association met on Capitol Hill, with representatives of five ex-spouse groups. The purpose was an attempt to reach some compromise on USFSPA reform legislation in response to a request by Chairman Dornan of the Military Personnel Subcommittee of the House National Security Committee.

The meeting met the expectations of the military veterans groups in that the ex-spouse groups were reluctant to give up any USFSPA benefits in exchange for amendments to the USFSPA which would render it fair to both divorcing partners. The veterans groups laid on the table three proposals for amendments:

1. Elimination of the "windfall benefit."
2. Establishment of a statute of limitations of two years on the time allowed to claim USFSPA benefits.
3. Termination of USFSPA payments upon the remarriage of the benefiting ex-spouse.

The ex-spouse groups countered with proposals for 17 amendments and refusal to consider any of the veterans groups' proposals. What this portends is a continuing effort to 'tighten the USFSPA noose.' The legislative history of the USFSPA to date suggests that this will be largely a 'stealth' activity, without public hearings or debate. In this environment it is clear that if military veterans relax their vigilance, the treatment they now consider to be unfair will become atrocious. There have already been some legislative forays. Some of these and others may be expected in the future.

- Presumptive entitlement to a pro-rata share of military retired pay.
- Render retroactive the redefinition of disposable pay in P.L. 101-510 as pre-tax to cover those ex-spouses divorced prior to 3 February 1991. (Rep. Schroeder introduced H.R. 2258 and H.R. 2790 in the 103rd Congress, to this effect).
- Provide shopping and other base privileges for 20/20/10's, 15's or 17's; that is, something less than 20.
- In the event of drawdowns, provide statutory entitlement of an ex-spouse to a share of the paydown

monies (i.e., VSI or SSB) as property. (Rep. Schroeder proposed this in H.R. 3574 in the 103rd Congress.[11])

• Eliminate the protection of disability pay now embodied in the USFSPA.

• Remove from the USFSPA all provisions providing the protections of jurisdiction so that an ex-spouse can sue for USFSPA payments in any state, at will.

• Eliminate the deduction of the cost of SBP premiums in calculating disposable pay.

For its part, the ARA will continue to press for the USFSPA reforms proposed in H.R. 2537 in the 105th Congress. No decision has been reached on amendments beyond that point. The most likely next objective would be an attempt to "level the playing field" in the SBP arena by modifying the law to permit SBP benefits to be divided between the first and subsequent spouses of military members.

It is worth repeating that the veterans' community can never relax its vigilance. It is essential that the ARA and its contemporaries in the national community of veterans' organizations remain abreast of what is being sought by ex-spouse groups, what is happening on Capitol Hill and the Pentagon and what can and must be done, either to quash the initiative or to reduce, and to acceptable proportions, its impact on military members. To repeat, ARA is seeking fairness in the law for both parties.

CHAPTER ENDNOTES

1. The change came in markup to the Defense Authorization Act.

2. The original entry was for the amendment to become effective

90 days after being signed into law. Unbeknown to its sponsor, Rep. Dornan, it was learned that another change had been slipped into the final version, delaying the effective date by two years.

3. On 25 May 1993, Rep. Schroeder introduced legislation (H.R. 2258) to make this provision apply retroactively to all military divorces. In other words, her bill would have allowed former spouses already awarded a portion of retired pay as part of the property settlement to go back to court to get the payments recomputed. Such payments would, however, be prospective and not retroactive. In the spring of 1993, this bill was withdrawn during subcommittee markup deliberations.

It would be totally unfair to the military member to change the wording in a decree that may have been issued years ago. People plan their lives based on the amount of income they are receiving, and such an enormous change could wreak havoc in a long-lasting domino effect: loan applications in progress, mortgage payments, child support and alimony payments to former spouses, share of college tuition expenses for children, and more. Whatever income the member might be receiving as a result of the definition for retired pay at the time of the divorce is, to be sure, taxed to the member. Where states allow spouses to reserve or apply for additional support based on changed circumstances, then such remedies are already available to the former spouse. We see here, once again, a situation where the federal government ought not to meddle in the domestic relations laws of the individual states.

4. The retiree's form 1099-R (the name of this form is Distributions from Pensions, Annuities, Retirement or Profit Sharing Plans, IRAs, Insurance Contracts, Etc.) shows taxes withheld for the amount of retired pay the retiree receives. The ex-spouse's form shows taxes withheld from any retired pay a military finance center pays to the ex-spouse as property divided under a court order. The amounts a retiree pays to a former spouse as alimony, child support, or as a voluntary allotment continue to be reported as income received by the retiree and appear on the retiree's 1099-R form.

5. This was a stand-alone bill, S. 3009, introduced by Senator Pete Domenici (R-NM).

6. Payments come out of funds in the Department of Defense Military Retirement Fund, as established by section 1461 of Title 10 U.S.C.

7. The Defense Department's family advocacy program stated there were 23,343 reports of child abuse in 1992, of which 44 percent were substantiated. There were also 23,872 cases of spouse abuse in 1992, of which 76 percent were substantiated. Additional bills targeting domestic violence in the military were introduced (summer 1993) by Rep. Jon Kyl (R-AZ), and some were included in the Defense Authorization Act for FY94.

8. This bill was revised and titled, "Divorced Military Members' Equity Amendments of 1993."

9. An example of this is: Parties assigned under orders to Alaska, consent to the jurisdiction of Alaska courts to secure a divorce decree. The court fails to divide retired pay. The service member subsequently retires and moves to Florida while the ex-spouse moves to a permanent residence in Massachusetts. Subsequent action by the ex-spouse to divided retired pay should be brought in Florida, not Alaska.

10. Many people do not think that their "one little letter" can make a difference, but it can. Constituency mail, obviously, does have an impact. A sincere, typed or handwritten letter is generally thought to be the most effective.

11. Rep. Schroeder introduced H.R. 3574 in the first session of the 103rd Congress. The bill would have amended Title 10, U.S.C., to provide improved benefits for former spouses of service members who are voluntarily or involuntarily discharged during the downsizing of the Defense Department. She proposed that the separation pay be subject to division as marital property in a divorce.

17

ABOUT THE ARA

What and Where

The American Retirees Association (ARA) was formed in 1984 to defend the rights of active duty, reserve, and retired service members in divorce. Since its inception, ARA has also been helping spouses and attorneys to understand the USFSPA as well. The ARA publishes a newsletter for members to keep them informed of pending legislation and other actions affecting the service member's retired pay relative to divorce.

ARA sends out special notices when it needs to alert the membership about an important congressional action or to write to Congress.

Chartered in California as a tax-exempt corporation #1551226, ARA has also been granted federal tax exemption status I.D. 33-0246746. Dues are tax deductible, as are any contributions to the ARA. The Washington operations office is staffed weekdays from 8:00 a.m. to 4:00

p.m., ET. Both ARA offices are staffed by volunteers. The addresses are:

Headquarters ARA
P.O. Box 2333
Redlands, CA 92373-0781
Tel: (909) 793-2424

Washington Operations ARA
2009 N. 14th St. Suite 300
Arlington, VA 22201-2514
Tel: (703) 527-3065

Web: www.American RetireesAssociation.org

If You Need Information

Inquiries relating to dues, membership, publications, etc., should be directed to the headquarters office in Redlands, CA. All other matters should be directed to the Washington operations office.

ARA maintains a website, address (see above). This is a comprehensive on-line source of information on the USFSPA and other aspects of military divorce addressed in this book. There are many people working on the Internet, several of whom are long on opinion and short on fact. If you are not satisfied with what is available on the ARA website, or you need to confirm information obtained elsewhere, please call ARA's Washington office.

The ARA's Platform

The ARA's pursuit of USFSPA reform is based on a platform of fairness and equity for *both* members of a military marriage that ends in divorce. The ARA believes that divorce settlements should be based on merit, need, and ability to pay—not blind adherence to an unfair, discriminatory law which implies that the military spouse is invariably blameless while the military member always "wears the black hat" in a divorce proceeding. This may change when affected (and possibly traumatized) female military members appear in divorce court to defend against making USFSPA payments to their civilian, male ex-spouses, but it has not happened yet.

ARA's Proposals for Reform of the USFSPA

The following proposals for reform are based on input from the military and civilian community.

1. Terminate USFSPA payments upon the remarriage of the benefiting ex-spouse. Terminate current payments to remarried former spouses not more than 180 days from the date of enactment of the amendment.
2. Restrict awards under the USFSPA to correspond to the military member's length of service and pay grade at the time of divorce, not at the time of retirement. USFSPA payments would, however, be adjusted to existing pay scales at the time of retirement.
3. Establish a statute of limitations giving former spouses two years from the date of a final divorce to seek a division of military retired pay under the USFSPA.
4. Reinforce that provision of the USFSPA which precludes the inclusion of disability pay in the calculation of disposable pay. Consider, however, the inclusion of disability pay where military retired pay is the *only* asset of the marriage.
5. Provide specific wording to protect active duty military personnel by precluding:

   - Involuntary court-ordered retirements in order to commence USFSPA payments.
   - Distribution of active duty pay pursuant to court

orders under the USFSPA.
- USFSPA payments after recall of retired military members to active duty.

6. Preclude retroactive application of the USFSPA for any divorce finalized prior to 1 February 1983, the effective date of the USFSPA. Public Law 101-510 (5 November 1990) prohibits retroactive opening of divorces final on and before 25 June 1981, one day before the U.S. Supreme Court *McCarty* decision. This denies relief for those divorced during the "gap" period between *McCarty* and the effective date of the USFSPA. The failure to grandfather the USFSPA was a manifest injustice to military people who had served honorably prior to 1 February 1983, and who were preemptively deprived of their matured right to *full* retired pay.

7. Require the leadership of the uniformed services to brief their personnel on the existence and significance of the USFSPA.

Afterthought

It is very important to constantly revisit the USFSPA and to reexamine the premises underlying its enactment. This should occur in the light of evolving social, economic, and cultural changes which have substantially altered the status of the military spouse of the early 1980s.

The history of the USFSPA provides irrefutable evidence that it unfairly discriminates against divorcing military marital partners who, manifestly, do *not* enjoy protection under the law equal to that provided their civilian counterparts. An interesting aspect of the USFSPA's treatment of military women is that virtually all the resistance to its reform emanates from the feminist sector.

An overwhelming majority of the national community of veterans' organizations, with an aggregate membership over 10,000,000, supports reform of the USFSPA to resolve its inequities. Some even advocate its repeal.

Somehow, members of the Uniformed Services of both sexes must convince their contemporaries that they are not looking for a *win* in a divorce court, just a *tie*.

18

RESTORING FAIRNESS AND EQUALITY TO THE MILITARY DIVORCE PROCESS

Why No Further Equity Changes to the USFSPA?

Perhaps you may be wondering why further equity changes have not been made to this law.

Congress does not operate in a vacuum. We find some lessons learned in the legislative process here. First, laws are not made without going through a very structured process. When the law is one that affects a lot of people, such as the COLA for military retirees, you can be sure that various military and veterans' organizations will not only be tracking such legislation, but will also be publicizing it to their membership. Indeed, rules and procedures[1] that further clarify whatever legislation is passed are first published (as well as proposed changes) in the *Federal Register*, during which time the general public has the opportunity to comment.

Thus, with regard to USFSPA, there was congressional testimony published[2] that anyone could have read, but evidently few did—or, if they did, decided the law was too unreasonable to have much chance of enactment.

Second, our elected officials need to hear from their constituents. The question you should be asking yourself then (be it the issue of divorce law or environmental problems) is: When was the last time you let your representative know how you stood on a particular issue? Further, do you know how that person feels about a particular issue or law? Is that individual even remotely aware a problem exists?

On 10 March 1993, the House Budget Committee first passed legislation calling for COLA caps for military retirees. Until 1 April 1993, when debates in Congress ended, your Pentagon leadership remained silent. Why? Lobbyists for organizations representing the service members and retirees said the reason was "the lack of support from uniformed and civilian Pentagon leaders."[3]

Civics 101—Congress Does Not Have to Be Consistently Fair

In the same media reports article on COLA caps, one can find another similarity to USFSPA. Some groups have been spared from COLA limits, just as some federal retirees (notably some employees of the Foreign Service and the Central Intelligence Agency) were exempt from having the payments to the former spouse deducted from their retired pay. This was another case of a similar program (i.e., Federal retirement) that was not extended to military retirees. Quoting retired Air Force Colonel Paul W. Arcari, director of legislative affairs for The Retired Officers Association, "The fact that federal police and air traffic controllers were protected but military members were not [the former were spared the COLA caps] is a sign that we did not get our message across."[4]

Read It in Your Military Newspaper First!

In some respects, then, the same thing (call it apathy in some cases) could be said regarding USFSPA recognition, although with some differences. First of all, while the coverage has been limited, the various service *Times* (Air Force, Army, Navy) have had a number of articles on USFSPA issues. Thus, there is little excuse for being "totally in the dark" on this subject. If you are like many of your military counterparts, you read the *Times*, or some other contemporary publication to learn what is really happening in the military.

"NIMBY" Syndrome

Despite whatever publicity proposed legislation gets, whether it affects the nation as a whole or just your local community, the general tendency is for people to "tune out" or turn their efforts elsewhere once the issue is resolved to their satisfaction. You might call this the NIMBY syndrome—not in my backyard. An example of this was the one major piece of legislation that has been passed since 1982 which addressed the problem of retroactivity of the USFSPA.[5]

Immediately following the enactment of the 1990 legislation, the ARA experienced a significant loss of members—presumably those who benefited from the passage of this amendment. Unfortunately, the subject of retroactivity is just one of several equity issues that need to be looked at in terms of reforming the USFSPA. Retirees should consider that without strength in numbers and continued efforts to work for reform for the benefit of all, not just a few, that any new legislation is doomed. This goes for any association you may belong to. Members who cease belonging should remember that others helped to get the retroactivity issue resolved for them; now they would like your support for further changes.

If the military member believes he or she is now "safe"—that is, has ceased making payments in accordance with what members and their attorneys believe is the correct interpretation of the 1990 amendment to the USFSPA, you both may want to reconsider joining the ARA after reading the following:

> *In a New Mexico case, a master sergeant and his wife were divorced in 1973, with the divorce decree making no reference to the retired pay. The ex-spouse filed a petition 16 years after the divorce, seeking a partition of the retired pay, and was subsequently awarded 42 percent of it. The sergeant continued making payments for two more years (until November 1992), and filed a petition with the NM courts seeking termination of the USFSPA payments on the basis of the 1990 congressional amendment. In June 1993, New Mexico's Second Judicial District Court, Bernalillo County, ruled against the retired sergeant, reasoning that under New Mexico law, there is a "limited reservation of jurisdiction" that is incorporated into every divorce decree issued in New Mexico. As such, New Mexico has ruled that the conditions of the congressional amendment do not apply and can never apply in New Mexico. The retiree's redress was in a federal court, which would have cost thousands of dollars.[6]*

The decision flies in the face of the intent of Congress and is in direct violation of federal law. Unfortunately, there have been similar decisions in California. The *only* way to stop the state courts from ignoring the federal law is for the federal courts to uphold the supremacy clause of the U.S. Constitution in this context.

Ignorance or Apathy?

The leadership at ARA notes that publicity surrounding the USFSPA, the military retiree, and former spouses, has been out there frequently, albeit not always making headline news. Retiree newsletters published by each of the services have addressed the issue; former spouses' groups have had their stories published in military and local newspapers; various publications[7] cover the subject, including SBP; and the veterans' organizations have devoted some attention to it as well. ARA's membership is less than three-tenths of one percent of the nation's USFSPA victims. Yet, single votes have turned the tide in many a law.

Ignorance and apathy do not apply only to the members or nonmembers of associations. Indeed, at the April 1990 hearings for reform of the USFSPA, the senior military leader (a flag officer) who testified was unaware that many reservists are not in paid billets and, therefore, do not receive money in return for their military duty (e.g., on the weekend). When questioned as to whether he had any reservists on his staff or whether any reservists had any substantive input to the law, relative to its inequity with regard to reservists, he said no. Why didn't he know that some reservists are not paid—he was on active duty at the time? Here was a law that significantly affected reservists, in some ways quite differently from the active duty personnel who retire in their late thirties, forties, or early fifties.

The Military Member Is Not the Lone Ranger . . .

The ARA is engaged in continuous dialogue on Capitol Hill and in the Pentagon. In efforts to come to a friendly meeting ground, ARA has also had discussions with EX-POSE.[8]

The ARA is a member of the National Military/Veterans Alliance (NMVA). The Military Coalition[9] has established a subcommittee for USFSPA reform. ARA is coordinating its efforts with the Coalition's. A key factor in the passage of any legislation is, first, DoD approval of the proposed law, and then White House approval of that.

With each election, new faces appear in the House,[10] where proposed legislation is first introduced in subcommittee. Through your membership in an organization like ARA, you can be kept informed. Use that information in contacting *your* representatives and senators in Congress and telling them what you want done about the situation. Ask them what their position is on it, and what they plan to do about it.

What You Can Do[11]

1. Keep yourself informed on USFSPA issues by becoming a member of at least one veterans' organization that is keeping up in this area.[12] By doing so you will be alerted when you need to shake up Congress with a letter.

2. Find out the position your elected representatives in Congress are taking on this or any other issue important to you. Be sure to let them know you will be keeping track of their interest and voting record (whether it is regarding the military retiree or the spouse). Keep in mind that the military member's objective—sustaining at least equal benefits for the

military retiree—is not the same as that of your elected officials—which is getting reelected.

3. Keep the heat on all the veterans' organizations of which you are a member. Find out where they stand on the USFSPA reform and what they are doing about it. Pressure them to press forward with some USFSPA initiatives of their own on Capitol Hill and cooperate with, and assist, the ARA with its legislative program.

4. By all means, become a member of ARA, actively participate in its activities, and financially support its operations.

5. NEVER GIVE UP!

CHAPTER ENDNOTES

1. An example of the rules and procedures would be the specific service rules that are cited in the *Code of Federal Regulations (C.F.R.)*. The particular process that the services follow with regard to processing USFSPA direct payments may be found in 32 C.F.R. §63. If you are interested in reading the original notice that was published in the *Federal Register*, look up 50 Fed.Reg. 2665 (1985). The procedures for processing child support and alimony are found in 5 C.F.R. §581.

2. It is not the authors' intent to turn this book into a legislative history of the USFSPA. However, for those who would like to read some of the testimony that was presented by the House of Representatives, including that by Rep. Schroeder (D-CO), you should consult the following in the *Congressional Record*: H.R. 6030—the debate on USFSPA—as found in 128 Cong.Rec. H4717 (daily ed. 28 July 1982) (reprinted in 1982 U.S. CODE CONG. & ADMIN. NEWS, 1596).

3. See: Rick Maze, "Military leaders mum during debate on COLA CAP," *Air Force Times* (19 April 1993): 16. This article details why there has been silence among the military leadership

regarding the COLA issue.

4. Ibid.

5. Former spouses are now prevented from having a divorce that was finalized before 26 June 1981 reopened to adjudicate the issue of military retired pay, thereby causing retirees to have to pay back retired pay as well as prospective payments. For example, a military member who had been divorced for 15 years, remarried, and retired, could (and did in many cases) find himself facing a judgment for back retired pay plus half of all prospective retired pay. Some in this situation were forced into bankruptcy because the state courts applied this law retroactively.

6. See Chapter 4, Endnote #2.

7. An example of such a publication is the *Retired Military Almanac*, published annually by the Uniformed Services Almanac, Inc., P.O. Box 4144, Falls Church, Virginia 22044. Telephone: (703) 532-1631. See Appendix P for other publications.

8. EX-POSE, the acronym for Ex-Partners of Servicemen (women) for Equality, is an organization primarily of women who are divorced from military members.

9. See Appendix K for a listing of military and veterans organizations.

10. See Appendix L on how to write your elected representatives effectively.

11. These steps apply equally to the service member and spouse.

12. Membership in most organizations is open to non-military people. Spouses are encouraged to join as well.

19

BITS AND PIECES

There are numerous other topics of which our readers should be aware that do not neatly fall into any particular subject area. You may never need this information, but information is power, and the basic premise in our first book, as well as this second book, is to provide information that your personnel, family support, and JAG offices may not furnish.

When the Service Member Might Lose Retired Pay

How many retirees have ever truly read, from start to finish, the fine print in their retired papers? Probably not many. If you were to do so, however, you might find that the member is under more restrictions than he or she ever imagined. If convicted by a court martial, you could be stripped of your pay and allowances, jailed, dismissed from the service, and ineligible to draw retired pay. If convicted by a court martial while on active duty (e.g., on charges of adultery, conduct unbecoming, dereliction of duty), prosecutors could ask that you be dismissed from the service and stripped of all pay, including retired pay. If you are already retired, you could be returned to active duty to stand trial for any charges, and a court could impose a sentence whereby you forfeit a portion of your retired benefits for a certain period. And, if the plaintiff feels that the court-martial was not enough, then that person could also sue in Federal Court. The point here is that it could happen and the retired pay would be in jeopardy. (Like many other things in the military, double standards exist vis-a-vis members of Congress, feminists, and others. If they commit a felony, they frequently can continue to receive their retired pay.)

Keeping Your Military Status Current

To receive benefits of any kind from the military, you must keep your status current. This begins with valid military and family-member I.D. cards and registration in the Defense Enrollment Eligibility Reporting System (DEERS) database. Please note: Renewing your I.D. card DOES NOT automatically update you in the DEERS database. You should verify that you are current in DEERS by calling their office: 800-334-4162 (California only), 800-527-5602 (Alaska and Hawaii only), 800-538-9552 (all other states).

Disbursement of Retired Pay

Military retirees and annuitants receive a form 1099-R every tax year, as do former spouses who receive a portion of a retired member's pay due to a court-ordered division of community property. This form is mailed to the home address on file with DFAS at the end of January for the previous tax year, another reason to make sure your address is current with everyone who has a need to know! If you are a former spouse who receives your portion of the service member's retired pay directly from the service member, the member can provide you with a substitute 1099-R. You will not receive any form from DFAS because of that pay arrangement. (ARA recommends that all retirees who are paying out of pocket a portion of their retired pay to a former spouse have an allotment go directly from DFAS to the former spouse.)

Pension Funds to Which You May Be Entitled

If you have been a trailing spouse to the service member, you have probably worked at a number of jobs and may be entitled to pension monies. The Pension Benefit Guaranty Corporation unveiled in 1996 a search database as a nationwide hunt for thousands of workers who have not received pension money due them. You can go online with the Pension Search Directory at (http://search.pbgc.gov or www.dol.gov). If you find your name in the list for companies whose pension plans have folded, E-mail the PBGC or write its Pension Search Program at 1200 K St NW, Washington DC 20005-4026. You can search by your name or company, whether you have reached retirement age or have relocated or switched employers several times.

Soldiers' and Sailors' Civil Relief Act

The Soldiers' and Sailors' Civil Relief Act of 1940 (SSCRA) was passed by Congress to provide protection for individuals entering or called to active duty in the military. It is intended to postpone or suspend certain civil obligations to allow service members to devote their attention to duty. It applies to active duty as well as reservists and members of the National Guard while on active duty.

It is important to note, however, that for provisions of the SSCRA to be of benefit to the service member, that member's ability to either defend or pursue an action must be materially affected by their military service. An example of this would be when the member is assigned overseas, and returning to the U.S. would be geographically prejudicial because of the service member's location. Further protection is extended to military members who are facing a default judgment for failure to respond to a lawsuit or to appear at trial. In such cases, the plaintiff must provide the court an affidavit stating the defendant is not in military service.

Courts can delay proceedings when the obligations of the military member prevent the member from asserting or protecting a legal right. This delay can last for the period of military service plus three months, unless the court finds that the member's ability to defend or pursue action is not materially affected by military service.

Further relief is available, and the service member and anyone filing a lawsuit (including a divorce action) against a service member should contact the local JAG office or seek competent legal counsel. In ARA's experience, the majority of service members cannot prove that they are materially affected as a result of their military service when a divorce action is filed against them; however, overseas duty could allow the service member to obtain a stay of proceedings temporarily.

Don't Stir the Pot

Most attorneys will immediately advise their clients to avoid any relationship (however innocent) with a member of the opposite sex while the divorce is pending. Unless you have a written agreement with your spouse that you can each see others, this is good advice you should not argue against. However (there is that ubiquitous however), ARA feels it is obligated to let you know that the timeworn cause of action, "alienation of affections," is alive and well, at least in North Carolina.

On 5 August 1997, a North Carolina verdict was handed down that awarded $1 million to a woman who sued another woman for luring her husband away. The husband and the other woman had an affair that culminated in his seeking a divorce and marrying the other woman. (If you are interested in this case, the plaintiff was Dorothy Hutelmyer, formerly the wife of James Hutelmyer; and the defendant, Margie Cox.) Two thirds of states bar the alienation defense.

One Final Thought or Two

We would like to leave you with some last thoughts. While you may think that you won't get through your divorce—you will, and we hope that this book will help you do so. And we want you to know that things could always be worse, and suggest that you not follow the example of Stanley and Dorothy Diller.

When the California couple split up in May 1984, after nearly 29 years of marriage, their net worth was between $10 and $15 million (not anyone we know!). But they were probably, we are happy to say, able to finance not only their attorneys' new homes, but the kids AND the grandkids' college educations (at no less than Harvard and Yale, plus graduate school), and yearly vacations to Europe for life! How did they do it? Stan and Dorothy ran up more than $3 million in legal fees fighting over everything from a missing silver tea set to their extensive real estate holdings.

Seven years after their divorce began, the couple finally did come to agreement on one thing—their lawyers charged too much. So, back to court they went, but not just any old court in California, but to the U.S. Supreme Court (nothing was too good for this couple). (No information on how things turned out, however.)

One thing that all of the many attorneys involved agreed was that this was one case in which the couple just should not have handled their affairs the way they did—"The couple wanted to fight like tigers," said one of the attorneys, "and they had the money to do it." Even the judge warned the couple they were running up huge legal bills (several days in court just to adjudicate the silver tea set alone!).

Both parties were described by the trial judge with words such as "avaricious, covetous, stubborn" (Stanley) and "frightened, bitter woman" (Dorothy), and that both their "venality and the unrelenting bitter belligerency" made the case "difficult, oppressive and frustrating for [everyone]." One trial, out of the 110 separate court hearings—even lasted 49 days! This was a divorce lawyer's dream.

So, let this be a lesson to you. If you do not know what you are doing and you let your emotions or lack of knowledge get the better of you, then you, too, could end up with a "divorce from hell." The courts are really the wrong place for revenge. And, as the old saying goes, "If you seek revenge, first dig two graves."

On that note, ARA has some advice on how to remain sane through the whole process. First, keep in mind that there is no clear-cut winner or loser. Only the attorneys come out ahead.

Second, don't fall for the mistaken belief that you have rights and they are written in concrete. If you have read any military newspaper or article in the last ten years, you know that what Congress gives to the Military Services, Congress can take away (or pretend it never existed).

Third, take a realistic look at what you have to divide. Do not let the courts and lawyers eat up what assets you have to divide. If your legal fees are approaching the value of the property you have to divide; if you are spending more time in court or on the phone with your attorney than you are at work; if the documentation you have amassed exceeds the shelf space in your den—then you are in deep do-do, and it is time to reevaluate what your objective was as you began this process. And, your strategy just might have to be that of the person who discovers he is riding a dead horse—sometimes the best thing to do is just dismount.

Finally, you need to take control of your case if you are ever going to control its costs—both financially and emotionally. Sometimes you may have to perform a cost-benefit analysis on the situation confronting you. Are the results worth the cost? More often than not, most of the decisions you and your spouse will make, with or without the attorneys, will require good old common sense. And, more often than not, you are better off going for being "happy" than being "right."

As the judge in an English case decided over 200 years ago, said: "Courts of Justice do not pretend to furnish cures for all the miseries of human life...and, as the happiness of the world depends upon its virtue, there may be much unhappiness in it which human laws cannot undertake."

There will always be a certain number of miseries in life. But it is up to each of us to recognize when laws, lawyers, the judges, and even ourselves, will only serve to make them more miserable. Don't forget the old canard: "As a *last* resort, use common sense—but only after having exhausted every other alternative."

APPENDIX A

THE UNIFORMED SERVICES FORMER SPOUSES' PROTECTION ACT

PUBLIC LAW 97-252
Title 10 U.S.C.

1408. Payment of retired or retainer pay in compliance with court orders

(a)   Definitions. - In this section:

(1) The term "Court" means-

(A)   any court of competent jurisdiction of any State, the District of Columbia, the Commonwealth of Puerto Rico, Guam, American Samoa, the Virgin Islands, the Northern Mariana Islands, and the Trust Territory of the Pacific Islands;

(B)   any court of the United States (as defined in section 451 of title 28) having competent jurisdiction;

(C)   any court of competent jurisdiction of a foreign country with which The United States has an agreement requiring the United States to honor any court order of such country; and

(D) any administrative or judicial tribunal of a State competent to enter orders for support or maintenance (including a State agency administering a program under a State plan approved under part D of Title IV of the Social Security Act), and, for purposes of this subparagraph, the term "State" includes the District of Columbia, the Commonwealth of Puerto Rico, the Virgin Islands, Guam, and American Samoa.

(2) The term "court order" means a final decree of divorce, dissolution, annulment, or legal separation issued by a court, or a court ordered, ratified, or approved property settlement incident to such a

decree (including a final decree modifying the terms of a previously issued decree of divorce, dissolution, annulment, or legal separation, or a court ordered, ratified, or approved property settlement incident to such previously issued decree), or a support order, as defined in section 453(p) of the Social Security Act (42 U.S.C. 653(p), which-

(A) is issued in accordance with the laws of the jurisdiction of that court;

(B) provides for-

(i) payment of child support (as defined in section 459(i)(2) of the Social Security Act (42 U.S.C. 659(i)(2)));

(ii) payment of alimony (as defined in section 459(i)(2) of the Social Security Act (42 U.S.C. 659(i)(2))); or

(iii) division of property (including a division of community property); and

(C) in the case of a division of property, specifically provides for the payment of an amount, expressed in dollars or as a percentage of disposable retired pay, from the disposable retired pay of a member to the spouse or former spouse of that member.

(3) The term "final decree" means a decree from which no appeal may be taken or from which no appeal has been taken within the time allowed for taking such appeals under the laws applicable to such appeals, or a decree from which timely appeal has been taken and such appeal has been finally decided under the laws applicable to such appeals.

(4) The term "disposable retired pay" means the total monthly retired pay to which a member is entitled less amounts which-

(A) are owed by that member to the United States for previous overpayments of retired pay and for recoupments required by law resulting from entitlement to retired pay;

(B) are deducted from the retired pay of such member as a result of forfeitures of retired pay ordered by a court-marital or as a result of a waiver of retired pay required by law in order to receive compensation under title 5 or title 38;

(C) in the case of a member entitled to retired pay under chapter 61 of this title, are equal to the amount of retired pay of the member under that chapter computed using the percentage of the member's disability on the date when the member was retired (or the date on which the member's name was placed on the temporary disability retired list); or

(D) are deducted because of an election under chapter 73 of this title to provide an annuity to a spouse or former spouse to whom payment of a portion of such member's retired pay is being made pursuant to a court order under this section.

[(E), (F) Redesignated (C), (D)]

(5) The term "member" includes a former member entitled to retired pay under section 12731 of this title.

(6) The term "spouse or former spouse" means the husband or wife, or former husband or wife, respectively, of a member who, on or before the date of a court order, was married to that member.

(7) The term "retired pay" includes retainer pay.

(b) Effective service of process--for the purposes of this section--

(1) service of a court order is effective if-

(A) an appropriate agent of the Secretary concerned designated for receipt of service of court orders under regulations prescribed pursuant to subsection (i) or, if no agent has been so designated, the Secretary concerned, is personally served or is served by facsimile or electronic transmission or by mail;

(B) the court order is regular on its face;

(C) the court order or other documents served with the court order identify the member concerned and include, if possible, the social security number of such member; and

(D) the court order or other documents served with the court order certify that the rights of the member under the Soldiers' and Sailors' Civil Relief Act of 1940 (50 U.S.C. App. 501 et seq.) were observed; and

(2) a court order is regular on its face if the order-

(A) is issued by a court of competent jurisdiction;

(B) is legal in form; and

(C) includes nothing on its face that provides reasonable notice that it is issued without authority of law.

(c) Authority for court to treat retired pay as property of the member and spouse--

(1) Subject to the limitations of this section, a court may treat disposable retired pay payable to a member for pay periods beginning after June 25, 1981, either as property solely of the member or as property of the member and his spouse in accordance with the law of the jurisdiction of such court. A court may not treat retired pay as property in any proceeding to divide or partition any amount of retired pay of a member as the property of the member and the member's spouse or former spouse if a final decree of divorce, dissolution, annulment, or legal separation (including a court ordered, ratified, or approved property settlement incident to such decree) affecting the member and the member's spouse or former spouse (A) was issued before June 25, 1981, and (B) did not treat (or reserve jurisdiction to treat) any amount of retired pay of the member as property of the member and the member's spouse or former spouse.

(2) Notwithstanding any other provision of law, this section does not create any right, title, or interest which can be sold, assigned, transferred, or otherwise disposed of (including by inheritance) by a spouse or former spouse. Payments by the Secretary concerned under subsection (d) to a spouse or former spouse with respect to a division of retired pay as the property of a member and the member's spouse under this subsection may not be treated as amounts received as retired pay for service in the uniformed services.

(3) This section does not authorize any court to order a member to apply for retirement or retire at a particular time in order to effectuate any payment under this section.

(4) A court may not treat the disposable retired pay of a member in the manner described in paragraph (1) unless the court has jurisdiction over the member by reason of (A) his residence, other than because of military assignment, in the territorial jurisdiction of the court, (B) his domicile in the territorial jurisdiction of the court, or (C) his consent to the jurisdiction of the court.

(d) Payment by the Secretary concerned to (or for benefit of)

spouse or former spouse--

(1) After effective service on the Secretary concerned of a court order providing for the payment of child support or alimony or, with respect to a division of property, specifically providing for the payment of an amount of the disposable retired pay from a member to the spouse or a former spouse of the member, the Secretary shall make payments (subject to the limitations of this section) from the disposable retired pay of the member to the spouse or former spouse (or for the benefit of such spouse or former spouse to a State disbursement unit established pursuant to section 454B of the Social Security Act or other public payee designated by a State, in accordance with part D of title IV of the Social Security Act, as directed by court order, or as otherwise directed in accordance with such part D) in an amount sufficient to satisfy the amount of child support and alimony set forth in the court order and, with respect to a division of property, in the amount of disposable retired pay specifically provided for in the court order. In the case of a spouse or former spouse who, pursuant to section 408(a)(3) of the Social Security Act (42 U.S.C. 608(a)(4)), assigns to a State the rights of the spouse or former spouse to receive support, the Secretary concerned may make the child support payments referred to in the preceding sentence to that State in amounts consistent with that assignment of rights. In the case of a member entitled to receive retired pay on the date of the effective service of the court order, such payments shall begin not later than 90 days after the date of effective service. In the case of a member not entitled to receive retired pay on the date of the effective service of the court order, such payments shall begin not later than 90 days after the date on which the member first becomes entitled to receive retired pay.

(2) If the spouse or former spouse to whom payments are to be made under this section was not married to the member for a period of 10 years or more during which the member performed at least 10 years of service creditable in determining the member's eligibility for retired pay, payments may not be made under this section to the extent that they include an amount resulting from the treatment by the court under subsection (c) of disposable retired pay of the member as property of the member or property of the member and his spouse.

(3) Payments under this section shall not be made more frequently than once each month, and the Secretary concerned shall not be required to vary normal pay and disbursement cycles for retired pay in order to comply with a court order.

(4) Payments from the disposable retired pay of a member pursuant to this section shall terminate in accordance with the terms of the

applicable court order, but not later than the date of the death of the member or the date of the death of the spouse or former spouse to whom payments are being made, whichever occurs first.

(5) If a court order described in paragraph (1) provides for a division of property (including a division of community property) in addition to an amount of child support or alimony or the payment of an amount of disposable retired pay as the result of the court's treatment of such pay under subsection (c) as property of the member and his spouse, the Secretary concerned shall pay (subject to the limitations of this section) from the disposable retired pay of the member to the spouse or former spouse of the member, any part of the amount payable to the spouse or former spouse under the division of property upon effective service of a final court order of garnishment of such amount from such retired pay.

(6) In the case of a court order for which effective service is made on the Secretary concerned on or after the date of the enactment of this paragraph and which provides for payments from the disposable retired pay of a member to satisfy the amount of child support set forth in the order, the authority provided in paragraph (1) to make payments from the disposable retired pay of a member to satisfy the amount of child support set forth in a court order shall apply to payment of any amount of child support arrearages set forth in that order as well as to amounts of child support that currently become due.

(7) (A) The Secretary concerned may not accept service of a court order that is an out-of-State modification, or comply with the provisions of such a court order, unless the court issuing that order has jurisdiction in the manner specified in subsection (c)(4) over both the member and the spouse or former spouse involved.

(B) A court order shall be considered to be an out-of-State modification for purposes of this paragraph if the order—

(i) modifies a previous court order under this section upon which payments under this subsection are based; and

(ii) is issued by a court of a State other than the State of the court that issued the previous court order.

(e) Limitations.—

(1) The total amount of the disposable retired pay of a member payable under all court orders pursuant to subsection (c) may not exceed 50 percent of such disposable retired pay.

(2) In the event of effective service of more than one court order which provide for payment to a spouse and one or more former spouses or to more than one former spouse, the disposable retired pay of the member shall be used to satisfy (subject to the limitations of paragraph (1)) such court orders on a first-come, first-served basis. Such court orders shall be satisfied (subject to the limitations of paragraph (1)) out of that amount of disposable retired pay which remains after the satisfaction of all court orders which have been previously served.

(3)(A) In the event of effective service of conflicting court orders under this section which assert to direct that different amounts be paid during a month to the same spouse or former spouse of the same member, the Secretary concerned shall—

(i) pay to that spouse from the member's disposable retired pay the least amount directed to be paid during that month by any such conflicting court order, but not more than the amount of disposable retired, pay which remains available for payment of such court orders based on when such court orders were effectively served and the limitations of paragraph (1) and subparagraph (B) of paragraph (4);

(ii) retain an amount of disposable retired pay that is equal to the lesser of—

(I) the difference between the largest amount required by any conflicting court order to be paid to the spouse or former spouse and the amount payable to the spouse or former spouse under clause (i); and

(II) the amount of disposable retired pay which remains available for payment of any conflicting court order based on when such court order was effectively served and the limitations of paragraph (1) and subparagraph (B) of paragraph (4); and

(iii) pay to that member the amount which is equal to the amount of that member's disposable retired pay (less any amount paid during such month pursuant to legal process served under section 459 of the Social Security Act (42 U.S.C. 659) and any amount paid during such month pursuant to court orders effectively served under this section, other than such conflicting court orders) minus—

(I) the amount of disposable retired pay paid under

clause (i); and

(II) the amount of disposable retired pay retained under clause (ii).

(B) The Secretary concerned shall hold the amount retained under clause (ii) of subparagraph (a) until such time as that Secretary is provided with a court order which has been certified by the member and the spouse or former spouse to be valid and applicable to the retained amount. Upon being provided with such an order, the Secretary shall pay the retained amount in accordance with the order.

(4)(A) In the event of effective service of a court order under this section and the service of legal process pursuant to section 459 of the Social Security Act (42 U.S.C. 659), both of which provide for payments during a month from the same member, satisfaction of such court orders and legal process from the retired pay of the member shall be on a first-come, first-serve basis. Such court orders and legal process shall be satisfied out of moneys which are subject to such orders and legal process and which remain available in accordance with the limitations of paragraph (1) and subparagraph (B) of this paragraph during such month after the satisfaction of all court orders or legal process which have been previously served.

(B) Notwithstanding any other provision of law, the total amount of the disposable retired pay of a member payable by the Secretary concerned under all court orders pursuant to this section and all legal processes pursuant to section 459 of the Social Security Act (42 U.S.C. 659) with respect to a member may not exceed 65 percent of the amount of the retired pay payable to such member that is considered under section 462 of the Social Security Act (42 U.S.C. 662) to be remuneration for employment that is payable by the United States.

(5) A court order which itself or because of previously served court orders provides for the payment of an amount which exceeds the amount of disposable retired pay available for payment because of the limit set forth in paragraph (1), or which, because of previously served court orders or legal process previously served under section 459 of the Social Security Act (42 U.S.C. 659), provides for payment of an amount that exceeds the maximum amount permitted under paragraph (1) or subparagraph (B) of paragraph (4), shall not be considered to be irregular on its face solely for that reason. However, such order shall be considered to be fully satisfied for purposes of this section by the payment to the spouse or former spouse of the maximum amount of disposable retired pay permitted under paragraph (1) and subparagraph (B) of paragraph (4).

(6) Nothing in this section shall be construed to relieve a member of liability for the payment of alimony, child support, or other payments required by a court order on the grounds that payments made out of disposable retired pay under this section have been made in the maximum amount permitted under paragraph (1) or subparagraph (B) of paragraph (4). Any such unsatisfied obligation of a member may be enforced by any means available under law other than the means provided under this section in any case in which the maximum amount permitted under paragraph (1) has been paid and under section 459 of the Social Security Act (42 U.S.C. 659) in any case in which the maximum amount permitted under subparagraph (B) of paragraph (4) has been paid.

(f) Immunity of officers and employees of United States.—

(1) The United States and any officer or employee of the United States shall not be liable with respect to any payment made from retired pay to any member, spouse, or former spouse pursuant to a court order that is regular on its face if such payment is made in accordance with this section and the regulations prescribed pursuant to subsection (i).

(2) An officer or employee of the United States who, under regulations prescribed pursuant to subsection (i), has the duty to respond to interrogatories shall not be subject under any law to any disciplinary action or civil or criminal liability or penalty for, or because of, any disclosure of information made by him in carrying out any of his duties which directly or indirectly pertain to answering such interrogatories.

(g) Notice to member of service of court order on Secretary concerned.—A person receiving effective service of a court order under this section shall, as soon as possible, but not later than 30 days after the date on which effective service is made, send a written notice of such court order (together with a copy of such order) to the member affected by the court order at his last known address.

(h) Benefits for dependents who are victims of abuse by members losing right to retired pay.—

(1) If, in the case of a member or former member of the armed forces referred to in paragraph (2)(A), a court order provides (in the manner applicable to a division of property) for the payment of an amount from the disposable retired pay of that member or former member (as certified under paragraph (4)) to an eligible spouse or former spouse of that member or former member, the Secretary concerned, begin-

ning upon effective service of such court order, shall pay that amount in accordance with this subsection to such spouse or former spouse.

(2) A spouse or former spouse of a member or former member of the armed forces is eligible to receive payment under this subsection if—

(A) the member or former member, while a member of the armed forces and after becoming eligible to be retired from the armed forces on the basis of years of service, has eligibility to receive retired pay terminated as a result of misconduct while a member involving abuse of a spouse or dependent child (as defined in regulations prescribed by the Secretary of Defense or, for the Coast Guard when it is not operating as a service in the Navy, by the Secretary of Transportation); and

(B) the spouse or former spouse—

(i) was the victim of the abuse and was married to the member or former member at the time of that abuse; or

(ii) is a natural or adopted parent of a dependent child of the member or former member who was the victim of the abuse.

(3) The amount certified by the Secretary concerned under paragraph (4) with respect to a member or former member of the armed forces referred to in paragraph (2)(A) shall be deemed to be the disposable retired pay of that member or former member for the purposes of this subsection.

(4) Upon the request of a court or an eligible spouse or former spouse of a member or former member of the armed forces referred to in paragraph (2)(A) in connection with a civil action for the issuance of a court order in the case of that member or former member, the Secretary concerned shall determine and certify the amount of the monthly retired pay that the member or former member would have been entitled to receive as of the date of the certification—

(A) if the member or former member's eligibility for retired pay had not been terminated as described in paragraph (2)(A); and

(B) if, in the case of a member or former member not in receipt of retired pay immediately before that termination of eligibility for retired pay, the member or former member had retired on the effective date of that termination of eligibility.

(5) A court order under this subsection may provide that whenever

retired pay is increased under section 1401a of this title (or any other provision of law), the amount payable under the court order to the spouse or former spouse of a member or former member described in paragraph (2)(A) shall be increased at the same time by the percent by which the retired pay of the member or former member would have been increased if the member or former member were receiving retired pay.

(6) Notwithstanding any other provision of law, a member or former member of the armed forces referred to in paragraph (2)(A) shall have no ownership interest in, or claim against, any amount payable under this section to a spouse or former spouse of the member or former member.

(7)(A) If a former spouse receiving payments under this subsection with respect to a member or former member referred to in paragraph (2)(A) marries again after such payments begin, the eligibility of the former spouse to receive further payments under this subsection shall terminate on the date of such marriage.

(B) A person's eligibility to receive payments under this subsection that is terminated under subparagraph (A) by reason of remarriage shall be resumed in the event of the termination of that marriage by the death of that person's spouse or by annulment or divorce. The resumption of payments shall begin as of the first day of the month in which that marriage is so terminated. The monthly amount of the payments shall be the amount that would have been paid if the continuity of the payments had not been interrupted by the marriage.

(8) Payments in accordance with this subsection shall be made out of funds in the Department of Defense Military Retirement Fund established by section 1461 of this title or, in the case of the Coast Guard, out of funds appropriated to the Department of Transportation for payment of retired pay for the Coast Guard.

(9)(A) A spouse or former spouse of a member or former member of the armed forces referred to paragraph (2)(A), while receiving payments in accordance with this subsection, shall be entitled to receive medical and dental care, to use commissary and exchange stores, and to receive any other benefit that a spouse or a former spouse of a retired member of the armed forces is entitled to receive on the basis of being a spouse or former spouse, as the case may be, of a retired member of the armed forces in the same manner as if the member or former member referred to in paragraph (2)(A) was entitled to retired pay.

(B) A dependent child of a member or former member referred

to in paragraph (2)(A) who was a member of the household of the member or former member at the time of the misconduct described in paragraph (2)(A) shall be entitled to receive medical and dental care, to use commissary and exchange stores, and to have other benefits provided to dependents of retired members of the armed forces in the same manner as if the member or former member referred to in paragraph (2)(A) was entitled to retired pay.

(C) If a spouse or former spouse or a dependent child eligible or entitled to receive a particular benefit under this paragraph is eligible or entitled to receive that benefit under another provision of law, the eligibility or entitlement of that spouse or former spouse or dependent child to such benefit shall be determined under such other provisions of law instead of this paragraph.

(10)(A) For purposes of this subsection, in the case of a member of the armed forces who has been sentenced by a court-martial to receive a punishment that will terminate the eligibility of that member to receive retired pay if executed, the eligibility of that member to receive retired pay may, as determined by the Secretary concerned, be considered terminated effective upon the approval of that sentence by the person acting under section 860(c) of this title (article 60(c) of the Uniform Code of Military Justice).

(B) If each form of the punishment that would result in the termination of eligibility to receive retired pay is later remitted, set aside, or mitigated to a punishment that does not result in the termination of that eligibility, a payment of benefits to the eligible recipient under this subsection that is based on the punishment so vacated, set aside, or mitigated shall cease. The cessation of payments shall be effective as of the first day of the first month following the month in which the Secretary concerned notifies the recipient of such benefits in writing that payment of the benefits will cease. The recipient may not be required to repay the benefits received before that effective date (except to the extent necessary to recoup any amount that was erroneous when paid).

(11) In this subsection, the term "dependent child", with respect to a member or former member of the armed forces referred to in paragraph (2)(A), means an unmarried legitimate child, including an adopted child or a stepchild of the member or former member, who—

(A) is under 18 years of age;

(B) is incapable of self-support because of a mental or physical incapacity that existed before becoming 18 years of age and is dependent on the member or former member for over one-half of the child's support; or

(C) if enrolled in a full-time course of study in an institution of higher education recognized by the Secretary of Defense for the purposes of this subparagraph, is under 23 years of age and is dependent on the member or former member for over one-half of the child's support.

(i) Certification date.—It is not necessary that the date of a certification of the authenticity or completeness of a copy of a court order for child support received by the Secretary concerned for the purposes of this section be recent in relation to the date of receipt by the Secretary.

(j) Regulations.—The Secretaries concerned shall prescribe uniform regulations for the administration of this section.

(k) Relationship to other laws.—In any case involving an order providing for payment of child support (as defined in section 459(i)(2) of the Social Security Act) by a member who has never been married to the other parent of the child, the provisions of this section shall not apply, and the case shall be subject to the provisions of section 459 of such Act.

APPENDIX B

McCarty v. McCarty, 1981

Extract From *The Supreme Court Reporter*

REFERENCE: 453 U.S. 210, 69 L.Ed.2d 589

Richard John McCARTY, Appellant

v.

Patricia Ann McCARTY.

No. 80-5.

Argued March 2, 1981.

Decided June 26, 1981.

A California Court of Appeal, First Appellate District, affirmed an award by a superior court to a wife on dissolution of marriage. On appeal, the Supreme Court, Justice Blackmun, held that, on dissolution of the marriage, federal law precludes a state court from dividing military nondisability retired pay pursuant to state community property laws.

Justice Rehnquist dissented and filed opinion in which Justice Brennan and Justice Stewart joined.

Syllabus*

A regular commissioned officer of the United States Army who retires after 20 years of service is entitled to retired pay. Retired pay terminates with the officer's death, although he may designate a beneficiary to receive any arrearages that remain unpaid at death. In addition there are statutory plans that allow the officer to set aside a portion of his retired pay for his survivors. Appellant, a Regular Army Colonel, filed a petition in California Superior Court for dissolution of his marriage to appellee. At the time, he had served approximately 18 of the 20 years required for retirement with pay. Under California law, each spouse, upon dissolution of a marriage, has an equal and absolute right to a half interest in all community and quasi-community property, but retains his or her separate property. In his petition, appellant requested, inter alia, that his military retirement benefits be confirmed to him as his separate property. The Superior Court held, however, that such benefits were subject to division as quasi-community property, and accordingly ordered appellant to pay to appellee a specified portion of the benefits upon retirement. Subsequently, appellant retired and began receiving retired pay; under the dissolution decree, appellee was entitled to approximately 45% of the retired pay. On review of this award, the California Court of Appeal affirmed, rejecting appellant's contention that because the federal scheme of military retirement benefits preempts state community property law, the Supremacy Clause precluded the trial court from awarding appellee a portion of his retired pay.

Held: Federal law precludes a state court from dividing military retired pay pursuant to state community property laws.

(a) There is a conflict between the terms of the federal military retirement statutes and the community property right asserted by appellee. The military retirement system confers no entitlement to retired pay upon the retired member's spouse, and does not embody even a limited "community property concept." Rather, the language, structure, and history of the statutes make it clear that retired pay continues to be the personal entitlement of the retiree.

(b) Moreover, the application of community property principles to military retired pay threatens grave harm to "clear and substantial" federal interests. Thus, the community property division of retired pay, by reducing the amounts that Congress has determined are necessary for the retired member, has the potential to frustrate the congressional objective of providing for the retired service member. In addition, such a division has the potential to interfere with the congressional goals of having the military retirement system serve as an inducement for enlistment and re-enlistment and as an encouragement to orderly promotion and a youthful military.

---

*The syllabus constitutes no part of the opinion of the Court but has been prepared by the Reporter of Decisions for the convenience of the reader.

APPENDIX C

Mansell Decision on Disability Retirement

Mansell v. Mansell, 1989
Extract From *The Supreme Court Reporter*

REFERENCE: 490 U.S. 581, 104 L.Ed.2d 675

Gerald E. MANSELL, Appellant
v.
Gaye M. MANSELL.
No. 87-201

Argued January 10, 1989.
Decided May 30, 1989.

Former husband sought modification of divorce decree by removing the provision that required him to share his total retirement pay with his former wife. The California Superior Court, Merced County, denied the request without opinion. Former husband appealed. The California Court of Appeal affirmed. The California Supreme Court denied the former husband's petition for review. Appeal was taken. The Supreme Court, Justice Marshall, held that military retirement pay that had been waived by the former husband in order to receive veterans' disability benefits was not community property divisible upon divorce.

Syllabus*

In direct response to *McCarty v. McCarty,* 453 U.S. 210, 101 S.Ct. 2728, 69 L.Ed.2d 589, which held that federal law as it then existed completely pre-empted the application of state community property law to military retirement pay, Congress enacted the Uniformed Services Former Spouses' Protection Act (Act), 10 U.S.C. Sec. 1408 (1982 ed.

and Supp. V), which authorizes state courts to treat as community property "disposable retired or retainer pay," 10 U.S.C. Sec. 1408(c)(1), specifically defining such pay to exclude, inter alia, any military retirement pay waived in order for the retiree to receive veterans' disability benefits, 10 U.S.C. Sec. 1408(a)(4)(B). The Act also creates a mechanism whereby the Federal Government will make direct community property payments of up to 50 percent of disposable retired or retainer pay to certain former spouses who present state-court orders granting such pay. A pre-*McCarty* property settlement agreement between appellant and appellee, who were divorced in a county Superior Court in California, a community property State, provided that appellant would pay appellee 50 percent of his total military retirement pay, including that portion of such pay which he had waived in order to receive military disability benefits. After the Act's passage, the Superior Court denied appellant's request to modify the divorce decree by removing the provision requiring him to share his total retirement pay with appellee. The State Court of Appeal affirmed, rejecting appellant's contention that the Act precluded the lower court from treating as community property the military retirement pay appellant had waived to receive disability benefits. In so holding, the court relied on a State Supreme Court decision which reasoned that the Act did not limit a state court's ability to treat total military retirement pay as community property and to enforce a former spouse's rights to such pay through remedies other than direct Federal Government payments.

Held: The Act does not grant state courts the power to treat as property divisible upon divorce military retirement pay waived by the retiree in order to receive veterans' disability benefits. In light of 10 U.S.C. Sec. 1408(a)(4)(B)'s limiting language as to such waived pay, the Act's plain and precise language establishes that 10 U.S.C. Sec. 1408(c)(1) grants state courts the authority to treat only disposable retired pay, not total retired pay, as community property. Appellee's argument that the Act has no preemptive effect of its own and must be read as a garnishment statute designed solely to limit when the Federal Government will make direct payments to a former spouse, and that, accordingly, 10 U.S.C. Sec. 1408(a)(4)(B) defines "disposable retired or retainer pay" only because payments under the statutory direct payment mechanism are limited to amounts defined by that term, is flawed for two reasons. First, the argument completely ignores the fact that 10 U.S.C. Sec. 1408(c)(1) also uses the quoted phrase to limit specifically and plainly the extent to which state courts may treat military retirement pay as community property. Second, each of 10 U.S.C. Sec. 1408(c)'s other subsections imposes new substantive limits on state courts' power to divide military retirement pay, and it is unlikely that all of the section, except for 10 U.S.C. Sec. 1408(c)(1), was intended to pre-empt state law. Thus, the garnishment argument misplaces its reliance on the fact that the Act's saving clause expressly contemplates that a retiree will be liable for "other payments" in excess of those made under the direct payment mechanism, since that clause is more plausibly interpreted as serving the limited purpose of defeating any inference that the mechanism displaced state courts' authority to divide and garnish property not covered by the mechanism. Appellee's contention that giving effect to the plain and precise statutory language would thwart the Act's obvious purposes of rejecting McCarty and restoring to state courts their pre-*McCarty* authority is not supported by the legislative history, which, read as a whole, indicates that Congress intended both to create new benefits for former spouses and to place on state courts limits designed to protect military retirees.

Reversed and remanded.

MARSHALL, J., delivered the opinion of the Court, in which REHNQUIST, C.J., and BRENNAN, WHITE, STEVENS, SCALLA and KENNEDY, J.J., joined. O'CONNOR, J., filed a dissenting opinion, in which BLACKMUN, J., joined.

---

*The syllabus constitutes no part of the opinion of the Court but has been prepared by the Reporter of Decisions for the convenience of the reader.

Additional Citations

> *Mansell v. Mansell (Forbes)*, 109 S. Ct. 2023 (1989), 104 L.Ed.2d 675 (1989), 57 U.S.L.W. 4567, 10 E.B.C. 2521. On remand *In re Marriage of Mansell* (1989, 5th Dist) 216 Cal.App.3d 937, 265 Cal.Rptr.227, 1989 Cal.App; 217 Cal. App.3d 319, 1989 Cal. App. (Prior history: 487 U.S. 1217, 101 L.Ed.2d 904, 108 S.Ct. 2868)

APPENDIX D

Barker v. Kansas

Barker v. Kansas

SUPREME COURT OF THE UNITED STATES
No. 91-611

KEYTON E. BARKER AND PAULINE BARKER,
ET AL.,
PETITIONERS v. KANSAS ET AL.

ON WRIT OF CERTIORARI TO THE SUPREME
COURT OF KANSAS
(April 21, 1992)

JUSTICE WHITE delivered the
opinion of the Court.

The State of Kansas taxes the benefits received from the United States by military retirees but does not tax the benefits received by retired state and local government employees. Kan. Stat. Ann. Sec. 79-3201 *et seq.* (1989).[1] The issue before us is whether the tax imposed on the military retirees is inconsistent with 4 U.S.C. Sec. 111, which provides:

"The United States consents to the taxation of pay or compensation for personal service as an officer or employee of the United States, a territory or possession or political subdivision thereof, the government of the district of Columbia, or an agency or instrumentality of one or

more of the foregoing, by a duly constituted taxing authority having jurisdiction, if the taxation does not discriminate against the officer or employee because of the source of the pay or compensation."

[1]As the Kansas Supreme Court explained, to arrive at the adjusted
gross income of a taxpayer under the Kansas Income Tax Act, the
starting point is the adjusted gross income under the federal Internal
Revenue Code, which includes retirement benefits received by retired
military officials and state and local government retirees. 249 Kan. 186,
190-101, 815 P. 2d 46, 49-50 (1991). As relevant for present purposes,
in calculating Kansas' adjusted gross income, the retirement benefits of
state and local governments are deducted and are exempt from taxation. See Kan. Stat. Ann. Sec. 79-32,117(c)(ii)(Supp. 1990); Sec. 74-
4923(b) (Supp. 1990); see also 249 Kan., at 190-191, 815 P. 2d, at 49-
50 (listing classes exempt from state taxation). Benefits received under the Federal Civil Service Retirement System and by retired railroad
employees are also exempt. Kan.Stat.Ann. Sections 79-32, 117(c)(vii)
and (viii) (Supp. 1990). Not deducted and hence taxable are benefits
received by retired military personnel, certain CIA employees, officials
serving in the National Oceanic and Atmospheric Association or the
Public Health Service, and by retired federal judges. See 249 Kan., at
205, 815 P. 2d, at 58.

Syllabus*
BARKER ET AL. v. KANSAS ET AL.
CERTIORARI TO THE SUPREME COURT OF KANSAS
No. 91-611. Argued March 3, 1992--Decided April 21, 1992

Title 4 U.S.C. Sec. 111 authorizes the States to tax federal employees'
compensation if the taxation does not discriminate against the employees because of the compensation's source. After *Davis v. Michigan*
Dept. of Treasury, 489 U.S. 803, invalidated, under Sec. 111 and the
doctrine of intergovernmental tax immunity, the Michigan income tax
imposed on the benefits of federal, but not state and local, civil service
retirees, petitioners filed suit in a Kansas state court challenging that
State's imposition of an income tax on federal military retirement benefits but not on the benefits received by retired state and local government employees. In affirming the trial court's grant of summary judgment for the state defendants, the State Supreme Court concluded that
military retirement benefits constitute reduced pay for reduced current
services, in contrast to the deferred compensation for past services
embodied in state and local government retirement benefits, and that
this "significant difference" justified the State's differential treatment of
the two classes of retirees under Davis, supra, at 816.
Held: The Kansas tax on military retirees is inconsistent with Sec. 111.

The State Supreme Court's conclusion that, for purposes of state taxation, military retirement benefits may be characterized as current compensation for reduced current services does not survive analysis on several bases. First, there are no "significant differences" between military retirees and state and local government retirees in terms of calculating retirement benefits. The amount of retired pay a service member receives is computed not on the basis of the continuing duties he actually performs, but on the basis of years served on active duty and the rank obtained prior to retirement. Military benefits thus are determined in a manner very similar to that of the Kansas Public Employee Retirement System. Second, this Court's precedents discussing military retirement pay provide no support for the state court's holding. The statement in *United States v. Tyler*, 105 U.S. 244, 245, that such pay is effectively indistinguishable from current compensation at a reduced rate was made in the context of the particular holding of that case, and cannot be taken as establishing that retirement benefits are for all purposes the equivalent of current compensation for reduced current services. And, although *McCarty v. McCarty*, 453 U.S. 210, 222, referred to *Tyler*, it did not expressly approve *Tyler's* description of military retirement pay, but specifically reserved the question whether federal law prohibits a State from characterizing such pay as deferred compensation and urged the States to tread with caution in this area. Third, an examination of other federal statutes treating military retirement pay indicates that Congress for many purposes does not consider such pay to be current compensation for reduced current services. See, e.g., 10 U.S.C. Sec. 1408(c)(1); 26 U.S.C. Sec. 219(f)(1). Thus, military retirement benefits, like the benefits paid to Kansas government retirees, are to be considered deferred pay for past services for purposes of Sec. 111. Pp. 3-10.

249 Kan. 186, 815 P. 2d 46, reversed and remanded.

WHITE, J., delivered the opinion for a unanimous Court. STEVENS, J., filed a concurring opinion, in which THOMAS, J., joined.

---

*The syllabus constitutes no part of the opinion of the Court but has been prepared by the Reporter of Decisions for the convenience of the reader.

APPENDIX E

**United States Court of Appeals
for the Federal Circuit**

"UNJUST TAKING" CASE
89-1106

ALBERT JOHN FERN, JR., JOHN T. FLANNAGAN,
ROBERT JEFFREY, DONNALD KIPPENHAVER,
JAMES H. POWELL, ROBERT LOUIS STIRM, MAX E.
THOMPSON,
JACK TRAHAN AND DAVID E. WALENTOWSKI,
Plaintiffs-Appellants,
v.

THE UNITED STATES,
Defendant-Appellee.

DECIDED: July 16, 1990

Before NIES, <u>Chief Judge*</u> NEWMAN and ARCHER,
<u>Circuit Judges</u>. NIES, <u>Chief Judge</u>.

This appeal is from the final judgment of the United States Claims Court,
Fern v. United States, 15 Cl. Ct. 580 (1988) (Lydon, J.), dismissing a
complaint which sought just compensation under the Fifth Amendment

to the United States Constitution arising from or as a result of the enactment of the Uniform Services Former Spouses' Protection Act, Pub. L. No. 97-252, 96 Stat. 718 (1985) (codified at 10 U.S.C. Sec. 1408(c)(1)(1988)) (hereinafter "the Act" or "FSPA"). appellants are retired members of the armed forces each of whom receive retired pay by reason of a least 20 years of satisfactory active duty service in the military. Each appellant seeks compensation from the United States for the portion of retired

---

* Chief Judge Nies assumed the position of Chief Judge on June 27, 1990.

---

pay which his former spouse has been awarded pursuant to a divorce decree. Appellants attribute their deprivation of part of their retired pay to the change made by FSPA in federal law. On cross-motions for summary judgment, the Claims Court held that FSPA did not effect a "taking" by the United States of appellants' property for public use within the meaning of the Fifth Amendment. We affirm.

I
Background

This appeal requires consideration of the interplay between the divorce laws of certain community property states and the federal statutes relating to military retired pay. The parties do not distinguish between specific state community property laws and, therefore, we will simply refer to California law.[1]

California treats property acquired during marriage as community property. When a couple divorces in that state, community and quasi-community property is divided equally between the spouses while each spouse retains full ownership of any separate property. In California, pension benefits are deemed property and, to the extent accrued during marriage, such property belongs to both spouses, as community or quasi-community property. California has applied these principles to military retired pay benefits the same as to any pension benefits and, upon divorce, has divided the benefits between the spouses, pro tanto. See McCarty v. McCarty, 453 U.S. 210, 216-18 (1981); In re Marriage of Fithian, 10 Cal. 3d 592, 111 Cal. Rptr. 369, 517 P.2d 449 (en banc), cert. denied, 419 U.S. 825 (1974); cf. Cearley v. Cearley, 544 S.W.2d 661 (Tex. 1976). In Fithian, the Supreme Court of California rejected the argument that, by federal statute, military retired pay had to be treated as the separate property of the retiree notwithstanding that community property laws of a particular state

---

[1] The appellants' divorces were granted under the laws of California, New Mexico, Texas or Washington.

generally required division of pension benefits. At the same time, Alaska, another state which also treats pension benefits as marital property, took the view that federal law regarding military retired pay did preempt state law, and prevented an award of any part of military retired pay to the ex-spouse of the service member. See *Cose v. Cose*, 592 P.2d 1230, 1232 (Alaska 1979). In *McCarty*, the Supreme Court resolved this conflict, holding that the federal statutes then governing military retired pay preempted state law and prevented state courts from treating military retired pay as marital property.

In direct response to the *McCarty* decision, Congress enacted FSPA which, in section 1408(c)(1), authorizes state courts to treat disposable retired pay as property solely of the retiree or as property of the retiree and his spouse. To this extent, the Act removed federal preemption retroactively to June 25, 1981, the day before the *McCarty* decision. See *Mansell v. Mansell*, 490 U.S. 581, 109 S. Ct. 2033 (1989).

All of the appellants here had received divorce decrees prior to the passage of FSPA. However, appellants classify themselves into three groups: (A) "final-decree" plaintiffs who had received divorce decrees that specifically refused to divide military retired pay with a spouse in view of *McCarty*; (B) "omitted-asset" plaintiffs where the decrees did not refer to retired pay; and (C) "pre-McCarty" plaintiffs whose decrees had divided retired pay, pursuant to a state's community property law, but who had stopped paying after the *McCarty* decision. Former spouses of (A) and (B) class plaintiffs successfully petitioned their respective divorce courts to reopen and modify outstanding final decrees to give them a right to proportionate shares of their husband's benefits. The former spouses of class (C) plaintiffs successfully brought enforcement proceedings on the original decrees after the enactment of FSPA. While there are factual differences between the groups, the differences are not legally significant to the arguments advanced for reversal of the Claims Court and, except where the text indicates otherwise, the same analysis is applied to all claimants. For convenience, we refer to all claimants as "Fern."

Fern's position is that the division of his retired pay benefits, albeit directly resulting from a state court decree, was made possible only by passage of FSPA. In Fern's view, the Act constitutes a taking of his property by the United States for which compensation must be paid under the Fifth Amendment. Fern identifies the "taken property" variously as his interest in the "final judgement" which was reopened because of the Act; "property entitlements of a final judgment"; "fully earned retired pay"; "vested property rights [in the] entirety of his retired pay"; and "impair[ment]" or "alteration of plaintiff's contractual rights" or "entitlements." The statute is constitutional, per Fern, but the government must pay the cost of the past and future benefits conferred on the former spouses by FSPA, not the retirees. In its simplest terms, Fern asks us to require the government to pay up to a pension and a half.

The government argues that Fern has not established a "taking" by the United States; that the challenged statute merely abrogates federal preemption of state law and allows state courts to apportion military retired pay benefits between spouses; that Fern has no property interest in federal preemption of state law; and that, if the statute were to be construed as directly reducing the amount of Fern's retired pay, Fern has, in any event, no property interest in the level of that pay. Accordingly, the government urges us to uphold the judgment of the Claims Court.

II

Issue

Is the United States required to pay just compensation under the Fifth Amendment to the extent of the economic effect on a retiree personally, resulting from a state court divorce decree following the withdrawal of federal preemption of state community property laws respecting military retired pay?

III

Opinion

The statute with which we are concerned, 10 U.S.C. Sec. 1408(c)(1) (1988) provides specifically in pertinent part:

Subject to the limitations of this section, a court may treat disposable retired or retainer pay payable to a member for pay periods beginning after June 25, 1981, either as property solely of the member or a property of the member and his spouse in accordance with the law of the jurisdiction of such court.

No facile formula is available for making the determination of whether a governmental "taking" of private property for public use has occurred within the meaning of the Fifth Amendment. *Connolly v. Pension Benefit Guar. Corp.*, 475 U.S. 211, 224 (1986). Rather, the Supreme Court stated therein, in connection with alleged takings by statute or regulation, that it "relied instead on ad hoc, factual inquiries into the circumstances of each particular case." Id. (citing *Ruckelshaus v. Monsanto Co.*, 467 U.S. 986, 1005 (1984); *Kaiser Aetna v. United States*, 444 U.S. 164, 175 (1979)). However, the Court "identified three factors which have particular significance in reaching a determination: (1) the economic impact of the [statute] on the claimant; (2) the extent to which the [statute] has interfered with distinct [and reasonable] investment-backed expectations; and (3) the character of the government action." Id. at 224-25 (internal quotation marks omitted). See *Monsanto Co.*,

467 U.S. at 1005; *PruneYard Shopping Center v. Robins*, 447 U.S. 74, 82-83 (1980); *Penn Cent. Transp. Co. v. New York City*, 438 U.S. 104, 124 (1978). As an initial matter, we note that both parties assume that when a statute or regulation does effect a taking without compensation which falls within the proscription of the Fifth Amendment, the remedy is compensation for the taking rather than a declaration that the statute is unconstitutional. Indeed, Fern insists that FSPA is constitutional although it would be unconstitutional, per Fern, if the government does not pay the amount "taken" from him by the divorce decree.

We do not find the case law so clear with respect to when a statute should be voided as violating the constitutional bar and when the availability of a Tucker Act claim would save the statute. Compare *Hodel v. Irving*, 481 U.S. 704 (1987), with *Preseault v. ICC*, ___U.S.___, 110 S. Ct. 914,___(1990). The availability of a Tucker Act remedy, here, may not afford the full relief requested by Fern with respect to past and future payments to his wife. It would require a rewriting of the statute to effectuate the system Fern seeks to have implemented, namely payment into the future of Fern's full amount of retired pay to him plus the amount of his ex-spouse's share as an addition thereto. However, in view of our ruling that there has been no taking by the United States, we need not decide whether the future relief Fern seeks would be appropriate.[2]

Before applying the above-quoted *Connolly* guidelines to determine whether a "taking" has occurred, it is necessary to analyze Fern's asserted "property." In effect, Fern argues that part of his military retired pay has been taken by FSPA because the benefits received must be divided with his wife.

---

[2] A computation of a lump sum evaluation of future payments (as an alternative to continuing future payments) would appear nebulous inasmuch as a military member has no entitlement to any continued level of retirement pay. Congress may alter and even eliminate military retired pay benefits whether classified as "current pay for reduced current services" or pension benefits. See *Hisquierdo v. Hisquierdo*, 439 U.S. 572, 575 (1979) (pension benefits); see also *Atkins v. Parker*, 472 U.S. 115, 129-30 & n.32 (1985) (pension benefits); *United States v. Larianoff*, 431 U.S. 864, 879 (1977) (reduction in pay); *Costello v. United States*, 587 F.2d 424, 426 (9th Cir. 1978) (en banc), cert. denied, 442 U.S. 929 (1979) (reduction in pay).

Fern's theory intermixes two separate and distinct bundles of rights-- his right to military retired pay vis-a-vis the government, a matter of federal law, and ownership of assets of a marriage vis-a-vis a former spouse, a matter of state law into a single sheaf.

With respect to Fern's entitlement to retired pay vis-a-vis the government, FSPA had no effect. Fern's "entitlement" against the government remained exactly the same before and after FSPA. Nothing was "taken" or "diminished" from the amount of military retired pay to which he was or may become entitled under federal law. It is immaterial whether such rights are deemed vested statutory rights, purported contractual obligations, or investment-backed expectations: Fern's asserted rights to benefits from the federal government have been fully satisfied and remain intact.

What has been affected by FSPA concerns ownership of military retired pay between Fern and his former spouse. Unless preempted, the laws of the states determine whether such retirement payments must be shared by marriage partners. Under the law of California and the other community property states involved here, individual pension benefits, accrued as a result of a spouse's employment during the marriage, are deemed the property of both spouses equally, to the extent accrued during the marriage. Thus, appellants had no ownership right in the entirety of their military retired pay vis-a-vis their spouses. A spouse, upon divorce, simply was barred from receiving a share of that asset, which the state otherwise would have recognized as her property, by the preemptive effect of the federal law. See McCarty, 453 U.S. 210 (1981); see also Mansell v. Mansell, U.S. , 109 S. Ct. 2033 (1989) (federal law continues to preempt division of military disability pay).

The lifting of that federal bar did not have the character or effect of a partial transfer of an appellant's military retired pay to his wife by the United States. That occurred only because a particular state in a particular divorce proceeding acted affirmatively to recognize the spouse's right to receive a share of her husband's retired pay as property of the marriage under state law.[3] It is true that Congress expected community property states would be likely to take steps to divide military retired pay between spouses under divorce decrees after enactment of FSPA. However, we cannot agree that the award of benefits to Fern's former spouse by the state became an act of the United States because Congress was aware that the community property states could take this action if Congress lifted the bar of preemption. Nor is the United States the actor with respect to the retroactive application of state law to payments Fern received after June 25, 1981. While allowing state law to be applied retroactively, FSPA itself had no direct effect, retroactive or otherwise, on division of the payments.[4] This decision was left entirely up to each state.

While Fern does not openly assert that he has a property right in continued federal preemption of state law, essentially that is a stick he would have to have in his bundles of rights to bar his former wife from sharing in his military retired pay. Lest there be any question, we reject the idea that continued preemption is a property right either as part of Fern's rights as against the government or his rights as against his wife. cf. *Duke Power Co. v. Carolina Env. Study Group*, 438 U.S. 59, 88 n.32 (1978); *New York Cent. R.R. v. White*, 243 U.S. 188, 197-98 (1917); *Second Employers'*

---

[3] California enacted a special statute to allow reopening of final decrees for this purpose. See Cal. Civ. Code Sec. 5124 (Deering 1984) (repealed by its own terms Jan. 1, 1986).

[4] We express no opinion on whether retroactive application of formerly preempted state law constitutes a taking by the state. Indeed, the legal effect of FSPA was not to abrogate completely the ban of federal preemption, but only to lift it as of June 25, 1981. Prior to that date, per *McCarty*, presumably preemption remains in effect.

Liability Cases, 223 U.S. 1, 50 (1911); *Munn v. Illinois*, 94 U.S. 113, 134 (1876) ("a person has no property, no vested interest, in any rule of common law. Rights of property which have been created [by common law] may not be taken away without due process; but the law itself, as a rule of conduct, may be changed at the will or even at the whim, of the legislature, unless prevented by constitutional limitations.").[5]

Summarizing the application of the three pronged test of *Connolly* (and other Supreme Court precedent) to Fern's "property" rights in retired pay, we conclude that the FSPA has no economic impact on Fern's rights to military retired pay vis-a-vis the United States and is at best an indirect cause of the reduction in the amount of retired pay he may keep for himself under his divorce decree. The action of the United States in enacting FSPA was correctly characterized by the Claims Court as a lifting of federal preemption of state law. That is not the kind of action which falls within the concepts of a "taking" of property.

IV
Conclusion

For the foregoing reasons, we hold that the United States has not taken Fern's property by enactment of FSPA. Accordingly, the judgment of the United States Claims Court is AFFIRMED.

NEWMAN, Circuit Judge, concurs in the result.

---

[5] Similarly, we reject the idea that any "property" right in the finality of a divorce decree was taken by the United States inasmuch as the subject divorce decrees were reopened pursuant to state action. See, e.g., Tex. R. Ct. 329b; N.M.R. Civ. P. Sec. 1-060; Wash. Ct. R. 60(b).

APPENDIX F

Treatment of Military Retired Pay

The following illustrate the various definitions used for military retired pay.

Uniformed Services Former Spouses' Protection Act Position

The USFSPA states, "Subject to the limitations of this section, a court may treat disposable retired or retainer pay..., either as property solely of the member or as property of the member and his spouse in accordance with the laws of the jurisdiction of such court."

Department of Defense Position on Military Retired Pay

The Department of Defense views military retired pay as reduced pay for reduced services. Military retired pay is defined in Federal statutes as income; it is treated as income in a tax court; and it is treated as income in a bankruptcy court. The distinction between the DoD position and the USFSPA on military retired pay is that state courts **may** treat it as property in a divorce action.

According to the Office of the Assistant Secretary of Defense for Military Manpower and Personnel Policy, "Military retired (and retainer) pay cannot be categorized as simply wages, pension, property, income, or any other single item. Military retired pay is a complex element of the compensation package used to help provide the quantity, quality, and mix of skilled personnel needed to meet national defense requirements. Although definition (27), Section 101, Title 10, U.S.C. states that "pay" includes retired pay and retainer pay, the complete definition of military retired pay can only be prescribed by the entire body of law that pertains to it."

Thus, military retired pay is the only form of compensation that is simultaneously treated as income and property. The treatment of military retired pay as (1) income for purposes of support and alimony (under the provisions of the state laws and under 42 U.S.C.§659 *et.seq.*, and as (2) property under the community property and equitable distribution laws of most states, raises the question: How can it be both?

McCarty Case (U.S. Supreme Court) and IRS Positions

In the *McCarty* decision, the U.S. Supreme Court said retired pay was "reduced compensation for reduced current services." The IRS says it is wages and, as such, is taxable as income. The IRS also treats that portion of retired pay which was divided as property and is received in the form of periodic payments by former spouses, as alimony and taxable as income. There are exceptions to this, of course, but generally the statement is true.

Comptroller General Position

The Comptroller General, in Decision B-221190 (11 February 1986), states, ". . . the Act in no way redefines retired pay but merely allows state courts to treat this current compensation as divisible property if permissible under state law."

Military Coalition Position and The Retired Officers Association

For years these two organizations' position on military retired pay is that it is "current reduced pay for current reduced services." Their rationale is "based in part on the fact that in cases of a national defense emergency, retirees could be recalled to active duty."[1]

TROA and other associations in The Military Coalition decided to support the Kansas military retirees in their appeal to the U.S. Supreme Court in *Barker v. Kansas.* (See below.)

Debates (3 examples) in Other State Courts[2]

Michigan. In 1989, the U.S. Supreme Court ruled as discriminatory a Michigan tax scheme that permitted the taxation of federal civilian retirees' retired pay while exempting its own state retirees from similar taxes.[3] This ruling forced tax law changes in dozens of states. As a result, military retirees in other states thought they, too, would be treated (for income tax purposes) as their civilian counterparts were treated.[4] This was not to be the case.

Kansas. On 12 July 1991, the Kansas Supreme Court declared that military retired pay is reduced income for reduced services to the government. In that action, the Kansas court denied an estimated $80 million in refunds to nearly 16,000 military retirees living in the state. In other words, Kansas upheld the state income tax levied on military retired pay, but not on most federal civil servants. The court felt that this was a permissible exception to the prohibition of the federal statute. Since Kansas did not believe the military retired pay was "legally" a pension, they felt justified in claiming that it did not fall under the 1989 U.S. Supreme Court ruling (that states must tax federal, state and local government pensions at the same rate).

In their reasoning, the Kansas Justices said that "military pensions are different because their recipients have not really retired but merely have stepped down from active duty, still subject to recall."[5] This case went all the way to the U.S. Supreme Court. (See below.)

Colorado. On 16 September 1991, the Colorado Supreme Court ruled that the military retired pay is a pension. Obviously, the military retirees who picked Colorado to settle down had something to celebrate about, for the ruling put as much as $5,000 back into their pockets in refunds for income taxes collected under a discriminatory tax law repealed in 1989.

Under the old law, retired people under the age of 55 could exclude $20,000 of their annual pensions from state income taxes, but military retirees were singled out and limited to a $2,000 exclusion.

U.S. Supreme Court and Kansas

On 27 November 1991, the justices agreed to review the Kansas decision (*Barker v. Kansas*) that held that retired pay is reduced compensation for reduced service, and not a pension. On 3 March 1992, the case was argued. Then, on 21 April 1992, the Justices handed down the following decision:

States may not tax military retired pay if they exempt state and local government pensions from state income tax.

The Court held that, for purposes of preventing discrimination against military retirees, military retired pay is to be considered deferred pay for past services, like the pensions of state and local government retirees. (See Appendix D.)

APPENDIX F ENDNOTES

1. See *The Retired Officer Magazine*, November 1991, page 12+.

2. The 5 July 1993 issue of the *Air Force Times* carried a state-by-state breakdown on the U.S. Supreme Court's June 18, 1993, ruling in favor of military and civilian retirees in Virginia. The Supreme Court has ruled that Virginia illegally taxed military (and federal) retirement pay while exempting the retirement income of state retirees. The most recent update on the various cases pending in the states appears in the January 24, 1994, issue (page 20) of the *Air Force Times*.

3. The Michigan case was *Davis v. Michigan*. The new law is found at 4 U.S.C. §111.

4. The U.S. Supreme Court ruling in *Davis v. Michigan* did not specifically mention military retired pay. It was widely assumed, however, that it would fall under the general heading of federal pensions.

5. *Barker v. Kansas*, 12 July 1992. Kansas also taxes the pensions of former foreign service officers, public health officers, and members of the Central Intelligence Agency. The Kansas Supreme Court said it would take another case to determine if those taxes are valid.

APPENDIX G

Public Laws Affecting Military Divorces

The following is a non-inclusive list of the major public laws affecting former spouses. (Some of these laws had expiration dates or inclusive dates for their applicability; thus, they may not apply to prospective divorces.) The remaining section identifies applicable portions of the *Code of Federal Regulations* that apply to related actions.

PL 97-248 (1982)**The Tax Equity and Fiscal Responsibility Amendment (TEFRA) of the Social Security Act**

Enables a former spouse of an active duty service member to file for involuntary allotments to be taken from the member's monthly pay for payment of overdue spousal and/or child support without having to pursue court proceedings.

PL 97-252 (1982) **The Uniformed Services Former Spouses' Protection Act**

Authorizes state courts to treat military retired pay in the same manner they treat other pensions; authorizes the retired pay to be treated as property (vs. income). Provides for direct pay from the military finance center of a percentage of the retired pay and/or for child/spousal support when the marriage lasted 10 years or more during shared active duty time of the member. Authorizes commissary, exchange, and medical care, including CHAMPUS, for unremarried former spouses who were married for at least 20 years during active duty service, if divorced after 1 February 1983. Authorizes naming the former spouse as SBP beneficiary.

PL 98-94 (1984) Defense Authorization Act

Allows military members who divorced before USFSPA to designate a former spouse as beneficiary of the SBP if member was a participant at the time of retirement.

301

PL 98-525 (1984) 1985 Defense Authorization Act

Extended military medical care and shopping privileges to 20-20-20s divorced before 1 February 1983 and medical care only to 20-20-15s divorced before 1 February 1983. Directed DoD to develop a plan for all former spouses to convert from military medical care to a private health insurance plan. Extended military care for two years or until the health plan was in place to 20-20-15s divorced after 1 April 1985. Enables the former spouse to ask for a "deemed election" of the SBP if the member does not file the application.

PL 99-145 (1985) 1986 Defense Authorization Act

Requires spousal concurrence for a member to waive SBP or select less than the maximum coverage. Creates a 2-tier system (55 percent until age 62, 35 percent after) for the SBP instead of a Social Security offset; benefits for those already enrolled are to be computed under the most favorable system. Creates new "former spouse" and "former spouse and child" categories with lower premiums than the former "insurable interest" category.

PL 99-661 (1986) 1987 Defense Authorization Act

Allows state courts[1] to order that a former spouse be designated as SBP beneficiary.[2] Extends medical coverage for 20-20-15s until a health plan is in place. Lowers the age at which a surviving spouse may remarry, without losing SBP benefits, from 60 to 55. Limits the deduction of Chapter 61 (DoD) (10 U.S.C. §1201 *et.seq.*) disability pay in determining disposable pay to be considered in the percentage awarded at the time of retirement. Eliminates the deduction for life insurance premiums in determining disposable pay. (The amendments made in this law apply to court orders issued on or after the date of the enactment of the Act.)

---

[1] Although state courts were authorized to order SBP, this did not mean that a state court would order it if the state law did not provide for such. For example, it was not until 1 July 1992 that Virginia passed such a bill. Before then, a court could not order the member to designate the former spouse as SBP beneficiary, even though the federal law allowed for it.

[2] Mandating SBP for the first spouse can present real problems in providing for a second spouse, particularly when the first spouse has already been awarded a share of the retired pay, and the second spouse could be the one who is married to the member longer.

PL 100-27 (1987) 1988 Defense Authorization Act

Extended medical care for certain spouses from 1 April 1988 until 31 December.

PL 100-456 (1988) 1989 Defense Authorization Act

Changes the cost of the SBP to a straight 6.5 percent except for a few with a low base amount who are grandfathered.[3]

PL 101-189 (November 1989) 1990 Defense Authorization Act

Authorized a supplemental Survivor Benefit Plan (changed 10 U.S.C. 1457 *et.seq.*, added Subchapter III to Chapter 73, Part II, of Title 10). Enables participants in the SBP to provide a supplemental annuity for the spouse or former spouse beginning when the participant dies or when the spouse or former spouse becomes 62 years of age, whichever is later, in order to offset the effects of the two-tier annuity computation under the SBP.

PL 101-510 (November 1990) 1991 Defense Authorization Act

Prohibits the reopening of pre-McCarty divorce cases for the purpose of dividing military retired pay. Placed a two-year limit (until November 1992) on payments to those who did reopen pre-McCarty cases and were awarded a share of the retirement pay. Redefines disposable pay to eliminate the deduction of taxes and personal debts for those divorced on or after 3 February 1991.

PL 102-484 (October 1992) 1993 Defense Authorization Act

Provides annuities for spouses or former spouses when military members lose eligibility for retired pay because of court-martial or law enforcement action and dependents can prove abusive behavior. (This annuity terminates upon the remarriage of the benefiting ex-spouse).

Amends 10 U.S.C. §1408 to allow DFAS to accept service via electronic mail or FAX.

---

[3]In most cases, this was a favorable change, as it reduced the monthly premium.

PL 104-201 (September 1996) 1997 Defense Authorization Act

Precludes circumvention of a divorce court order by military member's waiver of retired pay to enhance Civil Service retirement annuity. Authorizes the Director of OPM to deduct and withhold from the Civil Service retirement annuity payable to the employee an amount equal to that due an ex-spouse by reason of a prior USPSPA award under 10 U.S.C. §1408.

Provides former spouse access to disability pay to obtain payment of unsatisfied obligations to pay alimony and/or child support through garnishment, or other means, under either 10 U.S.C. §1408 or 42 U.S.C. §659.

Amends 10 U.S.C. §1408 to allow the Military Services to make payments for the benefit of former spouses directly to states in situations where the former spouse has assigned to a state the rights or such payments under a provision of the Social Security Act.

Amends 10 U.S.C. §1408 to disallow acceptance by the Service Secretary concerned for out-of-state modification, or to comply with the provisions of such a court order, unless the court issuing that order has jurisdiction in the manner specified by subsection (c) (4).

PL 105-85 (October 1997) 1997 Defense Authorization Act

Section 643 directs the Department of Defense to conduct a review of the history of the USFSPA and report to Congress not later than 30 September 1999. This was/is viewed by the veterans' community as providing an excuse for delaying Congressional Action on reform of the USFSPA unit not before year 2001.

PROCEDURAL REGULATIONS

The following citations are representative of some of the procedural regulations applicable to Uniformed Services retired pay. They are listed by U.S.C. title.

Title 26--IRS

Income Tax, Applicable rules relating to certain reduced uniformed services retirement pay, 26 CFR 1.122-1.

Title 32--National Defense

Eligible beneficiaries and health benefits authorized, 32 CFR 728.31.

Former Spouse Payments from Retired Pay, Definitions, 32 CFR 63.3.

Garnishment of pay of AF members and employees only for child support or alimony obligations, 32 CFR 818.20.

Title 38--Department of Veterans Affairs

Benefits at DIC rates in certain cases when death is not service connected, 38 CFR 3.22.

APPENDIX H

H.R. 2200 -- As Originally Proposed

102D CONGRESS
1ST SESSION
H.R. 2200

To amend title 10, United States Code, to revise the rules relating to the payment of retired pay of retired members of the Armed Forces to former spouses pursuant to court orders.

IN THE HOUSE OF REPRESENTATIVES
May 2, 1991

Mr. DORNAN of California introduced the following bill; which was referred to the Committee on Armed Services

A BILL

To amend title 10, United States Code, to revise the rules relating to the payment of retired pay of retired members of the Armed Forces to former spouses pursuant to court orders.

Be it enacted by the Senate and House of Representatives of the United States of America in Congress assembled,

SECTION 1. SHORT TITLE.

This Act may be cited as the "Uniformed Services Former Spouses' Protection Act Fairness Amendments of 1991."

SEC. 2. REVISION IN THE TERMINATION PROVISION FOR PAY-MENTS FROM DISPOSABLE RETIRED PAY.

(a) IN GENERAL.--Section 1408(d) of title 10, United States Code, is amended by striking paragraph (4) and substituting the following new paragraph:

307

(4)(A) Payments from the disposable retired pay of a member as a result of treating retired pay as property of the member and the former spouse pursuant to this section shall terminate in accordance with the terms of the applicable court order, but not later than the date of remarriage of the former spouse, the date of the death of the member or the date of the death of the spouse or former spouse to whom payments are being made, whichever occurs first. Payments under this section which are or have been terminated as the result of the former spouse's remarriage shall not be reinstated on account of the termination of the former spouse's subsequent marriage.

(B) Nothing in this section shall be construed to relieve a member of liability for the payment of child support required by a court order.

(C) The Secretary shall, within 90 days of the date of enactment of this Act, promulgate regulations establishing procedures for ascertaining the current marital status of former spouse's receiving payments of a member's retired pay under this section, and shall, with respect to former spouses who have entered into a remarriage, terminate such payments by not later than 180 days from the date of enactment of this Act".

(b) DEFINITION OF "REMARRIAGE."--Subsection (a) of such section is amended by adding the following new paragraph:

(7) The term 'remarriage' means any marriage subsequent to the termination by court order of a marriage between a member and his or her spouse, regardless of whether the subsequent marriage is terminated by (A) a court order or (B) death of the subsequent spouse.

(c) EFFECTIVE DATE.--The amendment made by subsection (a) shall apply with respect to payments of a member's retired pay by the Secretary payable 180 days after the date of enactment of this Act.

SEC. 3. AWARD OF RETIRED PAY TO BE BASED ON RETIREE'S LENGTH OF SERVICE AND PAY GRADE AT TIME OF DIVORCE.

(a) IN GENERAL.--Section 1408(c) of title 10, United States Code, is amended by adding a new paragraph (5) as follows:

(5)(A) In the case of a member as to whom a final decree of divorce, dissolution, annulment, or legal separation is issued before the date the member begins to receive retired pay, the disposable retired pay of the member that a court may treat in the manner described in paragraph (1) shall be computed based on the pay grade and lengths of service of the member while married that are creditable for purposes of calculating entitlements to basic pay and to retired pay on the date of the final decree. Amounts so calculated shall be increased by the cumulative percentage of increases in retired pay between the date of the final decree and the effective date of the member's retirement.

(B) With respect to payments to former spouses from a member's disposable retired pay pursuant to court orders issued prior to the effective date of this Act, the Secretary shall, within 90 days of the effective date of this Act, recompute the amounts of those payments in accordance with paragraph (A) hereof, and, within 180 days of the effective date of this Act, adjust the amount of disposable retired pay payable to the former spouse accordingly."

(b) EFFECTIVE DATE.--The amendment made by subsection (a) shall apply with respect to court orders issued on or after June 25, 1981.

SEC. 4. EFFECTIVE DATE; PROHIBITION OF CERTAIN RETRO-ACTIVE COURT ORDERS.

(a) IN GENERAL.--Subsection (e) of section 555 of Public Law 101-510 is amended by striking out "two-year" and inserting in lieu thereof "one-year."

SEC. 5. LIMITATION ON TIME FOR SEEKING DIVISION OF RE-TIRED PAY.

(a) IN GENERAL.--Subsection (c)(4) of section 1408 of title 10, United States Code, is amended to read as follows:

(4) A court may not treat the disposable retired pay of a member in the manner described in paragraph (1) unless--

(A) the court has jurisdiction over the member by reason of (A) his residence, other than because of military assignment, in the territorial jurisdiction of the court, (B) his domicile in the territorial jurisdiction of the court, or (C) his consent to the jurisdiction of the court. However, if the court, in the final decree, does not treat or reserve jurisdiction to treat the disposable retired pay of the member in the manner described in paragraph (1), then in any subsequent judicial proceeding to treat the disposable retired pay of the member in the manner described in paragraph (1), the jurisdiction of the court must be separately established at the time the subsequent judicial proceeding is initiated, based on the criteria in this subparagraph (A);

(B) the member's spouse or former spouse makes proper application to a court for division or partition of retired pay of the member as property of the member and the member's spouse or former spouse within two years of the date of a final decree of divorce, dissolution, annulment, or legal separation, including a court ordered, ratified, or approved property settlement incident to such a decree."

(b) EFFECTIVE DATE.--The amendment made by subsection (a) shall apply with respect to final decrees issued after the date of the enactment of this Act.

SEC. 6.TREATMENT OF DISABILITY PAY UNDER CHAPTER 61.

(a) IN GENERAL.--Subsection (a)(4)(E) of section 1408 of title 10, United States Code, is amended to read as follows:

(E) in the case of a member entitled to retired pay under chapter 61 of this title, are equal to the amount of retired pay of the member under that chapter computed using the percentage of the member's disability on the date when the member was retired (or the date on which the member's name was placed on the temporary disability retired list), and no court shall include amounts of disability pay so calculated as property of the member and the member's spouse or former spouse subject to division under this section.

(b) EFFECTIVE DATE.--The amendment made by subsection (a) shall apply with respect to court orders issued on, before or after the date of enactment of this Act.

SEC. 7.PROHIBITION ON DISTRIBUTIONS OF ACTIVE DUTY PAY.

(a) IN GENERAL.--Section 1408 of the title 10, United State Code, is amended—

(1) by striking in its entirety subparagraph (c)(3) and

(2) by adding a new subparagraph (c)(3) to read as follows:

(3) No court may, pursuant to this section, order a member to apply for retirement or retire at a particular time in order to effectuate any payment under this section, nor may any court order a member to make any payment pursuant to this section out of the member's active duty income earned on or after the date the member first becomes eligible for retirement, nor may any court order a member to make any pre-retirement payment equivalent to a payment which would otherwise be made pursuant to this section had the member retired and commenced receiving retired pay. A payment shall be deemed to be a pre-retirement payment prohibited by this subparagraph if the payment (i) is ordered by a court to be made by a member on active duty commencing on the date a member first becomes eligible to retire from military service and prior to actual retirement (ii) equals or approximates, in amount or percentage, the amount or percentage which would be paid to a former spouse had the member retired on or about the date the court orders payments to begin. Any retired member recalled to active duty after initial retirement shall not be ordered by any court to commence or continue payments to a former spouse resulting from the treatment of retired pay as property, while the member is on active duty."

(3) by adding at the end of subsection (d) the following new paragraph:

(6) In no event shall the Secretary make any payment under this section from a member's active duty pay."

(b) EFFECTIVE DATE.—The amendments made by subsection (a) shall apply to any payment prohibited by subsection (a) and due to be paid on or after the date of enactment of this Act pursuant to a court order.

APPENDIX I

H. R. 2537
Uniformed Services Former Spouses'
Equity Act of 1997

105th CONGRESS
1st Session

To amend title 10, United States Code, to revise the rules relating to the court-ordered apportionment of the retired pay of members of the Armed Forces to former spouses, and for other purposes.

IN THE HOUSE OF REPRESENTATIVES
September 24, 1997

Mr. Stump introduced the following bill, which was referred to the Committee on National Security, and in addition to the Committee on Ways and Means, for a period to be subsequently determined by the Speaker, in each case for consideration of such provisions as fall within the jurisdiction of the committee concerned.

A BILL

To amend title 10, United States Code, to revise the rules relating to the court-ordered apportionment of the retired pay of members of the Armed Forces to former spouses, and for other purposes.

Be it enacted by the Senate and House of Representatives of the United States of America in Congress assembled.

SECTION 1. SHORT TITLE

This Act may be cited as the "Uniformed Services Former Spouses' Equity Act of 1997."

SECTION 2.TERMINATION OF PAYMENTS UPON REMARRIAGE OF FORMER SPOUSE

(a) IN GENERAL -- Section 1408(c) of title 10, United States Code, is amended by adding at the end the following new paragraph:

> "(5) Payment from the monthly disposable retired pay of a member to a former spouse of the member pursuant to this section shall terminate upon the remarriage of that former spouse, except to the extent that the amount of such payment includes an amount other than an amount resulting from the treatment by the court under paragraph (1) of disposable retired pay of the member as property of the member or property of the member and his spouse. Any such termination shall be effective as of the last day of the month in which the remarriage occurs."

(b) EFFECTIVE DATE--The amendment made by subsection (a) shall apply with respect to marriage terminated by court orders issued before, on, or after the date of the enactment of this Act. In the case of such a court order issued before the date of the enactment of this Act, such amendment shall apply only with respect to amounts of a member's retired pay that are payable for months beginning more than 180 days after the date of the enactment of this Act.

SEC 3. AWARD OF RETIRED PAY TO BE BASED ON RETIREE'S LENGTH OF SERVICE AND PAY GRADE AT TIME OF DIVORCE.

(a) IN GENERAL -- Section 1408(c) of title 10, United States Code, as amended by section 2, is further amended by adding at the end the following new paragraph:

> "(6) In the case of a member as to whom a final decree of divorce, dissolution, annulment, or legal separation is issued before the date on which the member begins to receive retired pay, the disposable retired pay of the member that a court may treat in the manner described in paragraph (1) shall be computed based on the pay grade, and the length of service of the member while married, that are creditable toward entitlement to basic pay and to retired pay as of the date of the final decree. Amounts so calculated shall be increased by the cumulative percentage of increases in retired pay between the date of the final decree and the effective date of the member's retirement."

(b) IMPLEMENTATION--With respect to payments to a former spouse from a member's disposable retired pay pursuant to court orders issued before the date of the enactment of this Act, the Secretary shall--

> (1) within 90 days of such date, recompute the amounts of those payments in accordance with paragraph (5) of section 1408(c) of title 10, United States Code, as added by subsection (a); and

> (2) within 180 days of such date, adjust the amount of disposable retired pay payable to that former spouse accordingly.

(c) EFFECTIVE DATE--The amendment made by subsection (a) shall apply with respect to court orders issued on or after June 25, 1981.

SEC. 4. LIMITATION ON TIME FOR SEEKING DIVISION OF RETIRED PAY.

(a) IN GENERAL -- Subsection (c)(4) of section 1408 of title 10, United States Code, is amended to read as follows:

> "(4) A court may not after the date of the enactment of the Uniformed Services Former Spouses Equity Act of 1997 treat the disposable retired pay of a member in the manner described in paragraph (1) unless --

>> "(A) the court has jurisdiction over the member by reason of (i) the member's residence, other than because of military assignment, in the territorial jurisdiction of the court, (ii) the member's domicile in the territorial jurisdiction of the court, or (iii) the member's consent to the jurisdiction of the court; and

>> "(B) the member's spouse or former spouse obtains a court order for apportionment of the retired pay of the member not later than (i) two years after the date of final decree of divorce, dissolution, annulment, or legal separation, including a court ordered, ratified, or approved property settlement incident to such a decree, or (ii) the end of the six-month period beginning on the date of the enactment of the Uniformed Services Former Spouses Equity Act of 1997, whichever is later."

(b) EFFECTIVE DATE--The amendment made by subsection (a) shall apply with respect to final decrees of divorce, dissolution, annulment, or legal separation issued on or after June 25, 1981.

SEC. 5. LIMITATION ON APPORTIONMENT OF DISABILITY PAY WHEN RETIRED PAY HAS BEEN WAIVED

(a) IN GENERAL--Subsection (e)(4) of section 1408 of title 10, United States Code, is amended by adding at the end the following new subparagraph:

"(C) Notwithstanding any other provision of law, a court may not treat as part of the disposable retired pay of a member under this section or as part of amounts to be paid pursuant to legal processes under section 459 of the Social Security Act (42 U.S.C. 659) amounts which are deducted from the retired pay of such member as a result of a waiver of retired pay required by law in order to receive compensation under title 38."

(b) AMENDMENTS TO SOCIAL SECURITY ACT--Section 459(h) of the Social Security Act (42 U.S.C. 659(h)) is amended--

(1) in paragraph (1)(A)(ii)--

(A) by inserting "or" at the end of subclause (III);

(B) by striking out "or" at the end of subclause (IV) and inserting in lieu thereof "and";

(C) by striking out subclause (V); and (2) in paragraph (2) --

(A) by redesignating subparagraphs (E) and (F) as subparagraphs (F) and (G), respectively; and

(B) by inserting after subparagraph (D) the following new subparagraph:

"(E) are paid by the Secretary of Veterans Affairs as compensation for a service-connected disability under title 38, United States Code, when military retired pay has been waived in order to receive such compensation;"

(c) EFFECTIVE DATE--The amendments made by subsections (a) and (b) shall apply to court orders and legal processes issued on or after June 25, 1981. In the case of a court order or legal process issued before the date of the enactment of this Act, such amendments shall apply only with respect to retired pay payable for months beginning on or after the date of the enactment of this Act.

APPENDIX J

Survivor Benefit Plan (SBP)
Summary of Changes

The text for the SBP can be found in 10 U.S.C. §1448 *et seq.* The following summarizes the changes. (See Chapter 11 for further discussion of SBP.)

Approved Pub.L. 92-425 (1972). Amendments: Pub.L. 93-406 (1974) granted special tax treatment for SBP. Pub.L. 94-496 (1976) mandated certain deductions from retired pay. Pub.L. 95-397 (1978) eliminated the Social Security offset for a working widow not eligible to receive Social Security benefits because of her income from employment. A Reserve Component SBP was established. Pub.L. 96-402 (1980), among other changes, modified the Social Security offset; suspended voluntary SBP participation from certain disabled retirees. Pub.L. 97-35 (1981) authorized a one-year open enrollment period. Pub.L. 97-252 (1982) (and subsequent amendments to USFSPA) provided for former spouse coverage. Pub.L. 98-525 (1984) changed the Social Security offset rules, as did Pub.L. 99-145 (1985), which established a two-tier system relative to the Social Security offset. Pub.L. 99-145 also required spousal consent before the member can decline SBP or elect less than maximum coverage or coverage for a child only. Pub.L. 99-576 (1986) permits the deduction of SBP costs from VA disability compensation. Pub.L. 99-661 (1987), among other changes, authorized state courts to order members to participate in SBP. Pub.L. 100-224 (1987) allows for a concurrent increase in SBP base amount whenever military retired pay is increased. Pub.L. 100-456 (1988) makes changes relative to surviving spouses of members who died before November 1, 1953. Pub.L. 101-189 (National Defense Authorization Act for FY 1990) (1989) provides a revised premium computation for SBP annuities, to 6.5 percent of the amount selected. Those who became members of the uniformed services before March 1, 1990, are grandfathered, and have the option of whichever formula is more advantageous to them (provides the lowest cost).

317

APPENDIX K

Military/Veterans Organizations

Involvement on the Hill is Assumed and Necessary

Involvement of military organizations in defense legislation and national affairs is an accepted activity on the "Hill." The late Rep. Bill Nichols (D-AL), former Chairman of the House Armed Services Subcommittee on Military Personnel and Compensation, said of such involvement, "We are faced with a wide variety of issues, and it is very difficult for members of Congress to have detailed knowledge of all of them. Letters from military personnel and retirees assist in acquiring this knowledge. I think you serve as an important intermediary between your membership and the Congress. You take the expressed feelings of your members and focus those views on the legislation before the Congress."

Representing a combined membership of about 12 million active, reserve, national guard and retired military members and their families are the nationwide organizations which are united in their efforts to provide a strong voice in Congress and within the Department of Defense and the Department of Veterans Affairs on issues of importance to military personnel and their families. These are:

    The 26-member Military Coalition
    The 17-member National Military/Veterans Alliance
    The American Legion
    Disabled American Veterans (DAV)
    AMVETS

Members of the Military Coalition are:
    Air Force Association
    Army Aviation Association of America
    Association of Military Surgeons of the United States
    Association of the US Army
    Commissioned Officers Association of the
        US Public Health Service

319

CWO and WO Association of the US Coast Guard
Enlisted Association of the National Guard of the US
Fleet Reserve Association
Gold Star Wives of America
Jewish War Veterans of the USA
Marine Corps League
Marine Corps Reserve Officers Association
National Guard Association of the US
National Military Family Association
National Association of Battlefield Commissions
Naval Enlisted Reserve Association
Naval Reserve Association
Navy League of the US
Reserve Officers Association
The Military Chaplains Association of the USA
The Retired Enlisted Association
The Retired Officers Association
United Armed Forces Association
USCG Chief Petty Officers Association
US Army Warrant Officers Association
Veterans of Foreign Wars

Members of the National Military/Veterans Alliance are:

Air Force Sergeants Association
American Military Retirees Association
American Retirees Association
Class Act Group
Gold Star Wives of America
Korean War Veterans Association
Military Order of the Purple Heart
Military Order of the World Wars
National Association of Uniformed Services
Naval Reserve Association
Naval Enlisted Reserve Association
Non-Commissioned Officers Association
Society of Medical Consultants to the Armed Forces
The Retired Enlisted Association
Tragedy Assistance Program for Survivors
Veterans of Foreign Wars
Women in Search of Equity

AGENDAS OF THE NATIONAL COMMUNITY OF MILITARY/VETERANS ORGANIZATIONS

Each organization has its own agenda and the issue of divorce and military retired pay may not necessarily be the highest priority issue on every agenda. In early 1998, for example, the top priority on a majority of agendas was military health care. Nevertheless, the political process is quite dynamic and the focus on issues fluctuates in response to public reaction, pro tem party objectives and numerous other variables. While pursuing their agendas, veterans organizations remain alert for justification for shifting their focus to any area where an opportunity emerges to justify the advance of the priority of any item on their agenda. A good example is H.R. 2537, the "Uniformed Services Former Spouses' Equity Act of 1997," introduced in September 1997, which indicated a concrete possibility of reform of the USFSPA as compared with other issues still at the "talking stage." The result was that an overwhelming majority of the national community of military/veterans organizations visibly and vocally expressed their support for H.R. 2537 and turned to the ARA for leadership. In fact, the only organization which has been unvaryingly opposed to reform of the USFSPA is the National Military Family Association, which is unlikely to change its position.

ARA members who are members of any of the organizations listed above should make it their business to inquire--preferably at the local chapter level--as to the priority accorded to USFSPA reform by the national organization and the manifestations of active support. This ranges from the publication of articles in periodicals, through the adoption of national resolutions, and extends to lobbying or testifying on Capitol Hill. Much of what is accomplished in Washington originates at the 'grass roots' level--which is where many ARA members can be the most effective. Any reader of this book is encouraged to write to the ARA of the results of your representations to any other organization(s) and any recommendations for follow-up by ARA management.

One of the most important tasks to be performed by ARA members is to spread, throughout their sphere of acquaintances, information on the inequities of the USFSPA and the need to restore fairness and equity to the military divorce process. Throughout its existence the principal problems encountered by the ARA have derived from the lack of knowledge of the USFSPA by the parties to a military divorce, the uneven application of the USFSPA by state divorce courts, and the failure of military members to convey, to the American public, the unanticipated, adverse impact of a well-intentioned law. Concomitantly, these factors have contributed to a lack of widespread knowledge that there exists an organization (the ARA) committed to the address of the inequities of the USFSPA through a unified approach to its reform.

APPENDIX L

Contacting Your Elected Representatives

Why Your Input Is Needed

If you think that you are caught totally by surprise by some laws or complain that you just "didn't hear about it," then put yourself in the shoes of your elected officials, and consider that they, too, are uninformed and misinformed, even by their staff, on a lot that is happening. Impossible, you say? Consider that in an average year, the *Federal Register* alone turns out more than **63,000 pages** (9-foot high stack) on rules and procedures affecting all aspects of our lives.

It is impossible for your elected representatives to know everything that is going on—but, at the same time, it is possible for them to know something that is going on. And they learn it from their constituents— you. Our government needs the active participation of those who are directly affected by any proposed government legislation. Indeed, our legislators, their staff, and civil servants count on help from interested parties to resolve the issues that result in legislative compromises.

Before You Write or Visit

Just as you do when preparing for a job interview, you should gather as much information as possible about your senator's or representative's background. The information you acquire could be mentioned in your letter or during your visit. This includes their hometown, committee assignments, specific interests and background of those interests.

Once you have this information or find you have something in common (you admire their position on a particular issue), then say so in your letter or during your visit.

Writing a Member of Congress

Senators and representatives do pay attention to their mail—they know what it takes to get reelected! While they do receive form letters,

323

they are not nearly as effective as personal letters, where the constituent provides some personal information as to how or why a particular issue affects them. It goes without saying that the letter *must* be short, informed, and polite.

Here are some pointers that will help you make points with your congressmen and women:

1. Keep your letter to one typewritten page, two pages at the most. Never write on the back of a page. If you cannot type the letter, then write neatly in longhand, or better yet, print.

2. First paragraph—state your purpose and stick with only one subject or issue. The succeeding paragraphs must support your main topic.

3. If you are writing in response to a bill, cite it by name and number. If you do not know it, call Capitol Hill to find it out. The U.S. Capitol switchboard can be reached at (202) 224-3121.

4. Personalize your letter—cite facts and support your position about how the (proposed) legislation (will) affect you and others. Avoid emotional arguments or threats to withhold your vote in the next election.

5. If you have strong beliefs about the legislation and believe your official should oppose it, then state so, indicating the adverse effects it is likely to have. If you have a solution, propose it!

6. Ask your representative where he or she stands on the proposed legislation, but do not demand their support. Do not be surprised, however, when you receive a response that is neutral. Senators and Representatives must take into consideration the views of their entire constituency; perhaps your position will be heard the next time the issue is addressed.

7. Don't forget to provide your name and return address.

The address to write is:

The Honorable_____   The Honorable_____
U. S. Senate   U.S. House of Representatives
Washington DC 20510   Washington DC 20515

Dear Senator_____Dear Representative_____

Meeting a Member of Congress

Visiting your elected officials is a very effective way to take the letter-writing initiative one step further. A visit emphasizes your interest in a bill and reinforces your beliefs in the legislative process. Visiting, however, requires you to adhere to a particular set of courtesies.

1. Make an appointment--state your subject, the amount of time you will need, and anyone else who will be attending with you.

2. If a group is going, it is imperative that you select one person to be the spokesperson and that you all agree on what will be said. The representative will, in all likelihood, ask questions of individuals.

3. It is imperative that you **know the facts**. In this case, you must know the bill title and number, and its legislative content.

4. Your spokesperson must present the facts in a concise, organized, and positive manner.

5. Relate both the positive and negative impacts of the legislation, the problems it corrects and the problems it poses, along with a different approach, if possible.

6. Leave fact sheets or an information packet with your elected officials. Encourage the official and his or her staff to ask questions.

7. Your final requests when leaving are: ask for favorable consideration, thank the congressman/woman for their time and courtesy, and leave promptly.

On-Line Access to Congress

If you have access to a computer, you have a number of ways to contact your elected officials. They include e-mail, Web pages, and fax numbers. Many organizations also publish these addresses and telephone numbers. Because this information changes and is easily accessed elsewhere, we have not included that information in this book. (The ARA web site at *http://www.americanretirees.com* also lists and has links to mailing addresses and e-mail addresses for Congressional members.)

APPENDIX M

Checklist for Interviewing an Attorney

TYPE	QUESTIONS TO ASK AND ASSESS	+-

EXPERIENCE WITH MILITARY DIVORCES	1. How many military divorce cases has the attorney handled? How long in practice?
	
	2. What is his/her knowledge of the jurisdiction requirements for military personnel (if the member is on active duty)?
	
	3. Jurisdiction:
	  a. If yours is an out-of-state case (e.g., the spouse has had you served from another state), what is the attorney's experience in working with out-of-state attorneys?
	  b. What is the attorney's knowledge about the law in the other state (to give advice on whether to initiate a divorce suit in the member's current state or accept jurisdiction in another state)?
	
	4. What is the local court's track record regarding military retired pay division?
	
	5. How have the local courts treated the division of military retired pay for non-working spouses?
	
	6. What is the attorney's personal beliefs toward military spouses?
	
	7. How many cases has the attorney handled with the military member as the plaintiff? With the spouse as the plaintiff?
	
	8. What do they know about the USFSPA? SBP? Other insurance alternatives?	

TYPE	QUESTIONS TO ASK AND ASSESS	+-
FEES	1. Does the attorney require a written agreement before being retained? 2. Regarding the attorney's retainer: a. How much is it? b. Is any of it refunded if the divorce turns out to be processed quickly and without problems? c. What is the hourly fee? d. If the attorney has to appear in court for you, what are the rates? Is it an hourly fee or a flat rate? 3. Regarding the bill: a. Are you billed monthly? b. Is the entire amount required to be paid each month? c. Can you work out a payment schedule? d. What detail is included on the bills? e. Does the lawyer's fee include expenses (some do) or are expenses itemized separately? f. Are phone calls billed at a minimum of a certain time (e.g., 15 minutes)? 4. Does the attorney have a paralegal do any of the work? If so, are you charged less for the paralegal's services? (Some attorneys' fees are inclusive--their hourly rate covers the secretary and other staff.)	
GENERAL WORKING RELATIONSHIP	1. If necessary, will the attorney call you at your home instead of at work? 2. Will the attorney provide you (if you want) with drafts of all motions before they are signed and sent to the opposing attorney or court? 3. What is the attorney's opinion as to the difficulty of your case and what it might involve?	

TYPE	QUESTIONS TO ASK AND ASSESS	+-
YOUR SPECIFIC QUESTIONS	1.	
	2.	
	3.	
	4.	
	5.	
	6.	
	7.	
	8.	
	9.	
	10.	

Your suggestions or recommendations to improve this checklist are welcome. Is there any particular aspect about your attorney or the way your case was handled that could benefit others? If so, we would like to hear from you.

Please send your comments to ARA (Attn: Book Authors), PO Box 2333, Redlands, CA 92373-0781.

APPENDIX N

Preparing For Your Attorney:
What You Both Need to Know

TYPE	INFORMATION YOU NEED TO OBTAIN AND COMPILE	√
BASIC INFORMATION	1. Date & place of marriage 2. Prior marriage (& divorce) date 3. Birthdates/Ages of husband (H) & wife (W) 4. Children & their ages 5. Educational level of H & W 6. General health of H & W 7. General work experience of H & W 8. Total yearly income (last 3 years) for both 9. Unusual contributions (monetary & non-monetary) of both during the marriage 10. Standard of living established 11. Financial needs and resources of H & W 12. Any agreements between the H & W 13. Circumstances contributing to the divorce 14. Military pay grade and years of service 15. Estimated military retirement income	

MILITARY SUMMARY	1. Listing of all your military assignments
	    -when, where, how long
	    -accompanied or unaccompanied
	2. Indicate whether your spouse worked (and the approximately yearly income) for each assignment period, any pension plans
	3. Anticipating or already receiving VA disability compensation?
	4. Status of spouse (eligible for future military medical care, and commissary and exchange privileges?)	

TYPE	INFORMATION YOU NEED TO OBTAIN AND COMPILE	√

PERSONAL & REAL PROPERTY	Inventory all your assets--marital and non marital
	
	  automobiles
	
	  furniture
	
	  houses
	
	  land	

FINANCIAL STATUS For each account, provide the following: - date opened - beginning balance - current balance - average & frequency of deposits - yearly deposits	1. Complete an Income and Expense sheet (monthly budget). 2. Active Duty—a copy of member's Leave and Earnings Statement 3. Retiree—a copy of monthly retiree's account statement 4. Reservist—a copy of drill statements and the most recent point accounting statement. 5. Copy of the last three years income tax returns. 6. Other financial assets—e.g., savings accounts, credit unions, savings bonds. 7. Retirement plans (IRAs, 401k, TSP--if civil service, employer plan). 8. Outstanding debts (e.g., car loan, school loans, mortgage, credit cards). 9. Insurance policies (term, whole life and cash value, disability, property, supplemental health, etc.) 10. Estimate (both husband and wife) future income (e.g., selling a second home). 11. Estimate (both husband and wife) future expenses (e.g., college for the children, returning to school) 12. Statement on spouse's ability to afford an attorney.	

APPENDIX O

Family Law Quarterly
State Divorce/Support Criteria

The following charts, excerpted from pages 804-809 of the Family Law Quarterly, Winter 1997, are reprinted with permission from ABA Publishing, 750 North Lake Shore Drive, Chicago, Illinois 60611.

Appendix

Table 1—*Alimony/Spousal Support Factors*

STATE	Statutory List	Marital Fault Not Considered	Marital Fault Relevant	Standard of Living	Status as Custodial Parent
Alabama			X	X	
Alaska	X	X		X	X
Arizona	X	X	X	X	X
Arkansas		X			
California	X	X		X	
Colorado	X	X		X	X
Connecticut	X		X	X	X
Delaware	X	X		X	X
D.C.			X	X	
Florida	X		X	X	
Georgia	X		X	X	
Hawaii	X	X		X	X
Idaho	X		X		
Illinois	X	X		X	X
Indiana	X	X		X	X
Iowa	X	X		X	X
Kansas		X			
Kentucky	X	X		X	
Louisiana	X		X		X
Maine	X	X			
Maryland	X		X	X	
Massachusetts	X		X	X	X
Michigan			X	X	
Minnesota	X	X		X	X
Mississippi			X		
Missouri	X		X	X	X
Montana	X	X		X	X
Nebraska		X			
Nevada			X	X	X
New Hampshire	X		X	X	X
New Jersey	X		X	X	X
New Mexico	X	X		X	
New York	X		X	X	X
North Carolina	X	X		X	
North Dakota			X	X	
Ohio	X	X			
Oklahoma		X		X	X
Oregon	X	X		X	X
Pennsylvania	X		X	X	
Rhode Island	X		X	X	X
South Carolina	X		X	X	X
South Dakota			X	X	
Tennessee	X		X	X	X
Texas	X		X	X	X
Utah	X		X	X	
Vermont	X	X		X	X
Virginia	X		X	X	
Washington	X	X		X	
West Virginia			X		
Wisconsin	X	X		X	X
Wyoming			X		

Table 2—*Custody Criteria*

STATE	Statutory Guidelines	Children's Wishes	Joint Custody	Cooperative Parent	Domestic Violence	Health	Attorney or GAL
Alabama	X		X		X		
Alaska	X	X	X	X	X	X	X
Arizona	X	X	X	X	X	X	X
Arkansas							
California	X	X			X		X
Colorado	X	X	X	X	X	X	X
Connecticut		X	X				X
Delaware	X	X				X	X
D.C.	X	X	X	X	X	X	X
Florida	X	X	X	X	X	X	X
Georgia	X	X	X				X
Hawaii	X	X			X		X
Idaho	X	X	X		X	X	
Illinois	X	X	X	X	X	X	X
Indiana	X	X	X	X	X	X	X
Iowa	X	X	X	X	X	X	X
Kansas	X	X	X	X	X	X	
Kentucky	X	X	X	X	X	X	X
Louisiana	X	X	X		X		
Maine	X				X		X
Maryland			X		X		X
Massachusetts			X		X		X
Michigan	X	X	X	X	X	X	X
Minnesota	X	X	X		X		X
Mississippi	X		X				
Missouri	X	X	X	X	X	X	X
Montana	X	X	X		X		X
Nebraska	X	X	X			X	X
Nevada	X	X	X	X	X		X
New Hampshire	X	X	X		X		X
New Jersey	X	X	X	X	X	X	X
New Mexico	X	X	X	X	X	X	X
New York		X					X
North Carolina		X			X	X	
North Dakota	X	X			X	X	
Ohio	X	X	X		X	X	X
Oklahoma	X	X	X	X	X		
Oregon	X	X	X		X		X
Pennsylvania	X	X	X	X	X	X	X
Rhode Island		X	X	X	X	X	X
South Carolina		X	X	X	X	X	X
South Dakota		X	X	X			
Tennessee	X	X	X		X	X	X
Texas	X	X	X	X	X	X	X
Utah	X	X	X	X			X
Vermont	X		X		X		X
Virginia	X	X	X	X	X	X	X
Washington	X	X			X	X	X
West Virginia		X	X		X		
Wisconsin	X	X	X	X	X	X	X
Wyoming		X	X		X		

Table 3—*Child Support Guidelines*

STATE	Income Share	Percent of Income	Extraordinary Medical Add On*	Child-Care Add On*	College Support	UIFSA
Alabama	X		X	X	X	
Alaska		X	X			X
Arizona	X		X	X		X
Arkansas		X				X
California	X		X	X		
Colorado	X			X	X	X
Connecticut	X					
Delaware			X	X		X
D.C.		X		X	X	X
Florida	X		X	X		X
Georgia		X	X			
Hawaii				X	X	
Idaho	X		X	X		X
Illinois		X			X	X
Indiana	X		X	X	X	X
Iowa	X				X	
Kansas	X		X	X		X
Kentucky	X		X	X		
Louisiana	X		X	X		X
Maine	X		X	X		X
Maryland	X		X	X		X
Massachusetts		X	X		X	X
Michigan	X		X	X	X	X
Minnesota		X		X		X
Mississippi		X				
Missouri	X		X	X	X	X
Montana		X	X	X		X
Nebraska	X			X		X
Nevada		X	X			
New Hampshire		X			X	
New Jersey	X		X	X	X	
New Mexico	X		X	X		X
New York	X		X	X	X	
North Carolina	X		X	X		X
North Dakota		X				X
Ohio	X			X		
Oklahoma	X		X	X		X
Oregon	X		X	X	X	X
Pennsylvania	X		X	X		X
Rhode Island	X			X		X
South Carolina	X		X	X	X	X
South Dakota	X	X	X			X
Tennessee		X				
Texas		X	X			X
Utah	X		X	X		X
Vermont	X		X	X		
Virginia	X		X	X		X
Washington	X		X	X	X	X
West Virginia	X		X	X		
Wisconsin		X	X			X
Wyoming	X	X				X

* Source: Laura W. Morgan, Child Support Guidelines (1996).

Table 4—*Grounds for Divorce and Residency Requirements*

STATE	No Fault Sole Ground	No Fault Added to Traditional	Incompatibility	Living Separate and Apart	Judicial Separation	Durational Requirements
Alabama		X	X	2 years	X	6 months
Alaska		X	X		X	None
Arizona	X				X	90 days
Arkansas		X		18 months	X	60 days
California	X				X	6 months
Colorado	X				X	90 days
Connecticut		X		18 months	X	1 year
Delaware	X					6 months
D.C.	X			1 year	X	6 months
Florida	X					6 months
Georgia		X				6 months
Hawaii	X			2 years	X	6 months
Idaho		X			X	6 weeks
Illinois		X		2 years	X	90 days
Indiana		X			X	60 days
Iowa	X				X	None
Kansas			X			60 days
Kentucky	X				X	180 days
Louisiana		X		6 months	X	None
Maine		X			X	6 months
Maryland		X		2 years	X	1 year
Massachusetts		X			X	None
Michigan	X				X	6 months
Minnesota	X			60 days	X	180 days
Mississippi		X				6 months
Missouri		X		1-2 years	X	90 days
Montana	X		X	180 days	X	90 days
Nebraska	X				X	1 year
Nevada			X	1 year	X	6 weeks
New Hampshire		X		2 years		1 year
New Jersey		X		18 months		1 year
New Mexico		X	X		X	6 months
New York		X		1 year	X	1 year
North Carolina		X		1 year	X	6 months
North Dakota		X			X	6 months
Ohio		X	X	1 year		6 months
Oklahoma		X	X		X	6 months
Oregon	X				X	6 months
Pennsylvania		X		2 years		6 months
Rhode Island		X		3 years	X	1 year
South Carolina		X		1 year	X	3 months (both residents)
South Dakota		X			X	None
Tennessee		X		2 years	X	6 months
Texas		X		3 years		6 months
Utah		X		3 years	X	90 days
Vermont		X		6 months		6 months
Virginia		X		1 year	X	6 months
Washington	X				X	1 year
West Virginia		X		1 year	X	1 year
Wisconsin	X				X	6 months
Wyoming	X		X		X	60 days

Table 5—*Property Division*

STATE	Community Property	Only Marital Divided	Statutory List of Factors	Nonmonetary Contributions	Economic Misconduct	Contribution to Education
Alabama		X		X		X
Alaska		X	X	X	X	X
Arizona	X		X		X	X
Arkansas		X	X	X		
California	X		X	X	X	X
Colorado		X	X	X	X	
Connecticut			X	X	X	X
Delaware			X	X	X	
D.C.		X	X	X	X	
Florida		X	X	X	X	X
Georgia		X				
Hawaii			X	X	X	
Idaho	X		X			
Illinois		X	X	X	X	
Indiana		X	X	X	X	X
Iowa		X	X	X		
Kansas			X		X	
Kentucky		X	X	X	X	X
Louisiana	X					
Maine		X	X	X		
Maryland		X	X	X		
Massachusetts			X	X	X	
Michigan		X		X	X	X
Minnesota		X	X	X	X	
Mississippi						
Missouri		X	X	X	X	X
Montana		X		X	X	
Nebraska		X		X		
Nevada	X	X		X	X	X
New Hampshire			X	X	X	X
New Jersey		X	X	X	X	X
New Mexico	X					
New York		X	X	X	X	X
North Carolina		X	X	X	X	X
North Dakota				X	X	X
Ohio		X	X	X	X	X
Oklahoma		X		X	X	
Oregon				X		X
Pennsylvania		X	X	X	X	X
Rhode Island		X	X	X	X	X
South Carolina		X	X	X	X	X
South Dakota				X	X	
Tennessee		X	X	X	X	X
Texas	X				X	
Utah					X	
Vermont			X	X	X	X
Virginia		X	X	X	X	
Washington	X		X			
West Virginia		X	X	X	X	X
Wisconsin	X	X	X	X	X	X
Wyoming		X	X			

Table 6—*Third-Party Visitation*

STATE	Stepparents	Grandparents—Death of Their Child	Grandparents—Child Divorce	Out of Wedlock	Any Interested Party
Alabama		X	X		
Alaska	X	X	X	X	X
Arizona		X	X	X	
Arkansas		X	X		
California	X	X	X		X
Colorado		X	X	X	
Connecticut	X	X	X	X	X
Delaware	X		X		
D.C.					
Florida		X	X	X	
Georgia		X	X		
Hawaii	X		X		
Idaho			X	X	
Illinois		X	X	X	
Indiana	X	X	X	X	
Iowa		X	X		
Kansas	X	X	X	X	
Kentucky		X	X	X	
Louisiana		X	X		
Maine	X	X	X	X	
Maryland		X	X		
Massachusetts		X	X		
Michigan	X	X	X		
Minnesota	X	X	X	X	
Mississippi		X	X		
Missouri		X	X	X	
Montana		X	X	X	
Nebraska	X	X	X		
Nevada		X	X	X	
New Hampshire	X	X	X	X	
New Jersey	X	X	X	X	
New Mexico	X	X	X	X	X
New York	X	X	X	X	
North Carolina			X		
North Dakota	X	X	X		
Ohio	X	X	X		X
Oklahoma		X	X	X	
Oregon	X	X	X	X	X
Pennsylvania		X	X		
Rhode Island		X	X		
South Carolina		X	X	X	
South Dakota		X	X	X	
Tennessee	X		X		
Texas	X	X	X	X	X
Utah	X	X	X		
Vermont		X	X		
Virginia	X		X		X
Washington	X		X		
West Virginia		X	X	X	
Wisconsin		X	X		
Wyoming	X	X	X		X

APPENDIX P

Resources

This section is a list (by no means, inclusive) of sources of information that you may want to consult for further information. While some of the resources do not address issues related to military retirement, many contain information that is useful in establishing the positions of the parties in a divorce and sorting out the facts. This section is grouped according to the type of resource that is available. Some legal references are included for those who are interested in legal research. A specific listing does not imply endorsement by the American Retirees Association, the authors, or anyone associated with the publishing of this book.

Every attempt has been made to include valid addresses and telephone numbers. However, given their changing nature, we apologize for any errors you may find. (Let us know the correct data.)

1. AMERICAN BAR ASSOCIATION

750 North Lakeshore Drive Chicago IL 60611
Tel: 312-988-5603. ABA Service Center: 1-800-285-2221
ABA attorney Web site: http://www.abanet.org/home
ABA general public Web site: http://www.aba.net.org/genpublic

Within the ABA, Family Law Section, is the Military Law Committee. The chair is Marshal S. Willick, Esq., 3551 E. Bonanza Rd., Suite 12, Las Vegas, NV 89110-2198. Tel: 702-438-5311. (Note: This group was very pro-spouse regarding equity changes proposed in 1990.)

On-line you can see what has been published in its *Family Law Quarterly.* For example, the Spring 1997 issue (Vol. 31, No.1), published 6/17/97, contained an article by attorney Mark Sullivan on military divorce.

2. ASSOCIATIONS

American Retirees Association

PO Box 2333
Redlands, CA 92373-0781
Tel: (909) 793-2424
www.
AmericanRetireesAssociation.org

Washington Operations Office
2009 N. 14th St. Suite 300
Arlington, VA 22201-2514
Tel: (703) 527-3065

Women In Search of Equity for Military in Divorce (WISE)
P.O. Box 4383, Annapolis, MD 21403; E-mail: joinwise@aol.com

> WISE is an association formed by women who support the rights of military members in divorce and who are committed to equitable reform of the USFSPA.

EX-POSE, Ex-Partners of Servicemen (Women) for Equality
P.O. Box 11191, Alexandria, VA 22312; Tel: 703-941-5844

> Founded in 1980, active membership is around 3500. This organization serves the interests of the military spouse by educating them on legislation and benefits affecting military spouses who are divorcing or have divorced. It publishes a newsletter explaining current developments and the unique aspects of military divorce, and also publishes an excellent booklet entitled "A Guide for Military Separation or Divorce."

Men's Defense Association
17854 Lyons, Forest Lake MN 55025-8854
Tel: 612-464-7887; http://www.mensdefense.org/

> Founded in 1972, MDA has approximately 6000 members. MDA's purpose is to salvage the traditional family by obtaining equal (not necessarily identical) rights and equal dignity for men. Their monthly newsletter (approximately 28 pages), *The Liberator,* is full of issues related to divorce, particularly child support. They also publish a number of very inexpensive reference materials and a small divorce handbook, and are a major source for information on men and child custody problems. Some of the titles available are: "Divorce: What All Should Know," "Educate-a-Judge Package," "Alimony/Support Defenses," "Child Custody Preparation."
>
> MDA has a network of lawyers who charge reasonable fees, as well as a list of computer bulletin boards for legal issues related to men, divorce, and child custody cases. (If you do

write MDA, please mention you learned about them through
this book.)

Fathers and Children for Equality (FACE)
PO Box 16066 Columbus OH 43216
Tel: 614-275-6767

FACE's mission is to provide education, advocacy, and support to parents and children experiencing loss of the traditional
parent-child relationship.

Other Organizations

American Academy of Matrimonial Lawyers. 20 N. Michigan Ave, Suite 540, Chicago IL 60602. Tel: 312-263-6477.

You can call or write for a list of attorneys who specialize in
matrimonial law in your area. Also, you can research attorneys in the Martindale Hubbell reference book (in any library),
which is now on-line.

Divorce and Custody Instant Information Clearinghouse,
P.O. Box 1313, Waldorf MD 20604-1313; Tel: 301-843-9175, 888-
773-7444; Fax: 301-843-9484. This organization is currently
working on a fax-on-demand system to access various topics.

National Military Family Association, Inc. (NFMA) 6000
Stevenson Ave, Suite 304, Alexandria, VA 22304-3526; Tel: 703-
823-6632; Fax: 703-751-4857; E-mail: families@nmfa.org or
IamNMFA@aol.com

NMFA members receive Fact Sheets free of charge; nonmembers may order them by sending $1 for each sheet: Former
Spouse, Spousal Employment, Survivor Benefit Plan, Continued Health Care Benefit Program, and more.

3. BOOKS

Note: Do not be discouraged if you find that a listed book is out of
print (some are). Often, you can find them in used book stores.
One great source is Page One Too in Albuquerque, New Mexico.
For other out-of-print books, check Amazon.com on the Internet.
They can query a network of used bookstores and send you an
update.

DeAngelis, Barbara. *Are You the One for Me? Knowing Who's Right & Avoiding Who's Wrong.* NY: Bantam Doubleday Dell Pub. Grp., Inc. 1992.

This book can be found in used bookstores, and this one comes with my endorsement (M. Thole). If you don't do anything else after your divorce, you MUST read this book before you even think about getting involved with another person. Of all the 300+ books I have reviewed on relationships, this is the reference book you need to keep in your personal library forever. Not only will you learn why you chose the partner that you did, but you will learn how to make much better choices. In addition, you will learn the 10 types of relationships that won't work, and how to spot fatal flaws in a partner that will doom a relationship. You can also learn why you may be falling in love for the wrong reasons. There is a step-by-step guide for when and how to make commitments. In short, you will understand why your past choices were not right for you and learn how to make a healthy, successful choice in your next partner. An Albuquerque used bookstore, Page One Too, at 11200 Montgomery Blvd., NE, Albuquerque, NM 87111 (Tel: 505-294-5623), usually has a copy of this book.

E-Z Legal Forms. *E-Z Legal Guide to Divorce.* 384 So. Military Trail, Deerfield Beach FL 33442. Tel: 954-480-8933. Fax: 954-480-8906.

An excellent primer with everything you need to know to handle your own contested divorce. (Caution: Provisions for military related aspects are not included). Contains checklists, forms for legal paperwork and an excellent listing of divorce laws by state. ARA recommends that both the service member and the spouse use this book as a starting point to gather documentation and decide issues in preparation for meeting with your respective a attorneys.

Forer, Judge Lois G. *What Every Woman Needs to Know Before (and After) She Gets Involved with Men and Money.* Rawson Associates.

Gives advice on when to mediate and when to go to court.

Friedman, James T. *The Divorce Handbook—Your Basic Guide to Divorce.* NY: Random House, 1984.

This book is packed full of checklists, guides, sample schedules and worksheets for things such as assets and liabilities, child support schedules, initial interview sheet (what the lawyer will need from you), trial outline. It is presented in a question-and-answer format, and covers the topics of choosing a lawyer, discovery procedures, negotiation strategies, preparing for trial, child custody and support, financial hide-and-seek with your spouse, and much, much more. An excellent book to read *before* you pay your first visit to a lawyer.

HALT, *Divorce.* Washington, DC: HALT, 1612 K St. NW #510, Washington DC 20006. Orders only: Tel: 1-888-367-4258; Tel: 202-887-8255; Fax: 202-887-9699. http://www.halt.org; E-mail: halt@halt.org

HALT (an organization of Americans for legal reform) is very active in providing self-help legal resources for its members, and is the leading non-profit organization in seeking reform in state attorney discipline programs and exposure of outrageous legal practices by attorneys designed to prevent individuals from seeking or using self-help legal resources. HALT's Web site has the Legal Information Clearinghouse, featuring over 100 links to other legal reform and information sites.

HALT, *Using A Lawyer...And What To Do If Things Go Wrong.* Washington, DC: HALT.

By reading this book **before** you hire an attorney, you could very well avoid having anything go wrong (not agreeing with the law doesn't count). Besides telling you how to select an attorney and what to look for, it gives excellent coverage to the kind of problems that can develop (e.g., overcharging, overlawyering) and what you can do if you feel your lawyer is ignoring you.

Hunt, Morton. *The Affair.* NY: Signet.

The author has surveyed men and women who have experi enced every form of extramarital affair.

Hunt, Morton, and Hunt, Bernice. *The Divorce Experience.* NY: Signet,1977.

Helps explain the intensity of the divorce experience from the transition of separation to self-discovery and remarriage. It can answer some of those questions everyone seems to ask when their marriage falls apart—Why?

Joselow, Beth and Joselow, Thea. *When Divorce Hits Home: Keeping Yourself Together When Your Family Comes Apart.* Avon.

Although the introduction in this book says it is for children of people who are divorcing, it is recommended for parents, psychologists and teachers.

Kamm, Phyllis. *Remarriage in the Middle Years and Beyond.* Bristol Publishing Enterprises (Tel: 800-346-4889).

General advice for men and women.

Krantzler, Melvin. *Creative Divorce.* New York: M. Evans and Co., Inc., 1974.

Although this book was published years ago, the information in it is still relevant. For those who are having problems sorting out all the various dimensions of the divorce process, particularly the emotional aspects, this book can help. The book is available in many public libraries and can still be purchased at bookstores.

Krantzler, Melvin. *Learning to Love Again.* New York: Thomas Y. Crowell Co., 1977.

This is a companion book to the one mentioned above. For those who do not want to repeat the problems or mistakes in their previous marriage, this book can assist by identifying the differences and actions that may have taken place in your prior marriage and help you to understand them as differences, not problems to be ignored. This book is also available on audio cassette in libraries.

Moss, Anne E. *Your Pension Rights at Divorce—What Women Need to Know.* Washington, DC: Pension Rights Center (revised regularly).

Although this book is geared toward women, the plans identified (including military retired pay) are applicable to either spouse. Civil Service retirement plans are also covered. Order from the Pension Rights Center, 918 16th St. NW Ste. 704, Washington, DC 20006, Tel: 202-296-3776; E-mail: pnsnrights@aol.com.

O'Connell, Marjorie A. and Kittrell, Steven D. *Federal Retirement Plans: Division of Benefits and Divorce.* Washington, DC:

Divorce Taxation Education, Inc.

1730 Rhode Island Ave., NW Ste 809
Washington DC 20036
Tel: 202-466-8204; Fax: 202-466-4663

Publishes and sells several legal books for attorneys and professionals who plan financial settlements, tax returns, and divorce decrees.

Paul, Jordon and Margaret. *Do I Have to Give Up Me to be Loved by You?* Mpls, MN: Compcare, 1985.

This is an excellent book that everyone should read—especially if you feel that a divorce is the only solution to whatever is bothering you. It goes through the many struggles between couples and what is really going on behind the struggles. There are four patterns to the way people communicate, and the explanations in this book are in very easy-to-understand layperson's terms. A common feeling behind many actions is fear—fear of some loss. This book explains those feelings in a way that can help couples who do not wish to go to a professional therapist or cannot afford to do so.

Richman, Bruce L. *Tax and Financial Planning Strategies in Divorce.* Family Law Library, Wiley Law Publications. Tel: 800-879-4539.

This book is out-of-print.

Rosenberg, Stephen M., and Peterson, Ann Z. *Every Woman's Guide to Financial Security.* Capital Publishing.

From the calls that ARA has received, men could benefit from this book as well.

Schilling, Edwin III, and Wilson, Carol Ann. *Survival Manual for Women in Divorce.* Boulder CO: Quantum Press, 1991.

Schilling, Edwin III, and Wilson, Carol Ann. *Survival Manual for Men in Divorce.* Boulder CO: Quantum Press, 1992.

These two books are written in an easy-to-follow question-and-answer format. Indeed, the reader of either book could probably save some money on legal fees by reviewing these books and understanding the responses and the limitations placed on both parties and their lawyers.

Retired Air Force lieutenant colonel Edwin Schilling III adjudicated more than 6,000 USFSPA cases at the Air Force's finance center in Colorado, and advises attorneys and clients on the USFSPA. Carol Ann Wilson is a financial planner. She founded the Quantum Institute for Professional Divorce Planning in Boulder, CO.

Sheehy, Gail. *Passages: Predictable Crises of Adult Life.* NY: E.P. Dutton, 1974.

A classic still, you will see yourself at every stage in your lives—twenties, thirties, forties, etc., and the major events that occur during those periods.

Sitarz, Daniel. *Divorce Yourself. The National No-Fault No-Lawyer Divorce Handbook.* Carbondale, IL: Nova Publishing Company.

A wealth of detailed checklists. Includes an appendix of divorce laws in all 50 states.

Thorne, Julia, with Rothstein, Larry. *You Are Not Alone—Words of Experience and Hope for the Journey Through Depression.* NY: HarperCollins Publishers, Inc., 1993.

The former wife of a famous political figure, the author recovered from eight years of depression, and has described in her book, with the help of many others, how depression can affect every aspect of one's life. The book contains specific advice on how to make positive choices for recovery.

Tomes, Jonathan P., Lieutenant Colonel, US Army, Retired. *The Servicemember's Legal Guide,.* Harrisburg, PA: Stackpole Books. (The book is available in most military exchanges.)

This book is the only comprehensive one on just about every legal matter that a military member (and family) could be faced with. (The Reserves are also covered.) It contains chapters on divorce and separation, family members, military adoptions, and marriage (including overseas marriages). LTC Tomes currently has a law practice, Tomes and Dvorak, 5001 College Blvd. Ste. 214, Leawood KS 66211. E-mail: jon@tomesdvorak.com

Trafford, Abigail. *Crazy Time.*

This book, written in 1974 and updated, has become a standard on divorce reading recommendation lists. It is a near diary of the start to finish process known as the "emotional" divorce, which then moves into the "legal" divorce. Readers will see that their situation is not unusual—everyone becomes a little "crazy" during this time. Look for it in used bookstores.

Uniformed Services Almanac, Inc. publishes the following annual books: *Retired Military Almanac, Reserve Forces Almanac, National Guard Almanac, Uniformed Services Almanac* (for active duty personnel).

These annual publications cost less than $10 and are available in military exchanges or from the publisher: Uniformed Services Almanac, Inc. P.O. Box 4144, Falls Church, VA 22044, Tel: 703-532-1631, Fax: 703-532-1635. The one for retirees includes information in the USFSPA, SBP, state-by-state income tax information for retired military, TRICARE, and other retirement benefits. Both the military member and spouse should review the benefits in developing an asset/liability/income/expense accounting. For details on the various benefits in Chapter 9, readers can consult these almanacs. To order: Tel. 1-888-872-9698, Web: http://members @aol.com/usalmanac, E-mail: militaryalmanac@ erols.com.

U.S. Department of Health and Human Services, National Institute of Mental Health. *Caring About Kids: When Parents Divorce.*

Wallerstein, Judith S. and Kelly, Joan Berlin. *Surviving the Breakup—How Children and Parents Cope with Divorce.* New York: Basic Books, 1980.

This book, still considered a definitive body of research, was the first major study to document the immediate and long-range effects of family dissolution.

Weiner-Davis, Michele. *Divorce Busting: A Revolutionary and Rapid Program for Staying Together.* (Fireside)

There are many disadvantages to divorce, and this Woodstock, Illinois marriage and family therapist has a proven track record for keeping couples together (85% of those she counsels). Divorce rarely solves the problems people think it will, and the proof is in the breakup of second marriages as well. If you think you need to divorce to solve your problems, reading her book may just help you. In her experience, there is no difference in the number of problems you see in traditional marriages vs. two-career marriages.

4. MILITARY HEALTH CARE (CHAMPUS has been replaced by TRICARE)

For assistance with TRICARE, consult the Health Benefits Advisor at your nearest military treatment facility. The military health care program is managed out of Aurora CO 80045-6900.

5. CONGRESSIONAL RESEARCH SERVICE

These reports are available only through your elected representatives.

Report 88-215A, July 1988. *Treatment of Former Spouses Under Various Federal Retirement Systems.* By Marie Morris. No special situations such as disability are discussed.

Report 89-187F, March 20, 1989. *Military Benefits for Former Spouses: Legislation and Policy Issues.* This report was updated in CRS Report No. 92-557 F, July 13, 1992 (same title).

6. COURT DECISIONS — Federal

Comptroller General No. B-228790.2, 3/1/91. This ruling protects former spouses from owing a sudden debt to the government when the service member is awarded a retroactive increase in disability compensation.

Eatinger v. Commissioner of Internal Revenue, U.S. Tax Court Dkt. No. 16564-89. (1990) Military retirement benefits are included as gross income to the recipient spouse as well as the military member. The retirement income was characterized as deferred compensation to the military member and not a transfer of community property to the spouse. (*Tax treatment of military retirement benefits in a divorce*)

Fern v. U.S., C.A.F.C., No. 89-1106, July 16, 1990; 908 F.2d 955 (1990 U.S. App.), 12 E.B.C. 1936. 15 Cl. Ct. 580 (1988). (*The "Unjust Taking" case*)

Mansell v. Mansell (Forbes), 109 S. Ct. 2023 (1989), 104 L.Ed.2d 675 (1989), 57 U.S.L.W. 4567, 10 E.B.C. 2521. On remand In re Marriage of Mansell (1989, 5th Dist) 216 Cal.App.3d 937, 265 Cal.Rptr.227, 1989 Cal.App; 217 Cal. App.3d 319, 1989 Cal. App. (Prior history: 487 U.S. 1217, 101 L.Ed.2d 904, 108 S.Ct. 2868). (*VA Disability pay waived in lieu of retired pay is not a divisible marital asset*)

McCarty v. McCarty, 453 U.S. 210 (1981), 69 L.Ed.2d 589, 101 S. Ct. 2728, 49 U.S.L.W. 4850 (1981). (*Division of military retired pay as a marital asset*)

7. **COURT DECISIONS — State** (listed by issue). For a more detailed listing of specific state cases, see Chapter 12, "51 Flavors and Counting."

Civil Service Retirement (as a deduction from gross military retirement pay)

Gallegos v. Gallegos, 788 S.W.2d, 158 (1990). This appears to be the first case in Texas where the civil service salary paid to a military retiree at the time of the divorce must be deducted from the gross military retirement pay in order to determine what is "disposable" pay. (This case also affirmed that VA disability retirement is excluded from division.)

Computation of Military Retirement Benefits

Kniss v. Kniss, C.A. (2d App. Dist. Calif.), Case No. 2d Civil No. B040717, July 3, 1990: This is an unpublished case that can be entered as evidence in California cases for basing the award of retired pay on the grade and service time at the time of separation (or divorce) and not at the time of retirement. (When it is based on the date of retirement, the former spouse gets a "windfall" amount that should be the sole property of the retiree.) Kniss (now deceased) cited two Texas cases that ruled the same way.

Berry v. Berry, 647 S.W. 2d 945 (Tex. 1983), on valuation and apportionment (at time of divorce).

Busby v. Busby, 457 S.W.2d 551 (Tex. 1970) and *Cearley v. Cearley*, 544 S.W.2d 661 (Tex. 1976) state the formula for division of military retirement benefits between spouses as: months married/months in service X final benefit X 1/2. This formula allows for the division of future military retirement benefits.

Taggart v. Taggart, 552 S.W.2 422 (Tex. 1977). Pre-McCarty formula for apportioning community property interest in retirement benefits.

Direct Payment vs. Allotment

In re marriage of Wood, 767 P.2d 338 (Or. Ct. App. 1984). Distinguishes between court orders that provide for a specific amount or percentage of disposable retirement pay and court orders that merely give offsetting judgment awards.

Disability

Berry v. Berry, 7876 S.W.2d 672 (Tex. 1990). Retroactivity of the Mansell decision.

Busby v. Busby, 457 S.W.2d 551 (Tex. 1970). Disability compensation was community property prior to the McCarty decision.

Conroy v. Conroy, 706 S.W.2d 745 Tex. App. 8th Dist. 1986). Disability retirement pay is community property.

Miller v. Miller, 632 P.2d 732 (1981), 96 N.M. 497. The couple was divorced in NM, but stipulated that Texas law determined whether the disability compensation received by the husband could be characterized as community property. The Court ruled that the VA compensation was not subject to division, but that a trial court could award alimony where the sole source of funds for payments were disability benefits from the VA and Social Security.

Retroactivity

A New Mexico state court (2d Judicial District, Bernalillo County) decision on June 29, 1993 has ignored the 1990 amendment to USFSPA (to prohibit state courts from dividing retired pay for divorces occurring prior to June 25, 1981 and where the court did not treat the retired pay as joint property or reserve jurisdiction to do so—the retroactivity feature). The case in January 1994 involved retired Air Force Master Sergeant Lambert J. Gonzales of Albuquerque, in which he petitioned the NM courts to terminate USFSPA payments on the basis of the 1990 congressional amendment. The court reasoned that under NM law there is a "limited reservation of jurisdiction" that is incorporated into every divorce decree issued in New Mexico. Under this rationale, the conditions of the congressional amendment did not apply—and can never apply—in New Mexico. The facts of Sergeant Gonzales's case render it exactly the kind of situation Congress was trying to prevent by passing the amendment.

Unemployment Benefits (reduced) and Military Retirement

Kan v. Commonwealth of Pennsylvania, 530 A.2d 1023, 109

Pa. Commw. 184 (1987). The Unemployment Compensation Board of Review affirmed a referee's order reducing unemployment benefits by the entire amount of military retirement benefits. On appeal, the case was reversed and remanded for recalculation to deduct the amount going to the former spouse.

8. **GOVERNMENT AGENCIES** (See also other listings within this Appendix.)

Defense Finance and Accounting Service (DFAS). Commonly known as the finance center, each has attorneys on staff who are experts on USFSPA and SBP. Unlike the general toll-free telephone number that the centers have, however, most of these attorneys are not available via an 800 number. The finance centers were consolidated in 1992; retirees are paid out of Cleveland (Tel: 800-321-1080), and annuitants out of Denver (Tel: 800-435-3396). To contact DFAS: General on-line: http://www.dfas.mil

SBP: DFAS--Denver, Tel: 800-435-3396
Fax: 800-982-8459; Comm: 303 -676-6552
Address: DFAS-DE/FRB
6760 E. Irvington Place, Denver CO 80279-6000
E-mail: dfas-de-frb@cleveland.dfas.mil

Retired Pay: DFAS--Cleveland
Tel: 800-321-1080, (OH) 326-522-5955, Fax: 800-469-6559
Address: PO Box 99191, Cleveland OH 44199-1126
E-Mail: dfas_cleveland@cleveland.dfas.mil

Information on USFSPA: http://www.dfas.mil/money/garnish/index.htm. Address for sending DD Form 2293 (application for retired pay payments): DFAS, Cleveland Center, Code L, PO Box 998002, Cleveland OH 44199-8002, Customer Service: 216-522-5301, Fax: 216-522-5394. The application must be served personally, by facsimile or by mail. ARA recommends mailing with "return receipt requested." Internet users can obtain the form online.

SBP coverage: DFAS, Cleveland Center, Attn: Code FRB (for retired members) or Code FRABA (for active duty and reservists).

Applications for retired pay by the former spouse and for SBP must be submitted using precise procedures. You should be able to obtain forms from any military installation, or call DFAS. If you are the former spouse, it is a waste of time to write your Congressperson for help in dealing with the finance center or get them to do what you won't do yourself. The retiree cannot make application for you. Besides, receiving a response could take up to three months or more and in the mean time, with the use of certified-return-receipt-mail, you can do it yourself.

Military Family Resource Center. 4040 N. Fairfax Dr, Room 420, Arlington VA 22203-1635;Tel: 703-696-4555; Fax: 703-696-9062; DSN 426-9062; E-mail: mfrc@odedodea.edu

This office assists military personnel and their families with literature searches on various topics, including divorce. They publish a yearly demographics survey.

U.S. General Accounting Office—*Report to the Chairman, Subcommittee on Military Personnel and Compensation, Committee on Armed_Services, House of Representatives: Implementation of the Uniformed Services Former Spouses' Protection Act,* GAO/NSIAD-85-4, October 24, 1984.

> This report is a summary of the evaluation of how the Department of Defense and the Military Services were implementing PL 97-252. The report, besides describing the problems the services were having with implementing the law, provides some excellent examples of the tax withholding implications. If your divorce is pre-February 1991, you might find this report interesting reading.

Department of Veterans Affairs (VA)

> If a veteran or his dependents need information on what benefits they are entitled to, they now only have to make one phone call (800-827-1000 in the US, Puerto Rico, Virgin Islands) to reach the nearest VA regional office during normal office hours.

9. JUDGE ADVOCATE GENERAL

Every military installation will have a legal office with one or more "JAGs" and a (senior) Staff Judge Advocate. Although the military attorneys can provide some help with personal legal matters (e.g., you can get a will prepared free of charge, or a lease reviewed, etc.), the military member and the spouse are responsible for seeking a civilian attorney in divorce matters. The military attorneys can advise the military couple of their rights and benefits, provide checklists and forms for accomplishing a separation agreement, and can assist in helping obtain family support. This assistance will only be done in person and not over the phone.

10. LEGAL RESEARCH SOURCES

ADMINISTRATIVE REGULATIONS

The services have their own set of administrative regulations that covers various subjects related to SBP and USFSPA. Check for them in the Code of Federal Regulation. Not following the instructions precisely can result in delays or non receipt of the monies.

ENCYCLOPEDIC

Corpus Juris Secundum

6 C.J.S. *Armed Services* §§114, 116, 121, 255

These sections cover, in order above, the point that retired pay is not considered a pension, disability retirement, dual compensation, and disability compensation.

27C C.J.S. *Divorce* §557-559

General discussion on divorce and pensions. Includes military retired pay and disability.

American Jurisprudence, 2d

6 Am.Jur.2d *Attachment and Garnishment* §179.5

General law about garnishments and how states have applied it.

24 Am. Jur. 2d *Divorce and Separation* §909 and §911 (1983 and Supp.)

These two sections discuss military retired pay and disability benefits, respectively. Only very general information is given on *McCarty*, with some of it somewhat incorrect.

1 Am Jur Legal Forms 2d

For an extensive discussion of the federal tax aspects as they relate to property settlement agreements, see *Federal Tax Guide to Legal Forms, Alimony and Separation Agreements, (§110 et.seq.)*

§17:114 contains a form-drafting guide—Checklist—Matters to be considered in drafting a property settlement agreement. "Forms" are actually the paragraphs that go into the divorce decree and property settlement. The list is extensive and serves to provide a checklist where nothing is left out.

American Law Reports

Annotation, *Pension or Retirement Benefits as Subject to Award or Division by Court in Settlement of Property Rights Between Spouses,* 94 A.L.R. 3d 176 (1979) & Supp.

Annotation, *Federal Pre-Emption of State Authority Over Domestic Relations—Federal Cases,* 70 L.Ed.2d 895 & Supp.

Community Property Law and the United States. W. S. McClanahan, Lawyers Cooperative Publishing, Aqueduct Bldg, Rochester NY 14694. Tel: 716-546-5530.

This book is not readily available in law libraries, but can be purchased from the publisher (contains yearly supplements). Call 800-328-4880 to order from the publisher, West Group, or on the Web: http://www.westgroup.com.

Equitable Distribution Journal

Available at any major law library, this journal regularly discusses military retirement cases. A source of information in this publication and assistant editor and regular user of it, is Brett R. Turner, Senior Attorney with the National Legal Research Group, 2421 Ivy Road, P.O. Box 7187, Charlottesville VA 22906-7187; Tel: 800-446-1870; 804-977-5690; Fax: 804-295-4667); Web: http://www.nlrg.com; E-mail: nlrg1@aol.com.

LEGAL PERIODICAL LITERATURE

Articles (in alphabetical order by author)

Cardos and Sinnott, *The Uniformed Services Former Spouses Protection Act.* 33 Fed. Bar. J. 33, January 1986.

Defense Department Would Not Oppose Divorce Bill If Changes Made. 385 Pension Reporter 426 (March 22, 1982) (BNA). This article gives a good initial introduction to efforts to overturn *McCarty* and what led up to the FSPA.

Henderson, *Dividing Military Retirement Pay and Disability Pay: A More Equitable Approach,* 134 Mil.L.Rev. 87 (Fall 1991).

Hochman, *The Supreme Court and the Constitutionality of Retroactive Legislation,* 73 Harv. L.R. 663 (1960). While not specifically addressing the issue as it relates to USFSPA, this article is, nonetheless, interesting in getting a perspective as to why retroactivity was not excluded in USFSPA initially.

MacIntyre, *A Legal Assistance Symposium—Division of U.S. Army Reserve and National Guard Pay Upon Divorce,* 102 Mil.L.Rev. 23 (Fall 1983). Despite the date of this article, the information is still current. Hardships and inequities that were originally cited as the main reason in changing the law do not exist when the military member is a reservist. The author examines in detail the language of the original statute to determine whether reservists were ever meant to fall under this law. Problems are created in calculating the eligibility for direct payment of retirement benefits.

Shiles, *The Second Legal Assistance Symposium—Part III: Legal Assistance Overseas: Rights of Family Members Who Separate While Residing in the Federal Republic of Germany,*112 Mil. L. Rev. 131 (Spring 1986).This article discusses the basic rights of family members who separate from the military sponsor while residing in Germany.

Woldman, Elizabeth. *The Division of Military Pension Benefits in New Mexico in the Aftermath of Mansell.* Divorce Litigation, Vol. 1, No. 9, pp. S1 (3), November 1989.

WEST KEY-NUMBER DIGEST SYSTEM

Most of the cases in West digests can be found under the following Key Numbers, with the division of military retirement in a divorce appearing under "Divorce, 252.3."

Armed Services
Key 13.5	Retirement pay and disability retirement
Key 104	Compensation for disability

Divorce
Key 248	Disposition of property
Key 252	Division of property
Key 252.3	Insurance, retirement, or pension rights

Husband and Wife
    Key 240   Insurance & retirement benefits

ON-LINE LEGAL RESEARCH

LEXIS-NEXIS, the mega-database, is an excellent source for any legal research, however, it is not the most user-friendly. Larger law offices will have this system, as will law libraries. If you aren't an expert in search techniques, then check out the Web (http://10.86.12.119/lexnex1.htm). A professor at California State University, Bill Budge, has written an excellent tutorial.

WWW VIRTUAL LAW LIBRARY (http://www.law.indiana.edu/law/lawindex.html) is an enormous listing of on-line resources, from law firms to state agencies. Just consider the source of any of the resources that you might access, as the legal information posted may not be kept up with changes in the law. The best sources are those on federal government agencies (The Federal Web Locator: http://www.law.vill.edu/Fed-Agency/fedwebloc.html).

ARA has its own Web site at: http://www.americanretirees.com. By typing in "Military Divorce" in any search engine, you will get a plethora of sources.

CONGRESS has its own Internet service for legislative information (http://Thomas.loc.gov). This service has received many complaints, primarily claiming that the information is really for lobbyists, because all amendments are not put on it. (Congressional rules do not require advance disclosure to the committees, other members or the public. A member of Congress can show an amendment to anyone or to no one—it is the member's choice.) The Thomas system does upload the Congressional Record (the daily proceedings of the House and Senate, including speeches), all versions of bills introduced in Congress (searchable by keyword), and even C-SPAN's schedule.

FEDERAL PROGRAMS and activities can be accessed through Fedworld, a free on-line database (telenet fed-world.gov; Web users: http://www.fedworld.gov).

HALT is on the Internet, at http://www.halt.org. Their E-mail address is: haltfry@aol.com.

U.S. HOUSE OF REPRESENTATIVES Internet Law Library (for the U.S. Code): http:// law.house.gov/usc.htm.

LEGI-SLATE (800-733-1131) or (gopher.legislate.com[port 70]) is a call-in service and Internet database that provides information about all bills and resolutions introduced in Congress and the full text of all federal regulations since 1990. Prices vary.

OTHER LEGAL SELF-HELP SOURCES

The best mail-order source for self-help books is Nolo Press Self-Help Law Books and Software, 950 Parker Street, Berkeley, CA 94710. Their 24-hour order line: 800-992-6656. Customer Service: 800-728-3555, M-F, 9-5, PT. FAX orders: 800-645-0895, 548-5902 in Area Code 510. Order by E-mail: cs@nolo.com. When you order, you receive a free 2-year subscription to their excellent newsletter and catalog, *Nolo News*. Their list of publications (which includes those by non-Nolo staff) includes: *How to Raise or Lower Child Support in California, Smart Ways to Save Money During and After Divorce, Child Custody* (with checklists and blank agreement), *The Living Together Kit, California Marriage Law, Practical Divorce Solutions, Good Divorce, A Guide to Divorce Mediation, Clinician's Guide to Child Custody Evaluations, California Divorce Course* (video), *How to Do Your Own Divorce* (in California and Texas).

OTHER RESEARCH SOURCES

If you are interested in reading some of the papers written by the late Justice Thurgood Marshall (who played an important part in the USFSPA), and you are in the Washington DC area, you can read his papers at the Library of Congress manuscript reading room, 1st floor of the Madison Building, 101 Independence Ave SE., Washington DC. Researchers are asked to obtain a library user's card, which requires them to show a photo identification card, and to describe the general purpose of their work.

Congressional Voting Records: If you want to know how your elected officials have voted contact Project Vote Smart, 129 Northwest 4th St., Ste 204, Corvallis OR 97330, Tel: 800-622-7627), a nonpartisan organization that provides free information. You can even find out about ratings from special interest groups that have evaluated the federal lawmakers' voting records: http://www.vote-smart.org, E-mail: comments@vote-smart.org.

11. ## LEGISLATION — FEDERAL

5 C.F.R. §581 — processing of garnishments for child support and alimony.

5 C.F.R. §831 — waiving military retirement in favor of a civil service pension based upon both periods of service combined.

32 C.F.R. §48 — procedures for administering the Retired Serviceman's Family Protection Plan (RSFPP), which was the forerunner of the Survivor Benefit Plan (SBP). (SBP replaced RSFPP in 1972.)

32 C.F.R. §63 — procedures for processing USFSPA direct payments.

10 U.S.C. §1401 — states that military retirement pay is not a pension or annuity.

10 U.S.C. §1408 — Uniformed Services Former Spouses' Protection Act, Pub.L. 97-252, 96 Stat. 730 (1982). This is the initial Act, as part of the Department of Defense Authorization Act of 1983. It amends 10 U.S.C. §1002, Ch. 71.

10 U.S.C. §1448 (b)(2) and §1450(f) — sets forth eligibility requirements for members who may elect or are required to elect SBP for former spouses or to both a former spouse and child.

38 U.S.C. §3101 [amended by Pub.L. 99-576 §503 (October 28, 1986)] — permits the VA to deduct SBP costs from VA compensation when military retired pay is waived for such compensation.

42 U.S.C. §665 (1988) — involuntary allotments from pay for child and spousal support.

38 U.S.C. §1115, 1135 — additional VA compensation for dependents; if rated equal to or greater than 30 percent, the member receives additional money for dependents.

50 U.S.C. §501 et. seq. — Soldiers' and Sailors' Civil Relief Act of 1940. Whenever a service member is involved in a legal action, certain rights must be complied with. (§513-Protection of persons secondarily liable; §520-Default Judgments; affidavits; bonds, attorneys for persons in service; §521-Stay of proceedings where military service affects conduct)

The Code of Federal Regulations is available on-line at: http://www.access.gpo.gov/nara/cfr/cfr-table-search.html.
The U.S. House of Representatives Internet Law Library (for the U.S. Code) is on-line at: http://www.law.house.gov/usc.htm.

12. LEGISLATIVE HISTORY

Pre-1989 History:

S.2248 (H.R.6030): House Reports: No. 97-482 accompanying H.R. 6030 (House Armed Services Committee) and No. 97-749 (Conference Committee).
Senate Report: No. 97-330 (Senate Armed Services Committee).

128 Cong.Rec. (1982): May 3-6, 11-13, considered and passed Senate. July 19-22, 27-29, H.R. 6030, considered and passed House; S.2248, amended, passed in lieu. Aug. 17, Senate agreed to Conference Report. Aug. 18, House agreed to Conference Report.

Hearings (information found in CIS)
H201-17 Benefits for Former Spouses of Military Members, 11/5/81. Committee Serial HASC No. 97-70 before Subcommittee on Military Personnel and Compensation to consider: H.R. 3039 (entitle spouses to pro rata share of military retirement), H.R. 1711 (require DoD compliance with state divorce court decisions),

H.R. 1540: authorize medical and dental care in DoD medical facilities for certain former spouses.

H.R. Rep. No. 749, 97th Cong, 2d Sess (reprinted in 1982 U.S. CODE CONG. & ADMIN NEWS, 1569-1573).

Other testimony:

Cong. Rec. 15721, (daily ed. July 14, 1981). H.R. 1711, H.R. 3039.

128 Cong.Rec. H4717 (daily ed. July 28, 1982) (reprinted in 1982 U.S. CODE CONG. & ADMIN NEWS, 1596). H.R. 6030 - the debate on USFSPA.

S.Rep.No. 502, 1982 U.S. CODE CONG. & ADMIN NEWS, 1617.

Post-1989 Legislation:

H.R. 3525, introduced October 8, 1991, by Rep. Schroeder: a bill to apply the expanded definition of disposable retired pay to divorces retroactively. ARA believes that if the definition of disposable retired pay as defined in Public Law 101-510 were applied retroactively, military members (as well as their spouses) would have their divorce cases readjudicated where the parties had already agreed to the division in good faith.

H.R. 3915, introduced November 25, 1991, by Rep. Schroeder: a bill to amend 10 U.S.C. to provide commissary and exchange privileges to all former spouses who meet at least a 20/20/15 standard, regardless of the date of the divorce. If passed, former spouses would have had more privileges than former military members, including reservists, who are now out of uniform and for whom such benefits were originally intended.

H.R. 4138, introduced January 29, 1992, by Rep. Schroeder provided taxpayer-subsidized survivor benefits to certain former spouses of members who were eligible to participate but who did not or could not designate a former spouse as a beneficiary.

H.R. 2200, introduced May 2, 1991, by Rep. Dornan (see Chapter 16 and Appendix H).

[These bills, introduced in the 102d Congress, did not pass.]

Union List:

Other legislative history on USFSPA, Public Law 97-252, Department of Defense Authorization Act, 1983, 96 Sta. 730 can be obtained from the *Union List of Legislative Histories*, 5th ed., 47th Congress, 1881-98th Congress, 1984: Van Ness, Feldman, Sutcliffe, Curtis & Levenberg, 1050 Thomas Jefferson St. NW, Washington DC 2000, Tel: 202-298-1800. Library: Tel. 202-298-1901; Fax: 202-338-2361.

13. USAA FOUNDATION

800-531-8857 (in San Antonio, 210-498-6661). A full-service insurance company serving the military community, USAA publishes a series of educational booklets for its clients through the USAA Foundation. Some you may find helpful are: "New Beginnings: When Your Marital Status Changes," "Financial Guide for Retirement," and "The Surviving Spouse."

14. PERSONNEL OFFICES (AT MILITARY INSTALLATIONS)

The Military Personnel Office at the local military installation will usually have two offices that can assist with USFSPA information and SBP. Help is available either in the Retirement Section or the Personal Affairs Section.

Once retired, a military member will receive some newsletter from his service. For example, the Air Force publishes AFRP 30-16. "Afterburner—USAF News for Retired Personnel." The Army publishes "Army Echoes." The Navy publishes "Shift Colors." Information on USFSPA and related matters is published in these newletters, along with updates on legislation and telephone numbers for assistance with retiree matters. Many of these hardcopy newsletters, though, are being eliminated in favor of an on-line version. Without a computer and access to the Internet, you may not be able to effectively keep up in the future with changes that affect you.

15. **SERVICE PROCEDURES & REGULATIONS**

Each of the uniformed services has information or fact sheets on both USFSPA and SBP. You can obtain information sheets from several sources—the active duty military personnel office, the base or post legal office, the retiree center

The best aggregate source for information on the various finance centers, is a book titled, *Retired Military Almanac*. It is published annually by the Uniformed Services Almanac, Inc. Copies are sold in military exchanges. They can also be ordered directly from the publisher: P.O. Box 4144, Falls Church Virginia 22044, Tel. 888-872-9698.

16. **SUPPORT GROUPS**

More so today, there are many groups available to both the husband and wife when it comes to seeking help with domestic issues. These groups, staffed often by volunteers, have a wealth of literature available, including statistical information. Do not overlook such organizations as an inexpensive source of group support.

One excellent source of support in coping with the trauma of divorce as well as the rebuilding process, are three programs sponsored by the Roman Catholic archdiocese called Coping, Rebuilding, and Beginning Experience. (You do not have to be Catholic to attend, and the programs are offered around the country.) Both men and women attend, and the support and learning that result can be worth savings of hundreds of dollars over one-on-one psychotherapy.

Many active duty military members are reluctant to seek professional help for fear of their security clearances or other reasons. Those who feel that way would be interested in programs such as these. The cost is either free (for Coping) or minimal for a 10-week seminar in Rebuilding. The text used in Rebuilding is one of the most comprehensive books one will ever come across in explaining the entire emotional process of divorce.

17. PUBLICATIONS—MILITARY SPECIFIC

The Retired Officers Association publishes an excellent booklet entitled "SBP Made Easy." It costs less than $5 and is available from TROA, 201 N. Washington St. Alexandria VA 22314-2539. Tel: 800-245-TROA, 703-549-2311. The publication has an extensive section on the Social Security Offset issue. It can serve as a basic guide for retirement planning, particularly in calculating financial interests. The guide is also helpful in presenting the facts regarding SBP coverage when you waive military retired pay in favor of a combined military/civil service retirement.

The *Army Air Force Mutual Aid Association* (AAFMA), located at 102 Sheridan Ave., Ft. Myer VA 22211 (Tel. 800-336-4538, Fax: 703-522-1336, http://www.aafma.com, E-mail: info@aafma.com), reviews with its active, reserve/guard, retired members (officers, NCOs corporal and up, warrant officers), financial or separation (from service) options to provide free unbiased counseling and detailed forecasts of the effect on your benefits, including options relative to SBP. You can receive information on what your projected costs will be, and what the value of the SBP is to the spouse. If you are an active reservist (in a billet), the services AAFMA provides can be invaluable, including keeping track of your accumulated retirement points. (Unfortunately, if you are an active reservist in a non-pay category, you are not eligible to join AAFMA. We would like to see AAFMA revise its membership policy to include all reservists, whether in a pay billet or non-pay status.)

The *Navy Mutual Aid Association* serves the Navy, Marine Corps, Coast Guard, Public Health, and NOAA uniformed personnel and their families, Tel: 800-628-6022.

The *Uniformed Services Almanac, Inc.,* publishes a variety of almanacs that contain estate planning tips related to the uniformed personnel and their families. Publications include: *National Guard Almanac, Reserve Forces Almanac, Retired Military Almanac,* and *Uniformed Services Almanac (Active Duty).* They are revised yearly and can be found in military exchanges and clothing sales stores.

18. PUBLICATIONS—USAA

The USAA Educational Foundation publishes a number of informational booklets for educating its members on consumer issues. Among them is "When Your Marital Status Changes," publication #541. Members can call the USAA TouchLine at 800-531-6194 to obtain this free publication.

19. PUBLICATIONS—VETERANS AFFAIRS

The VA offers a number of publications, including, "Federal Benefits for Veterans and Dependents," GPO Stock #051-000-00202-4. Sometimes you can get their publications free by walking into your local VA office or hospital. Others cost a small fee.

20. PUBLICATIONS—MISCELLANEOUS

Domestic Violence. An excellent booklet for anyone in need of a safety plan to escape domestic violence is called, "Striving to Be Violence Free...A Guidebook for Creating a Safety Plan." It is written and published by an award-winning, nonprofit agency called Perspectives, Inc., in St. Louis Park MN. You can order this book by sending $4 to: Perspectives, Inc., 3381 Gorham Ave, St. Louis Park MN 55426 (Attn: Guidebook). Include your name and address printed clearly on an address label, or a 3x5 card or a sheet of paper, and allow 4-5 weeks for delivery.

Document Room, U.S. House of Representatives. To order documents published by the House, contact the Office of the Doorkeeper, Washington DC 20515-6622, Tel: 202-225-3456; Fax: 202-226-4362.

21. HOW TO FIND SOMEONE

ON-LINE Resources. If you are trying to find someone (e.g., to serve divorce papers on), consider the following World Wide Web sources: Switchboard, *http://www.switchboard.com*; Four11, *http://www.four11.com*

Professional Services. For a fee (and expect to pay up to $125 an hour or more), you can hire someone to locate someone else, perform manual searches (e.g., public court records in a county), or do on-line research for you (e.g., searching motor vehicle records). Some professional fee-for-service companies include: Find People Fast, 800-829-1807; Infoquest, 800-562-7547; and Old Friend Information Services, 800-841-7938.

These companies use public information that you can search yourself. However, if you are not familiar with this specialized search process, your money may be well spent. And, if you are wanting information in another locale, you may have no choice but to go through a third party.

How to Find Missing Persons: A Handbook for Investigators. Loompanics, Unlimited, PO Box 1197, Port Townsend WA 98368; Tel: 206-385-2230.

How to Locate Anyone Who Is or Has Been in the Military, Armed Forces Locator Directory, by Lt Col Richard S. Johnson, AUS-Ret.. Published by Military Information Enterprises, Box 5143, Burlington NC 27216. ($23 PP)

American Foreign Conflicts Electronic Library and Veteran Locator, 25601 Narbonne Ave, Suite 6, Lomita CA 90717; Tel: 310-530-0177. This is a computer database service.

22. HOW TO CONTACT THE FINANCE CENTERS

Retired Pay Accounts. DFAS—Cleveland Center, Code RO, PO Box 99191, Cleveland OH 44199-1126; Tel: 800-321-1080; Fax: 800-469-6559. Casualty Notification: 800-269-5170.

Annuitants (SBP). DFAS—Denver Center, DFAS-DE/FRB, 6760 E. Irvington Place, Denver CO 80279-6000; Tel: 800-435-3396; Fax: 800-982-8459

The best time to call the DFAS is between 8 AM-10AM and 3 PM-6 PM. Nonpeak times are the 2nd, 3rd, and 4th weeks of each month, and Thursdays and Fridays.

U.S. Public Health Service. Compensation Branch, Parklawn Building, 5600 fishers Lane, Rockville MD 20857; Tel: 800-638-8744; 301-443-2475.

U.S. Coast Guard Pay & Personnel Center (C.G. & NOAA); Tel: 800-772-8724

23. PENSION VALUATION

Value of Pensions in Divorce (with annual supplements), by Marvin Snyder. Wiley Law Publications, 7222 Commerce Center Drive, Colorado Springs CO 80919-9810. Mr. Snyder, a pension actuary, is an expert witness and consultant to professionals and clients in the areas of pension valuation, structured settlements, QDROs and COAPs (Court Order Acceptable for Processing—the document used to divide pensions of federal employees as property in divorce under the Civil Service Retirement System and the Federal Employees Retirement System, FERS), and lost wages. He can be reached at Marvin Snyder Associates, Inc. 2100 Timer Rose Drive, Las Vegas NV 89134; Tel: 702-869-0303; Outside a.c. 702, 800-806-3759.

24. **STATISTICAL DATA ON MILITARY RETIREMENT SYSTEM**

DoD Statistical Report on the Military Retirement System, FYXX. (Data for the previous fiscal year is normally released in May of the following year.) You can obtain a copy of this actuarial table by writing to: Department of Defense, Office of the Secretary of Defense, Personnel and Readiness, Office of the Actuary; 1555 Wilson Blvd, Suite 701, Arlington, VA 22209-2405; Tel: 703-696-7400, DSN 426-7400. For technical questions related to specific data in the report, call Richard Allen, 703-696-7409, DSN 426-7409. This publication contains every number you would want to know about retirement data, including the number of retirees on the rolls (by age, rank, and sex), and where retirees live, both here and abroad. Planners in the Pentagon and Congress use the numbers to project future outlays for retired pay and survivor benefits.

25. **RESERVE AND GUARD**

Reserve Forces Almanac. Published yearly by Uniformed Services Almanac, Inc., Falls Church VA.

19XX Handbook for the Guard and Reserve Forces Almanac. Published yearly by the Army Times Publishing Co., Springfield, VA, as a supplement to the *Army Times, Navy Times*, and *Air Force Times.* To purchase copies: Call 800-368-5718; or write to Army Times Publishing Co., Customer Service Dept, Springfield VA 22159; E-mail: pmyers@atpco.com.

Communicating with Your Reserve Service. Many agencies no longer are publishing hardcopy updates or newsletters to keep the reservist up to date. Going on-line is your only way to communicate with your service, other than by telephone. For example, to reach the Air Force Reserve: AFRES Home Page: http://www.afres.af.mil. To access the ARPC/IMA Home Page, go to the AFRES Home Page and click on the ARPC/IMA button, or type: http://www.afres.af.mil/arpc-ima/

26. CONGRESSIONAL & OTHER LEGISLATIVE INQUIRIES

All the services have an office, sometimes within the Public Affairs section, that is responsible for responding to congressional inquiries. For example, in the Air Force Reserve, you could contact AF/REI (Policy Integration Division), 703-693-2452, fax: 703-697-9103. When you write your elected officials with your questions on USFSPA, don't forget these other sources to make your concerns known.

27. OTHER AGENCIES

Department of Veterans Affairs. For the nearest regional office, call 800-827-1000.

*Department of Veterans Affairs—Insurance Center (NSLI & USGLI);*Tel: 800-669-8477.

Office of Servicemembers' Group Life Insurance (SGLI & VGLI); Tel. 800-419-1473.

Social Security Administration, Tel: 800-772-1213.

28. RETIREMENT & RESERVE MATTERS—SERVICE SOURCES

Army. Retirement Services Division, Community and Family Support Center, Alexandria, VA 22331-0521; Tel: 800-336-4909.

Army Reserve Personnel Center (ARPENCEN). Retirement Points Accounting Section, Tel: 800-325-8311. Service Computation Section/DEERS, Tel: 800-648-5487. Retiree Mobilization; Tel: 800-325-2660.

Navy. Dept of the Navy, Bureau of Naval Personnel, Retired Activities Section, PERS-662C. Washington DC 20370-6620; Tel: 800-255-8950.

Air Force. Air Force Military Personnel Center, DPMARA, 550 C St. West, Suite 11, Randolph AFB TX 78150-4713; Tel: 800-531-7502 (Tues-Thurs, 1-3 PM).

Air Reserve Personnel Center. Denver, CO 80280; Tel. 800-525-0102.

Marine Corps. Commandant, USMC, Retired Affairs Office

(Code MMSR-6), Washington DC 20380-0001; Tel: 800-336-4649.

Coast Guard. Commanding Officer (RPD), USCG Pay & Personnel Center, (PPC-USCG), 444 S.E. Quincy St., Topeka KS 66683-3591; Tel: 800-772-8724.

29. SURVIVOR BENEFIT PLAN (SBP)

The Retired Officers Association publishes an excellent booklet entitled "SBP Made Easy." See Section 17, this appendix.

The Army Air Force Mutual Aid Association (AAFMA). See Section 17 for information on AAFMA's Services regarding SBP.

****

This resource listing is but a small compilation of reference materials. If you know of other sources that should be included, please let the authors know. You can also e-mail updates or changes to:

mthole_TheWriter@bigfoot.com.

UPDATES

In order to provide current and accurate information, some changes which have occurred since the original printing of *Divorce and the Military II* appear below. Please note, however, that it is impossible to keep up with constantly changing information in Appendix P, and we encourage you to notify us when you find corrections.

Legislative Update (Chapter 16)

H.R. 1111, the Uniformed Services Divorce Equity Act of 2003, was introduced in the 108th Congress by Rep. Cass Ballenger (R-NC) on 6 March 2003. This proposed amendment takes a new approach to reform of the USFSPA by relating the period of payments to the duration of the marriage. Just as the service member must serve 20 years to qualify for retired pay, so would a former spouse have to be married for 20 years while the member was serving in order to receive payments for life. In addition, H.R. 1111 would:

- Eliminate the Windfall Benefit,
- Establish a two-year statute of limitations on the time allowed a former spouse to claim USFSPA benefits after a divorce, and
- Reiterate and reinforce the USFSPA's protection of disability pay.

DFAS Contact Information Update (Resource #22, page 366)

The main telephone numbers for DFAS have not changed; however, the addresses to which a correspondence is sent have. Be sure to include the Social Security Number and a signature in all correspondence.

Retirees:	DFAS, U.S. Military Retired Pay, PO Box 7130
	London KY 40742-7130 Fax: 1-800-469-6559
Annuitants:	DFAS, U.S. Military Annuitant Pay, PO Box 7131
	London KY 40742-7131 Fax: 1-800-982-8459

You may also contact DFAS online. MyPay is a secure, DFAS-operated Web site that lets active duty, National Guard and Reserve service members, civilian employees, and military retirees and annuitants take charge of their pay accounts online. The DFAS MyPay Web site is found at https://mypay.dfas.mil/. Email inquiries take up to seven business days. Be aware of look-alike websites.

DEERS Verification changes for Unremarried Former Spouses (page 132)

As of 1 October 2003, DEERS will reflect TRICARE eligibility for unremarried former spouses by using their own SSN and not the former sponsor's. Health care information will be filed under the unremarried former spouse's own SSN and name. These beneficiaries will now use their own name and SSN to schedule medical appointments and to file TRICARE claims. The current Uniformed Services Identification and Privilege Card, DD Form 1173, is still valid until it expires. Upon renewal, the unremarried former spouse will be issued a replacement DoD/Uniformed Services Identification and Privilege Card, DD Form 2765. Contact or visit the nearest identification card issuing facility (locations may be found online at www.dmdc.osd.mil/rsl) for questions or assistance.

ORDER FORM

QUANTITY	PRODUCT	PRICE	COST
	Book: DIVORCE AND THE MILITARY II	19.95 each	(1)
	ARA Member Discount (on books only): 10% for 1-9 books; 20% for 10+:		(2)
	Shipping & Handling (books shipped via Priority Mail) $4.95 for first book; $4.40 for each additional book.		(3)
	22% additional postage (on lines 5 + 6) for foreign addresses (excluding APOs):		(4)
	Subtotal (lines 1 - 2 + 3 + 4):		(5)
	California residents add 7.50% sales tax on amount in line (5):		(6)
	TOTAL ENCLOSED (lines 5 + 6):		$

For telephone orders call (909) 793-2424. Have your VISA or Mastercard ready.

—OVER—

MAIL FORM TO: ARA, P.O. Box 2333, Redlands, CA 92373-0781.

Name(print) _____ Rank/Rate _____

Company/Organization _____ Telephone (____) _____

Address _____ City/State _____

ZIP+4 _____

If paying by credit card: ☐VISA ☐Mastercard   Card Number: _____ Exp. Date _____

Name of Cardholder: _____   Signature: _____

Please take a moment to check your status in each column, as applicable:

___ USAF	___ Active Duty	___ Officer
___ USA	___ Retired	___ Enlisted
___ USMC	___ Reserve/Guard	___ Warrant Officer
___ USN	___ Retired Reserve/Guard	___ Officer (prior enlisted)
___ USCG	___ Spouse of Active Duty	___ Other Dependent
___ PHS	___ Spouse of Retiree	___ Lawyer (___ Former JAG)
___ NOAA	___ Spouse of Reserve/Guard	___ Other _____

ARA Membership Application

Dues $25/year (includes newsletter)	$
Contribution	
Pledge Monthly _____	
Canada/Foreign addresses add $12/year (for postage)	
TOTAL AMOUNT ENCLOSED	$

Dues and contributions are tax deductible.
Send payment (no cash) and this form to ARA corporate headquarters:

ARA
P.O. Box 2333
Redlands, CA 92373-0781

Name (please print)_____

Rank/Rate _____Male_____Female_____

Company/Organization_____

Address_____

City/State_____ **ZIP+4**_____

Telephone (____)_____(Day___Evening__)

Credit Card Payment   ❑**Visa**   ❑**Mastercard**
Card No. _____ **Expiration Date** _____

Cardholder's Signature _____

Please check your status in each column, as applicable:

___USAF	___Active Duty	___Officer
___USA	___Retired	___Enlisted
___USMC	___Reserve/Guard	___Warrant Officer
___USN	___Retired Reserve/Guard	___Officer (prior enlisted)
___USCG	___Spouse of Active Duty	___Other Dependent
___PHS	___Spouse of Retiree	___Lawyer(___former JAG)
___NOAA	___Spouse of Reserve/Guard	___Other_____

Mail inquiries relating to dues, membership, and publications to the California office. Direct all other matters to:

ARA Washington Operations Office
2009 N. 14th St., Ste. 300
Arlington, VA 22201-2514
Telephone (703) 527-3065   Fax (703) 528-4229